BEYOND CONTINUITY

A guide to the craft of script supervising, the updated second edition features practical instruction through real-world examples that demonstrate and explain the skills needed by a professional script supervisor.

Author Mary Cybulski, one of Hollywood's premier script supervisors, imparts her sage wisdom as she walks you through the process of training and working as a professional script supervisor, covering the basic skills of breaking down a script, taking notes on set, matching, cheating, determining screen direction, and knowing what the director, actors, and editor expect from a script supervisor. She also details many of the subtler, but just as important skills—how to get a job, how to think like an editor, how to tell what is important in a script and on set, how to get along with the cast and crew, and how not to get overwhelmed when there is too much information to process. This second edition has been fully updated throughout to address significant changes to workflow as script supervisors utilize new technologies, software, and apps. The book also provides brand new coverage on how the role varies when working on episodic TV, commercials, and lower budget film projects.

Ideal for aspiring, early career, and established continuity and script supervisors, as well as filmmaking students wanting to gain a better understanding of script supervision and film continuity.

Accompanying support material features downloadable versions of the various forms, templates, logs, and checklists used by professional script supervisors.

Mary Cybulski is a script supervisor with more than 30 years' experience. She has learned and invented techniques that have made her one of the most skilled and valued script supervisors in the US. She is the first call for many of our most inventive directors: John Sayles, David Mamet, Jane Campion, M. Night Shyamalan, Ang Lee, Charlie Kaufman, Michel Gondry, and Tony Gilroy. She has worked on numerous A-list films such as *Life of Pi*, *Eternal Sunshine of the Spotless Mind*, *Michael Clayton*, and *Syriana*. During these years she has developed her craft by both learning and creating professional techniques.

BEYOND CONTINUITY

Script Supervision for the Modern Filmmaker

Second Edition

Routledge
Taylor & Francis Group

LONDON AND NEW YORK

Mary Cybulski

Front cover image: supplied by the author

Second edition published 2023
by Routledge
4 Park Square, Milton Park, Abingdon, Oxon, OX14 4RN

and by Routledge
605 Third Avenue, New York, NY 10158

Routledge is an imprint of the Taylor & Francis Group, an informa business

© 2023 Mary Cybulski

First edition published by Routledge 2014

British Library Cataloguing-in-Publication Data
A catalogue record for this book is available from the British Library

ISBN: 978-0-367-42336-0 (hbk)
ISBN: 978-0-367-42337-7 (pbk)
ISBN: 978-0-367-82366-5 (ebk)

DOI: 10.4324/9780367823665

Typeset in Optima and Utopia
by Apex CoVantage, LLC

Access the Support Material: www.routledge.com/9780367423377

Contents

Foreword

David Mamet

Orson Welles, 29 years old, was directing his first film: *Citizen Kane*. His photographer was the great Gregg Toland. Orson proposed a shot, and Toland told him it could not be done. Orson asked "why?" "Because," said Toland, "it won't cut."

Welles was the greatest stage director of his day, but this was his first run-in with the requirements of continuity. Toland taught Welles for an hour, covering the blackboard with many diagrams, arrows, and stick figures. Welles didn't understand and said he had to go home until he did. He closed down the set and came back three days later. "Alright," he said, "I've figured it out. Thank you. Now we can continue."

Hemingway said that he always regretted not having written about aviation.

He did write about many other romantic activities: sailing, fishing, hunting, bullfighting and, of course, war.

As a practitioner or aficionado, he understood the romance as resident in the technical aspects of these demanding activities. And he understood that he couldn't, as a non-pilot, do aviation justice.

To write about technical activities absent a knowledge of technique is certainly to risk devolving toward the purple—the only interesting description of a sunset I could imagine would be that written by a meteorologist.

Movie making is a completely technical process. The *result* is an attempt at romance, but the process is concerned solely with parameters: the aperture opening, the budget, travel time, the requisite number of pages per day, and so on.

Movies are made only by those who understand their particular technique (cutting, shooting, designing, scheduling, painting, building), and well-made only by those who love it.

The different pieces of the film, the shots, the music, the effects, and so on, are designed only to fit together at the last minute—the elements are like the ancient wooden ships, laid out, in construction, on the ground in pieces, and hoist and pinned together only at the end of the process—their conjunction only then recognizable as a ship.

The inspired director is, perhaps, in love not primarily with assembly, but with *disassembly*. He first plans the shot, in conjunction with the editor, camera and a.d. departments, and he and they deconstruct the story (called the script), into jobs connected not by their place in the plot, but by their logistical similarity. (Shots taking place in the same location, but at opposite ends of the film, will, of course, be filmed at the same time; an actress with a limited availability may have her scenes scheduled in a compressed continuous period, and so on.)

It is evident that there will be not one, but *many* logistical necessities, but that many will be mutually exclusive. (The actress may be available only for two weeks, but some of her scenes may be scheduled in locations unavailable during the same time period, and so on.) It is the job of the line producer and the first assistant director to make all the compromises necessary to accommodate the logistical requirements of the script. This process is far more difficult than all peace and disarmament compromises, as, at the end of the film planning, one will have arrived at an actual solution: a plan (called the day-out-of-days).

The continuity person is charged with ensuring the "cuttability" of shots filmed hours, or, indeed, months apart. (Does the actor's hair match? What about the state of the costumes? The props on the table, the actor's gestures, and eyeline?) If these (among other) elements are not consistent, the film will not "cut," the audience, that is, will be jarred out of involvement in the story. (In the first shot the actress wore a wristwatch on her left wrist, in the second, contiguous, shot, it is on her right.)

The continuity person is also in charge of that most Ancient and Sacred of Film Mysteries, THE LINE.

The Line is the connection between one actor and the next. If the actor is looking, in his single, to his left, the corresponding single of the actress must show her looking to the right. (If not, both appear to be talking to some third person. Try it.) This is fairly straightforward, but becomes intricate when there are more than two actors, and when there is movement. Many a fine morning has been spent on the set, as the director, the DP and the continuity person tried to figure out "The Line," while the cast and crew looked on, and the clock ticked and ticked.[1]

If the continuity ain't right, the scene is ruined, and the finest acting the world has ever seen gets bad laughs because the sword he so grandly flourishes in the first shot is a goblet in shot number two. (Could it happen? Of course, the shots were taken months apart, the Goblet Scene was rewritten, and ten weeks later no one remembered. It does not happen all the time, but it happens all the time if there is no one *devoted* to continuity.)

In the Old Days, the appearance of which, you, the canny reader, have most likely anticipated in this foreword, the script supervisor sat, or more often crouched, by the camera, next to the director. Both were watching the actors, close-up, which proximity they, correctly, understood as essential to their job. But in those days of yore there was no video playback. Now this technology is as dated as its terminology. There has long been through-the-lens video feed to monitors, set up some distance from the set in "Video Village." Here, deluded moderns watch neither a film nor the making of a film, but a television show, compressed, in size and complexity resembling only remotely that image which may be seen on the Big Screen.

This compression endangers not only minute nuances of acting, and gesture, but correct placement of props and set dressing. The continuity person at the video monitor misses the minutia which, on the Big Screen, will be minute no longer, but several feet across and evident to all: the coffee cup handle is turned the wrong way. It is a foot wide on the big screen. On the monitor it was invisible. No less importantly (this the choice of director), the performance in Take Three is vastly better than that in Take Five: the difference would have been apparent on the set, and will be apparent in the projected film, but can't be seen on the monitor.

Oh both boo and hoo, for the days gone by; but they have gone, and film today is not even film, and is seldom actually seen on the Big Screen, and (for the fans of Alexander Korda) "that's the law in Holland."

The culture of filmmaking is changing, as any culture does; but as any evolving culture, it can only build upon the ingrained knowledge of the Past. (The Bolsheviks replaced the Tsar with Joe Stalin and the Communists, and have replaced the Communists with Putin. What actually changed?)

Show business, as always, is made of hucksters, bankers, artists, and technicians. In any business "Where there's cash, there's theft," and "Foreign Sales" is just the Fifth Cash Register by another name.[2]

But the necessity of technique remains, as does the devotion, among the crafts, to technical perfection. This devotion prompted Mary Cybulski to write this book, God bless her.

I worked with Mary on several films. It was a treat to spend those days next to her, crouching under the camera. I learned a lot.

Over my desk is a small, stamped tin star on a safety pin. This is a "continuity star," awarded to me by Mary Cybulski. The award, of her invention, was issued to anyone on the set, cast or crew, who detected an error in continuity. The award was highly prized, and the vigilant received both the star and set-wide recognition which inspired all to pursuit of perfect continuity. She made it fun and we taught *ourselves* to look.

That is one smart woman. On which subject: Continuity Supervisor used to be known as "Script Girl." Why? As for the first 80 years, the position was always filled by a woman.

Why a woman? Probably because of the association of women with secretarial work. Is this to be decried? I hardly think so. It was a foot-in-the-door for women. As was the job of film-colorist.

Many silent films had sequences hand-tinted. This work was all done by women, who, it was thought, had more precise fine-motor skills. Because the women were involved in post-production, it was natural for them to migrate from tinting to editing, and, later, from editing to directing.

Ms. Cybulski has branched out into directing, writing, and still photography, and has taken the time to write on continuity for those who come after her.

Her book, like her daily film reports, is perfectly clear, easy to follow and completely thorough. It is now the go-to treatise on the subject, and will remain so as long as films are both shot and cut. Anyone seriously interested in shooting and/or cutting will read it and use it as a basis for application and study. She just wrote the bible of continuity.

Acknowledgments

FIRST EDITION

It is impossible to name everyone who has helped to shape this book after a career as long as mine.

It starts with John Tintori who was the editor for most of the first dozen films I script supervised. His instant, clear, and kind feedback saved me from repeating the many mistakes I made. Tim Squyres and Barbara Tulliver graciously continued that conversation for decades.

I have learned something profound from every director I have worked beside. In particular: (chronologically) Nancy Savoca, whose absolute emotional support allows actors to be their bravest; John Sayles, who designs so beautifully that he can tell complicated and compelling stories with almost nothing; Stephen Frears, who is a genius of subtext; Ang Lee, who gives his whole heart to each of his movies and gets it back again, even bigger; Jane Campion, who is the master of tone and all things female; David Mamet, a magician who can add three and two to make sixteen, right in front of you, and you believe it; Michel Gondry, whose playfulness makes us swoon; Stephen Gaghan, who is so audacious that he shows us our history as it is happening; M. Night Shyamalan, who sees the work of all his crew and makes us glad to come to work every single day; Tony Gilroy, who is the is the master of tone and and all things male; Charlie Kaufman, whose heartbreaking inventions take us places and tell us truths about ourselves we would never have guessed.

Hundreds of my fellow crew members have made my understanding of our work stronger and my life better. Among them are Maggie Renzi, Peggy Rajski, Sarah Green, Jennifer Fox, David Lee, Ellen Kuras, Bob Marshak, Drew Kunin, and Avy Kaufman.

Securing the rights to use my forms was as essential as it was difficult. James Shamus and Elizabeth Gabler did me the great favor of being the first executives to speak up for me, making it easier for the many others who followed, including Kim Cooper, Dede Gardner, Frank Marshall, Sarah Green, Anthony Bregman, Laurie Parker, Maggie Renzi, and Jean Doumainian. I am grateful to you all. Judy Noack, Spencer Bastian, Roni Lubliner, Jim

Tauber, Lynn Hendee, Cameron McCracken, Gursharm Khaira, Morgan Pollitt, and John Rusk aided this work. Thanks.

Big thanks to David Mamet for the gift of his wonderful foreword. And thanks to Suraj Sharma for letting me use his likeness. Thanks to Josh Muzaffer for technical information and Tara Dean Pietri for legal help. Thanks to Dina Goldman and Drew Kunin for help with the title.

Thanks to Focal Press, in particular Cara St. Hilaire and Carlin Bowers for their patience as I passed deadline after deadline.

Thanks to my readers, Sarah-Violet Bliss, Carol Dysinger, and John Tintori, who devoted many days to help make this book comprehensible.

Thanks to the Brooklyn Writer's Space, the Brooklyn Public Library, and New York University's Bobst Library for putting me up. And to my dear friends who are real writers, Charles Siebert, Bex Brian, Francisco Goldman, and John Sayles for letting me know what I was in for. My deep gratitude to Karyn Kusama and Kristen Kusama-Hinte, who were part of our family for many years and will remain dear friends forever.

Thanks to my mom, Carolyn Wescoat, and my sister and brother, Kath Schiffer and Steve Cybulski, for understanding when I went MIA because of work.

My infinite gratitude and love to the best husband and kids ever, ever, ever. John Tintori. Ray Tintori. Sophia Tintori.

SECOND EDITION

I wrote the first edition of this book at the end of my 25-year career as a script supervisor. My goal was to put my experience in a time capsule I could hand off to whoever might find it helpful. Since then, I have been working on set as a unit still photographer, where I have been watching the digital and streaming revolutions bring so many changes to the craft, that I knew it was time to update this book.

Whenever I am on set, I like to see what the script supervisor is up to. How are they adapting to the changes: what procedural adjustments are they making, what tools do they find most useful? This new edition began with these on-set conversations. Mary Bailey, Thomas Johnston, Belle Francisco, and Anna Lomakina have been particularly helpful in this regard.

Thanks to The New York Script Supervisors' Network, especially the NYSSN leaders, Sharon Watt and Diane Hounsell, who worked with me to organize a casual conversation about digital workflow, to send out a comprehensive survey and to organize six panels of industry experts who discussed a wide variety of digital workflows and how they relate to various types of production. I am grateful to the NYSSN members who shared their work experiences and discoveries with me and their fellow NYSSN members: Sharon Watt, Diane Hounsell, Diana Shoykhet, Cheryl Malat, Marianna Hellmund, Michele Tedlis, Jodi Domanic, Lori Grabowski, Sean Pollock, Alia Azamat, Thomas Johnston, Anna Lomakina, Heather Quick, Claudia Beesley, Nick Stergiopoulos, Devin Smith, Belle Francisco, and Alisa Traskunov. The following editors kindly took part in a panel to discuss what makes our notes most useful in post-production: Kate Sanford, Michael Taylor, Tim Squyres, and Andy Keir.

Script supervisors Roe Moore and Patti Mustari invited me to their excellent workshop where I got a solid, basic understanding of script supervising for multi camera projects, both sit-coms and live/live-to-tape.

When I needed a digital file to illustrate the exact opposite of a data bank, I thought immediately of my friend, Catherine Kunicki, whose beautiful digital drawings are unmistakably the product of a human eye and a human hand. Thank you, Catherine for making a drawing especially for this book. It is perfect.

Thanks to my very patient editors at Taylor and Francis, Sarah Pickles and Gennifer Eccles.

Finishing this edition was made more difficult by my working while dealing with a serious health issue. When I needed help, Holly Unterberger jumped in without hesitation to organize and coordinate a league of script supervisors and software developers who generated the digital forms and reports that inform the new edition: Peter Skarratt and Lori Grabowski for Peter Skarratt; Anthony Pettine and Jodi Domanic for ScriptE; Sean Pollock for MovieSlate 8; Sharon Watt for Microsoft Excel. Thanks to you all, now I know, really know, what a superpower it is to have a script supervisor helping me get the job done.

Even more essential to this project are Ray Tintori, Sophie Tintori, Mark Iosifescu, Jess Pinkham, and John Tintori, aka The Book Club, who organized themselves into a shadow writer, letting me know if what I wrote made sense or not; helping me find a better way to get my ideas across when it didn't; even reading chapters out loud to me when I couldn't see a computer screen. They all have demanding and important work of their own; still they graciously carved out time to help me finish this book, never letting on what it cost them in their own work.

Huge thanks to the cavalry of doctors, scientists, and medical professionals who came to my rescue: the doctors Joseph, Dan, and Melissa, Dr. Jennifer Moliterno Gunel, Dr. Ranjit Bindra, the irrepressible Dr. Nicholas Blondin and his right hand, Nurse Vanessa Nevins, all from Yale New

Haven Hospital. Thanks to my long time dear friend Michael Preston, who kept me upright and flowing. More thanks to my even longer time dear friend, Dr. Pearl Huang, and my daughter, Dr. Sophia Tintori, who helped me understand the otherwise incomprehensible mechanisms of what was going on in my brain and with my treatments.

The domestic cavalry, led by Maggie Renzi, has too many members to name. You are a rich collection of family, friends, and neighbors, gathered over decades, adventures, and continents. Thank you all for showing up to help me.

As always, my greatest love and appreciation to John, Ray, and Sophie, who made this last year not only possible, but beautiful.

NOTES

1   Q. How do you make Wild Rice?
    A. Take regular rice, and talk to it about continuity.

2   A bar owner knew his income was short. He suspected his bartenders were cheating him, and employed a private detective. The detective reported back after a week that every cent went into the five cash registers. The owner replied: "Five? I only have four cash registers."

Chapter 1
Introduction

WHAT'S SO GOOD ABOUT BEING A SCRIPT SUPERVISOR?

I am a script supervisor, outside, on location. It's 4:30 in the morning. I've been up for 20 hours. The sun will rise before we can finish the scene, which is making everybody grumpy. It's so cold that my hands hurt. I've needed to pee for the last three hours. It starts to rain. I will get ten hours off, including travel to and from home. I will come back the next day to do it again. Why do I like this so much?

Every member of the cast and crew contributes to a film's production, but script supervising is one of the few jobs on set where you can see—and are able to understand and help shape—the big picture. I used to work in the camera department. In between my work, I would try to get a little time to watch the director, actors, and cinematographer, hoping to understand what they were up to. These chances were rare, as they are for most of the crew. Now that I am a script supervisor, that stuff is exactly my territory.

As collaborative as filmmaking is, everyone on the shooting crew ultimately serves the director. For that to work, the director needs many lieutenants. There is a web of authority that centers on the director and spreads out to the shooting crew. The camera, electric, and grip crews get direction through the cinematographer; the set dressers get their direction by way of the production designer, etc. Each department has a head that works with the director.

Even though we don't have a department, script supervisor is one of those positions near the director. Just as the assistant director oversees the physical production for all the departments, the script supervisor oversees the story and narrative context for all the departments. We sit next to the director all day. We understand how they want the story to flow. We articulate and influence that flow. We manage and facilitate the information necessary to make that happen and pass this information on to the rest of the crew.

DOI: 10.4324/9780367823665-1

This is the best thing about being a script supervisor: our specialty is storytelling. It is our job to understand the bones and the spirit of the story. We imagine all the little bits of the movie we are making: what they look like and sound like, how they move, and how they impact each other when they are put together. We carry around a living, growing movie in our imagination. This is continuity, and a whole lot more.

> We carry around a **living, growing movie** in our imagination.

WHAT A SCRIPT SUPERVISOR DOES

There are three basic parts to our job. First, we analyze and supervise the script. Second, we are in charge of continuity. Third, we are technical advisors for the grammar of filmmaking. The sort of project we are supervising and the needs and sensibilities of our fellow filmmakers will affect the specifics of these tasks.

Supervising the Script

A typical feature film will take months to shoot. A long-running episodic drama may take years. During that time, the cast and crew will make tens of thousands of decisions. It is easy for anyone to get lost in the details. Scripts are the road maps of the story, and we script supervisors help our fellow filmmakers stay on course.

> **Our job:**
> 1. Analyze and supervise the script
> 2. In charge of continuity
> 3. Advisors for the grammar of filmmaking

At the most basic level, supervising the script is "holding book," as they say in the theater, following the dialog and action in the script as it is being performed on set. We remind the cast and crew what is on the page and what happens just before or after the current scene in the script. We note changes in the script as they happen.

The more sophisticated part of supervising is analyzing the script. Before shooting starts, we study the script for clues that reveal how the story moves through time, space, and emotion. We note key moments in the storytelling, flagging and resolving discrepancies. We understand the director's intent for each story beat and disseminate key information to crew members.

During shooting, we make sure that whatever is important in the director's vision of the script gets into the finished product in an appropriate manner. We track what is recorded and adjust the road map as the story evolves.

In Charge of Continuity

Movies are almost never shot in story order. Instead we record little bits of picture and sound whenever it makes the most financial sense. Shooting this way makes it easy to record media with small variations that are unremarkable on set but jarring (or worse) when the movie is cut together. It is the script supervisor's job to recognize variations in the material and to know which will be trouble and which will be okay.

There are two kinds of continuity: matched action, which is continuity within a scene; and progressive action, which is continuity between scenes. Both kinds have many aspects, which we will cover later in detail. Here is a short introduction.

CONTINUITY WITHIN A SCENE: MATCHED ACTION

Script supervisors match action within scenes, so that two or more camera angles taken at different times appear to be different views of the same moment. This includes matching the movement and dialog of actors, the placement and handling of props and set dressing, the choice and arrangement of wardrobe, of makeup and hair, and sometimes of light and atmospheric conditions.

CONTINUITY BETWEEN SCENES: PROGRESSIVE ACTION

We track big dramatic arcs from scene to scene. We chart physical, emotional, and logical developments from the beginning to the end of the story. Script supervisors make a timeline for the story that includes every scene, and sometimes action that happens outside the script. The entire crew will use this timeline to plan lighting and wardrobe changes, set dressing, makeup design, and the like.

Technical Advisor for the Grammar of Filmmaking

There is a language of cinema that, like all languages, has grammatical rules. Each film uses grammar differently, in its own fashion. This difference is one of the things that makes filmmaking an art. We script supervisors are the on-set authority of standard film grammar and a backup for our own project's unique film grammar.

BASIC SCRIPT SUPERVISING SKILLS

Understanding Cinematic Language

It is essential that script supervisors understand how films are constructed and how the director sees the particular material at hand. From the outside, it might look like script supervisors are secretaries taking dictation. Some people think of us as taskmasters who try to make everyone follow "the rules" of coverage. We do take a lot of notes and we do know the rules. But if we wrote down everything we saw in front of us, our notes would be too vast and chaotic to be of any use. If we followed the rules by rote, we would foster frustration and tedious filmmaking. Our fluency and mastery of cinematic language is the foundation that makes us valuable to our cast and crew.

> **Basic script supervising skills:**
> 1. Understanding cinematic language
> 2. Artistic and personal sensitivity
> 3. Good organization
> 4. Paying attention for long periods of time
> 5. Intensity and ease
> 6. Thick skin

Artistic and Personal Sensitivity

Because we act as a safety net for the cast and crew, including all of the big creative players, we often have to bring to their attention mistakes they have made or things they have forgotten. This takes a lot of tact and personal as well as artistic sensitivity. We need to know how to approach as an ally, not a critic. We need to recognize when to give a note so it doesn't interrupt an actor or crew member's concentration.

Good Organization

Script supervisors track thousands of details. All those details have to be understood and organized so that important information is quickly available on set and clear in the editing room. A script supervisor needs to be attentive, logical, and creative, able to follow, adapt, and design systems, and must be succinct in spoken and written language.

Paying Attention for Long Periods of Time

Most filmmakers have a rhythm of intensely focused work broken by periods of downtime. That is almost never the case for script supervisors. We pay attention all day long. When we are not shooting, we are prepping, reviewing, or writing notes. A good script supervisor will use breaks in the action to anticipate a problem or question before it is asked, and will be ready with the answer as soon as a question comes up.

Intensity and Ease

We script supervisors don't have an area of our own authority. We watch and assist everyone else's work. This takes a delicate balance between intensity and ease, which is essential to almost every task we do. We rely on critical thinking but never display a critical attitude.

We must be able to think on our feet, track every aspect of production, and react in real time. Often there is a question that only we can answer, the entire crew waiting to hear what we say before they can resume work. Sometimes we have a technical objection that stops the work cold. We must speak up and be clear and confident in our opinions. We must also be ready to let go of our objections entirely when the director does not share them.

Thick Skin

You may work with a director or actor who is stressed and shoots some of that your way. Creative work sometimes makes it necessary to operate from emotion, which can get out of hand. Script supervisors need to be able to distinguish process from abuse, support the former, and walk away from the latter.

Chapter 2
Getting Started

BUILDING SCRIPT SUPERVISING SKILLS

Most filmmaking crafts are learned by apprenticeship. New filmmakers start as production assistants (PAs) in the camera or prop department and advance within that department. Script supervisors are almost always a department of one. There are very few chances for us to apprentice. We usually start working on small projects with other beginners and move up project by project instead of within a department. For the most part, we are responsible for training ourselves.

Getting Basic Skills

We learn basic skills from reading books like this, talking to more experienced script supervisors, taking workshops (in person or online), and volunteering on student movies, micro-budget features, web shows, promotional pieces, and podcasts. There are several robust script supervisor communities on social media that are willing to answer questions from beginners. They present a nuanced picture of the profession and are worth following even if you don't have any immediate questions. There are many video tutorials and other online postings about specific topics. Check the experience and credibility of the author before you take what they have to say seriously.

The New York Script Supervisors Network and the Los Angeles Script Supervisors Network are both excellent resources for new and experienced script supervisors alike. I encourage anyone working in the field to join one of these supportive and inspiring organizations. The film union IATSE also has lots of educational programs. Once you are up and running, joining the union is beneficial to you personally and to the craft in general.

Putting Your Skills to Work

Chances are, if you are thinking about being a script supervisor, you have some filmmaking experience already. Maybe you know something about setting shots, editing, crew dynamics, performance, etc. All these

DOI: 10.4324/9780367823665-2

experiences will help you be a better script supervisor. If you are working on a production as you read this book, you can multiply your knowledge by relating what you are reading to what is happening on set. If you direct little movies, think about what you would like from a script supervisor.

If you are working as a production assistant on a film that has a script supervisor, they may be able to answer some questions or let you look over their notes. Do this only when things are not busy. Keep your questions as specific as possible. If you are working on a non-union shoot, and there is a second unit or VFX crew, volunteer to take notes on that splinter unit. If you have more experience, knowledge, or interest than anyone else available, you may get a chance to work under a more experienced script supervisor.

If you make friends with a working script supervisor, they may be in a position to have you shadow them at work. If that happens, you are lucky. Be gracious. Stay close enough to follow the work, but be sure you do not get in the way.

> **Building basic skills:**
> 1. Read books like this and search the internet
> 2. Talk to script supervisors on set and in professional organizations
> 3. Take workshops
> 4. Work on small projects
> 5. Watch what is happening on set
> 6. Volunteer to keep notes on a splinter unit

HOW TO GET A JOB

Hiring in the film business is mostly done through networking. Someone knows someone who needs a script supervisor. Someone else knows someone else who wants to work as a script supervisor. If you want to be a script supervisor, tell everyone you know.

My husband, John Tintori, got his first job on a feature film from a guy who was a cook in the restaurant where I was waitressing. The cook's dad was an expat Russian film director driving a cab in New York City. The cook was going to be the production manager of a small film made by a bunch of his dad's friends. This turned out to be the cult classic *Liquid Sky*. John was hired as the key grip and his feature film career was launched. So really—tell everyone. You never know where your first job will come from.

If you can afford it, volunteer as a script supervisor on small projects. Student films, independent labors of love, and internet content often need lots of free help, and are usually pretty forgiving about beginner's mistakes. If you do, a few good things will happen: you will get practice, you will build a

résumé, and you will meet people who are making content. If
you do a good job, the next time
someone on the crew is looking for a script supervisor, your
name will be mentioned. Try
to find projects and crews that

> **Getting the first job:**
> 1. Tell everyone you know
> 2. Volunteer on small projects
> 3. Get other work on movie sets

match your sensibilities. New contacts are built on old contacts. Careers
have momentum. When you can, try to steer your work towards a career
that you think will be satisfying.

If you can't work as a script supervisor right away, try to get some other
work on a movie set, TV show, or commercial. This will introduce you to more
filmmakers and give you a chance to watch how films are made. Production
companies are looking for smart, hard workers with practical skills. Do you
have a driver's license? Can you build things? Paint? Sew? Do you know Photoshop? If you work well in any capacity, people will notice. Make yourself
valuable and tell everyone, "But what I really want to do is script supervise."

WHAT SORT OF PROJECTS ARE RIGHT FOR YOU?

There are many types of projects that use script supervisors. Once you start
making connections, whatever work you do will lead to more work of the
same. Knowing the options early on can help you craft a professional path
that provides you with a happy life.

Feature Films

I have spent my career in feature films. This book is centered on this sort
of script supervising. I like working on features because they provide an
opportunity to dig deep into the story and the craft of each project. Production lasts anywhere from 20 to 120 days, long enough to absorb and live in
the movie as it is being assembled. Script supervisors work next to the director and can share a great deal of the director's process.

The main drawback of this work comes from the same place. Working
on features is very intense. Work takes over your life during production. The
hours are long and hard, leaving very little time and energy between shoot
days. Very often, you have to travel away from home for months at a time.

Single-Camera Episodic and Serials

These are the sort of TV shows that look like a series of short movies. We call
them "single-camera" (even when there is more than one camera shooting

at once) to distinguish them from multi-camera series, below, which use a very different production method.

Working on single-camera episodics is similar to working on features. The prep and daily rhythm of rehearsal and shooting are the same. Script supervisors can have the same intimacy with the story, but since most shows (not all!) have guest directors, there is less chance to mind-meld with the director. The showrunner is the leading creative. This may be a producer or head writer. Actors on a series have more creative power than on features, and there is an opportunity to work more closely with them. If the showrunner recognizes the script supervisor as a filmmaker who understands a long-running show, there is sometimes an opportunity to move into directing.

Old-fashioned TV shows were made of episodes that stood alone, like a series of shorts. More common these days are episodes that work together as a serial, each episode building on the story from the last. Practically, this makes one very long script for us to track. It is hard work made harder by the practice of "cross-boarding," shooting material for more than one episode at a time.

The crew is hired for the season, so a single project can last for several months. When a series runs for many seasons, it can mean years of steady work with a crew you know and work with well. A typical episode will shoot for ten days. The hours can be just as grueling as a feature. The practice of "Fraturday" (a Friday that doesn't end until Saturday) started in episodic and is too often a standard of the production schedule. Some shows split the work, using two crews—one crew prepping while the other shoots. This gives you a few days off between episodes, which may keep you from burning out. Most of the shooting will be in one production center, so there is very little out-of-town travel.

Multi-Camera Sitcoms

These are the sort of comedy series that look like they happen on a stage. Three or four cameras shoot at the same time in one basic direction, with lighting that works for all cameras. Production is organized by acts instead of set-ups. The cameras adjust position in real time as the action continues.

The script supervisor's work is tailored especially for this method. In general, we are the liaison between the set and production. We make the official notes for the writers during rehearsal and make sure the set crew has the latest rewrites. Along with the script, the most important breakdown we make is the "rundown," a document that lists each scene in order with running times. The entire shooting crew will use the rundown as a guide during rehearsal and shooting. Exact timing is important for shows that have commercial breaks, and continuity is less concerned with matched action than setting up each act properly.

The standard production period is five days for each episode, and works like a cross between a movie and a play. The first day may only last a few hours for a script supervisor—just a table read and production meeting. The work builds throughout the week with rehearsals, rewrites, and tech runs. The fourth day is long and the script is finalized with live run-throughs and pre-shoots. Day five is short but intense, with more pre-shoots and the final performance in front of a live audience.

This schedule can be very satisfying. The work builds to a crescendo of teamwork every week, followed by some easy days. A long-running show with a tight cast and crew can give you a stable professional base and a work community that feels like a theatrical production company.

Multi-Cam Live/Live-to-Tape

Live/live-to-tape shows are productions that contain elements of unscripted action, such as news broadcasts, talk shows, game shows, variety, and award shows. They may be a series or stand-alone events. Production on these shows is sort of a cross between a movie, a play, and a documentary. The set is configured similarly to a multi-cam sitcom shoot: many cameras shooting into a stage-like area.

Here, production is organized by segments. Blocks of time are scheduled for introductions, musical performances, comedy skits, playback clips, or interviews. The rundown is central for live/live-to-tape shows, and is the most helpful breakdown during the preproduction period. Script supervisors create detailed rundowns and format scripts which the production team will use when rehearsing and shooting. We are responsible for making sure the teleprompter operator is current, and taking notes for the editor. Shows that have lots of fast rewrites sometimes have more than one script supervisor at once.

The advantages to this work are similar to working on a multi-camera sitcom: a physically comfortable work environment, steady work with a familiar team, and the rush of putting out live content.

Commercials and Promos

Commercials come in all styles, shapes, and sizes: tabletop, testimonial, documentary, dramatic, comedy, avant-garde, anything! Mostly, they have short production schedules and pay very well. The crew is hired for each spot, but commercial houses like to keep a group of familiar crew members, so if you are associated with a commercial house that works a lot, you can have steady work with time off between projects. The work is generally very straightforward and can pay better than any other area of script supervising.

MEETING THE DIRECTOR

Script supervisors work with a lot of people on set, but the people they interact with most are the director (on a movie) and the lead producer or showrunner (on a series). That's why, on feature films, it is almost always the director who will hire you. On a series

> **What the director/showrunner is thinking:**
> 1. Is this person competent?
> 2. Does this person understand what I am trying to achieve?
> 3. Can I stand being next to this person for 14 hours a day?

or commercial, it will be the producer or showrunner. Someone from production will call you to set up an interview.

When the director or showrunner meets you, they will be thinking about three things: "Is this person competent?" "Does this person understand what I am trying to achieve?" and "Can I stand being next to this person for 14 hours a day?" Your job in the interview is to convince the director "yes," "yes," and "yes." Here's my strategy:

Read the script(s) at least twice. Knowing the script gives you and the director/showrunner some common ground to talk about. I find that without a script to refer to, the interview becomes all theory and gossip. This is not how you want to present yourself. If a production is afraid of script bootlegging and won't send scripts out, ask if you can come to the production office and read them in-house. As you read, look for questions that can lead to a good discussion in the interview: is there something interesting in the time structure, visual effects, or tone? Whatever draws you to the script is worth talking about, and that conversation will give you a better understanding of what is important to the director.

Find out everything you can about the director/showrunner's work. If they have made other projects, watch them. If not, what other work is there that can give you a clue to their aesthetics? A person who comes from writing will have scripts or books. An actor will have performances. A cinematographer will have content that they have shot. Think about how that past work could relate to the script you are reading. You won't know exactly, of course, but you will know enough to ask the questions that could lead to an understanding. Also, doing that research will give you additional material in common, providing more opportunities for engaging conversation. Make sure to mention your own past work if it relates to an issue at hand.

Your research will also pay off during the shoot. The more you understand the project's aesthetic, the less will have to be explained to you. This is a big plus for everyone. If they get the feeling in the interview that you understand or will understand what they are up to, they will know everyone's day on set will be a lot easier, and they will want to hire you.

Remember, even if you don't get the job, you've just met a new group of filmmakers. If they thought enough of you to set up an interview, they will probably hold on to your résumé for another time.

> **Make the most of your interview:**
> 1. Know the script(s)
> 2. Find out about the director/showrunner's work
> 3. Relate past work to the current script

Getting hired on a short, micro-budget feature or web series is not that different. If there isn't a finished script to read, see if you can get a written treatment, lookbook, or a list of other reference material—anything that can give you some understanding of the work ahead.[1] If the director or showrunner doesn't have previous work, ask whoever you know on the production what they have learned about the project. The director or showrunner may have an internet presence that could tell you something. The goal is the same—to walk into the meeting with some idea about the project that can lead to an interesting and lively conversation.

If you are up for a job with an established episodic series, watch previous episodes. Think about what makes the series special. Which characters, dramatic elements, and themes do you find compelling? Why?

Live/live-to-tape shows and sitcoms sometimes hire script supervisors from inside the company. If you are working on a show and have a good working relationship with the creative producer or head writer, there may be a chance to move into script supervising. Make sure the people doing the hiring know that you are hoping to do that. Understanding a show from the inside is a big advantage, for both the hiring and the actual work.

MAKING YOUR DEAL

Even if the director/showrunner hires you, a producer or production manager will call and offer you the job. Be prepared for this call by figuring out what you will ask for ahead of time. If you are in a union, it makes things easier. There is a minimum hourly rate, adjusted for budget and format, which will probably be what they offer. If you are experienced and in demand, you can ask for more than the minimum, but not a lot more.

Keep notes about what was agreed upon in this conversation. When you go to the production office, you will fill out a crew deal memo and should have the details of your deal at hand.

Hourly Rate

If you are talking about a non-union job, the rate could be anything. Think about how much (or little) you want the job, what you want to be paid, and what you would settle for. Remember to include time for preproduction, daily homework, and wrap. Are they paying by the hour or a flat daily rate? What is the overtime provision? If it is a flat rate, is there a maximum number of work hours allowed? Will there be travel involved? If so, will you be paid for your travel time?

Kit Rental

One way script supervisors raise their rate is by asking for a kit fee, also called a "box rental." This is an additional payment charged per day or per week that helps to maintain and replace the equipment we own and use for the job. The kit fee is not in the union contract, so it is more negotiable than most of the other points of your deal.

As electronics have become a bigger part of our job, our kit fees have gotten bigger. If the production is fully funded, and you are using your own computer, tablet, software, scanner, and printer, a kit fee of $10 a day is minimum. It can go to $100 a day or more for an experienced, in-demand script supervisor with a lot of equipment.

Equipment houses usually price their rentals on the "100 day rule," which says that the value of the equipment should equal 100 days of rental fees. Production is used to this formula, so it is a good place to start. It can

---

Be prepared to make a deal:
1. Rate
2. Include prep, homework, and wrap
3. If flat rate, what are the maximum hours?
4. If hourly, what's the overtime rate?
5. Travel
6. Kit fee
7. Keep notes about what was agreed

be adjusted by the size of the production and the experience of the script supervisor. You will need a list of all your equipment, including the serial numbers and value of each piece.

YOU HAVE THE JOB

Knowing the Script

Regardless of format, it's your job to know the script better than anyone else on set.

FEATURES

Read a feature script at least three times before you start your breakdowns. Read it front to back, all in one sitting. Give some time between reads. Each time you read it, you will notice something new. If you've read it twice before meeting the director, your next read will incorporate what you've learned from your interview. You should have at least a week to understand and learn the script before shooting starts.

EPISODIC

Episodic scripts are sometimes written as an entire season before any shooting starts. An established show might be more spontaneous, with new scripts published during production and tweaked at the last minute. Script supervisors generally have three days of prep per episode but that is not an absolute rule. You may, at times, get a script on the first day of shooting and subsequent rewrites all week. Knowing the world of the show (its characters, visual style, and dramatic tensions) gives you a head start and can make this situation workable, if not ideal.

MULTI-CAMERA

A multi-camera live show, like a game show, news, variety, or sitcom, will be rewritten every day, sometimes several times a day. You might get the first draft the morning of your first day or the night before. You will keep notes during rehearsals and make the official changes to the script yourself.

COMMERCIALS

Likewise, commercials scripts and storyboards will come to you at the last minute. You will spend your set-up time in the beginning of the day studying them.

The Production Office

By the time the script supervisor is hired, the production office is up and running. During production, I will be in constant contact with the office, but there are surprisingly few chances to spend time there interacting face to face, so even if I start doing my breakdowns at home, I like to go in and say hello to everyone before shooting starts.

PRODUCTION OFFICE STAFF

See the production office coordinator (POC) and set up a procedure for distributing your daily reports and notes. If you are working with pen and paper, there will be someone on set, usually the second second assistant director (2nd 2nd AD) or the Director's Guild trainee, taking information from you for production (see more about this in Chapter 9, "Lunch" on page 305, and "End of the Day Notes" on page 307). The production office will keep a copy of your notes on file and distribute other copies to the edit room, producers, and the studio—anyone who needs them. If you are distributing your notes electronically, coordinate with the POC as to who gets what notes, what method you will use, and when that will happen.

The production office will supply you with expendables: office supplies, exterior drives, photo paper, anything that you need and will use up or turn in on this project. This doesn't include equipment like scanners, computers, printers, and the like. These are part of the kit you will rent to production for your kit fee. Most productions have an account with an office supply store and prefer you to order from them, through the office. The assistant production coordinator (APOC) can tell you which office production assistant is in charge of that. If you need something unusual or hard to find, ask if you can get it yourself and get reimbursed.

PAYROLL

The first time you visit the office, you will get a packet of start paperwork from the payroll accountant. This will include a deal memo, the first week's time card, equipment rental forms, tax forms, and information sheets about company policies. A US production will ask for proof that you can work in the United States, so bring ID. A passport, or a driver's license plus a social security card, will do for a US citizen. If you are not a US citizen, you will need work papers. They are very strict about this. Look over everything before you leave and ask the payroll accountant about anything that isn't clear to you.

ASSISTANT DIRECTORS

The assistant directors (ADs) start work long before we do and will already have all sorts of breakdowns that show how they're thinking about the project. I take anything that might help get me up to speed. This includes shooting schedules, location breakdowns, cast lists, and the like. Ask the first AD if they have any immediate concerns about the timeline of the script. If there is a concern, try to resolve it early in your prep period.

I also pick up a crew list and try to start learning names.

OTHER DEPARTMENTS

Introduce yourself to the other department heads who are working at the production office, particularly the costume designer, the heads of the hair and makeup departments, the prop master, and production designer. If any of them have continuity or story time concerns, it is helpful to have advanced notice.

NOTE

1   A lookbook is a collection of images that is assembled in prep to illustrate the visual tone and themes of a project.

Chapter 3
A Note about Digital Workflow

PAPER IS THE NEW PAPYRUS

In the foreword of this book, David Mamet reminds us that technology must be used mindfully. For example through-the-lens video feed can be helpful, even necessary, but it encourages the bad habit of setting up monitors away from set, where "deluded moderns watch, neither a film nor the making of a film, but a television show, compressed, in size and complexity resembling only remotely that image which may be seen on the Big Screen." Nuance and liveliness get lost in compression.

Mr. Mamet wrote that foreword before digital tablets were available and WiFi was ubiquitous. At that time he sent me a note that included a wry exaggeration of this situation: "Paper is the new papyrus." Ten years later, that world is here. A huge amount of the work we used to do on paper we now do on digital devices. This future, showing up so soon, is my motivation for writing this new edition.

TWO CAMPS ABOUT DIGITAL WORKFLOW

As I started the research for this edition, in early 2020, I met with members of the New York Script Supervisors Network to find out what digital applications they were using and how satisfied they were with the various options. Members—mostly younger and newer members—shared dozens of applications, applications that most everyone else—digital users and not—had never heard of. Older, more experienced members seemed skeptical about the entire digital workflow idea. It became clear that there were strong, opposing opinions around this issue.

One camp argued that a digital workflow is the only way to work. Digital applications automatically complete tasks that are tedious and time-consuming, leaving more time for the nuanced part of our work.

The other camp argued that the practice of using digital applications is perverting our craft. Because digital systems are really good at the record-keeping part of our job, record-keeping has started to overshadow

DOI: 10.4324/9780367823665-3

the more important filmmaking and storytelling parts. Even worse, some new script supervisors learn how to use a digital platform and believe they are trained as script supervisors.

A lot has changed since that meeting. The most profound difference is that during the COVID-19 pandemic, script supervisors used their time away from set to explore various digital systems, to talk to each other, and to share information and recommendations. As part of this educational push, the New York Script Supervisors Network and I organized six panel discussions about working with a digital workflow. That was early in the lockdown. Since then, the script supervising community has held dozens of workshops, educational conferences, and tutorials. The conversation has evolved from two opposing camps into a very nuanced and sophisticated understanding about how and when to integrate digital components into our work.

EVERYONE USES EVERYTHING

The first big surprise in my research was that all script supervisors use a combination of digital applications *and* pen and paper. I expected those who use ScriptE or Peter Skarratt would use those systems exclusively. I thought script supervisors who preferred pen and paper would have no digital components in their workflow. I was wrong on both counts.

It is common for a ScriptE enthusiast to use the back of their sides to take scratch notes. Most devoted pen and paper users carry previous drafts or completed episodes as digital files. Almost everyone uses a separate spreadsheet application of some kind for at least some of their breakdowns. There is every variation of digital/analog workflow that you can imagine. No two are the same.

THERE IS NO STANDARD PLATFORM

The second surprising thing we found was that everyone has been patching together their own way of working, keeping their ears open for applications that sound promising, then trying them out, more or less on their own.

This makes sense. At this writing, there is no industry standard for us, no Final Draft or Movie Magic. Our craft is complicated. We use a wide array of skills: accounting, story analysis, precise observation, visual imagination, matching, interpersonal communication, the ability to make difficult judgment calls, and concise, clear writing. It will take a long time to develop a perfect digital fit for our incredibly wide skill set.

The good news is that application designers are making their systems better every day. More good news: they want feedback from script supervisors working in the field. You are invited to help shape your favorite applications by using them deliberately (with understanding and creativity) and maintaining an open and intelligent conversation with the designers and coders who make those systems.

DEVELOPING YOUR WORKFLOW

If you are just starting to work as a script supervisor, keep your on-set technical game as simple as possible. Use pen and paper for the first year or so and focus on your storytelling and filmmaking skills. You do not want to be in the middle of production trying to figure out why your application went south while the director, actors, or crew members are asking you for information or advice. You can build digital skills later, after you have mastered the more essential skills of observation and memory.[1]

Whatever digital systems are available by the time you are reading this, a general understanding of digital workflow systems will help you select which applications will be a good fit for the way you work and the task at hand. The most important concepts to understand are the differences between data banks and graphic-based functions and how they work together. Here is an explanation of this dynamic. I will try to keep the jargon to a minimum.

DATA BANKS VS. GRAPHIC-BASED FUNCTIONS

Data banks and graphic-based functions are two different ways of organizing and presenting information. Every application we use relies on both, in different combinations.

How Data Banks Work

Data banks are systems that organize information in a series of *cells* (aka *fields*, or *boxes*), which are assigned *categories* (aka *variables*, or *characteristics*), that are then filled with *values* (aka *information*, both numbers and words).

Fig. 3.1a Digital address book input page.

Fig. 3.1b Digital address book with input data.

August 10, 2020

Local 161
630 Ninth Avenue; Suite 1103
New York NY 10036

Dear Colleen;

Fig. 3.1c Letterhead.

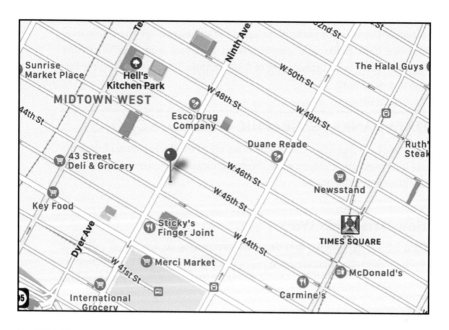

Fig. 3.1d Map.

A digital address book is a familiar example of this. It has a series of cells, and each cell is assigned a category: *First name* is one category; *Last name* is another; *Street, City, State, ZIP, Email address, Phone number*, etc., are all categories. These categories are filled with an appropriate value for each of our friends, relatives, and business contacts.

If you fill in the boxes correctly for each category, the values have meaning (see Fig. 3.1a). When a contact is saved, both the values and categories are included in the contact's data (see Fig. 3.1b). Now you have a sort of holding area, a bank of data, that can be exported in a number of different formats (sometimes called "reports"). Here are examples of two different formats for exporting the same data: a letterhead and a map (see Figs 3.1c and 3.1d). Notice how the graphic elements of the map increase our understanding of the data. The application recognizes the category (street address) and applies the value that was entered in those fields (street number and name, city, etc.). Another example of a report is the generation of a new text message. When you click on the *message* icon, a texting application opens, recognizes the category of *phone number* and uses the number logged in that field. If you click on the *mail* icon, an email application opens, using the contact's email address.

What Data Expression Means to Us

The ability to export data in a variety of different expressions is incredibly valuable for us. It can save hours of re-logging the same information on various reports. Information that is recorded on a facing page can be automatically exported as an editor's report or added to a daily production report. The set-up number entered in a lined script page may automatically show up on the facing page.

How Graphic-Based Functions Work

Graphically based systems work with visual information, not values like numbers and letters. For our purposes, you might think of data banks as having embedded information that can be displayed in a variety of formats without changing the essential value of that information. Graphic-based values are the display itself.[2]

> Data banks have embedded information which can be displayed in **a variety of formats** without changing the essential value of that information. Graphic-based values are the display itself.

Fig. 3.2 A digital drawing by Brooklyn artist Catherine Kunicki

This digital drawing by Brooklyn artist Catherine Kunicki is full of digital (visual) information. This visual information, detailed and specific, is not organized by categories, fields, or values, and will not be exported into reports as a data bank can.

How Data Banks and Graphic-Based Functions Work Together

Breakdowns that use spreadsheets are an easy-to-understand example of data and graphics working together.

The spreadsheet's data functions provide the categories: page count, running time, scene number, etc. Every scene has a line on the spreadsheet, with a cell for each category. Those cells are filled with meaningful values. Each value is expressed in a specific form: eighths for pages, minutes and seconds for time, numerical for scene numbers, etc. Just like the data in the digital address book, the data can be exported in several ways.

The grid layout is a graphic function that makes it easier to see relationships within the information set. Reading across a row helps us connect the various categories of information of each scene. Reading down a column connects all the scenes in a particular category. Understanding the relationships within the data is very important for the work we do, which is why the graphic elements of our breakdowns and reports are so important.

Below is a spreadsheet in its most basic form.

Master Breakdown

Sc	Pages	Run Time	SC #	I/E	D/N	Location	Characters	Action	Props/Set Dec/ VFX	Costume	Match
1	0.125	00:05	1	EXT	Dawn	Town Green		Town Green at dawn	Sprinkler on lawn		
1	0.125	00:10	2	EXT	Dawn	Town Green	Rosie, Petunia	Elderly woman walks a dog	Sprinkler on lawn, Very long leash	Baby blue sweater with sparkles	
1	0.250	00:13	3	EXT	Dawn	Coffee Shop	Rosie, Petunia	Rosie ties up Petunia and enters shop	Very Long leash	Baby blue sweater with sparkles	
1	0.375	00:20	4	INT	Dawn	Coffee Shop	Rosie, Petunia, Clerk	Rosie greets clerk and orders her regular.	Rosie's name on cup	Baby blue sweater with sparkles	
1	0.625	00:30	A4	INT	Dawn	Back Room	Stan, Lou	Stan and Lou unpack boxes. Lou tells Stan about his mom.	Boxes piled high		
1	0.500	00:32	5	EXT	Dawn	Coffee Shop	Rosie, Petunia	Rosie feeds Petunia her muffin. They walk away. Lou is watching Rosie.	Rosie's name on cup. Extra big muffin	Baby blue sweater with sparkles	
1	0.125	00:10	6	INT	Day	YMCA	Lou	Lou is working out	200# weights	Very sweaty gym clothes	
7	2.125	02:00									

Fig. 3.3 Basic spreadsheet.

Adding More Graphic Elements

Additional graphic elements can help us make more connections and distinctions within a data bank. These may include text styles, color fill, and outline options. These graphic elements do not change the value of the information.

Unlike the information in a data bank, you cannot sort based on graphic elements. They are display characteristics, attached to each cell, not to the data.

Here is the same spreadsheet with some added graphic elements.

Master Breakdown

Sc	Pages	Run Time	SC #	I/E	D/N	Location	Characters	Action	Props/Set Dec/ VFX	Costume	Match
1	0.125	00:05	1	EXT	Dawn	Town Green		Town Green at dawn	Sprinkler on lawn		
1	0.125	00:10	2	EXT	Dawn	Town Green	Rosie, Petunia	Elderly woman walks a dog	Sprinkler on lawn, Very long leash	Baby blue sweater with sparkles	
1	0.250	00:13	3	EXT	Dawn	Coffee Shop	Rosie, Petunia	Rosie ties up Petunia and enters shop	Very Long leash	Baby blue sweater with sparkles	
1	0.375	00:20	4	INT	Dawn	Coffee Shop	Rosie, Petunia, Clerk	Rosie greets clerk and orders her regular.	Rosie's name on cup	Baby blue sweater with sparkles	
1	0.625	00:30	A4	INT	Dawn	Back Room	Stan, Lou	Stan and Lou unpack boxes. Lou tells Stan about his mom.	Boxes piled high		
1	0.500	00:32	5	EXT	Dawn	Coffee Shop	Rosie, Petunia	Rosie feeds Petunia her muffin. They walk away. Lou is watching Rosie.	Rosie's name on cup. Extra big muffin	Baby blue sweater with sparkles	
1	0.125	00:10	6	INT	Day	YMCA	Lou	Lou is working out	200# weights	Very sweaty gym clothes	
7	2.125	02:00									

Fig. 3.4 Basic spreadsheet with added graphic elements.

Let's look at how these added graphic elements make it easier to navigate and understand the relationships within the data bank.

- The sheet's title, "Master Breakdown," presented here in the largest and boldest text, surrounded by lots of negative space, draws our attention first. Without even thinking, we recognize which breakdown this is.
- The column headings have a contrasting background shade to separate the heading row from the body of the sheet—an easy-to-find reference while looking around the form to compare and contrast values.
- Presenting the scene numbers as bold and larger than the rest makes them stand apart and serve as a spine for all the other information on this sheet. Whatever we are tracking in this breakdown, it is easy to spot the relevant scene number, helping us remain oriented as our eyes hop around the sheet. Giving this column a right justification helps set it apart too.
- In this particular breakdown, I have used the background shading of the scene rows to differentiate the interior and exterior scenes. This may be useful to track if the exterior scenes are on location and the interior are on a stage.[3]

Master Breakdown

Sc	Pages	Run Time	SC #	I/E	D/N	Location	Characters	Action	Props/Set Dec/ VFX	Costume	Match
1	1/8	00:05	1	EXT	Dawn	Town Green		Town Green at dawn	Sprinkler on lawn		
1	1/8	00:10	2	EXT	Dawn	Town Green	Rosie, Petunia	Elderly woman walks a dog	Sprinkler on lawn, Very long leash	Baby blue sweater with sparkles	
1	2/8	00:13	3	EXT	Dawn	Coffee Shop	Rosie, Petunia	Rosie ties up Petunia and enters shop	Very Long leash	Baby blue sweater with sparkles	
1	4/8	00:32	5	EXT	Dawn	Coffee Shop	Rosie, Petunia	Rosie feeds Petunia her muffin. They walk away. Lou is watching Rosie.	Rosie's name on cup. Extra big muffin	Baby blue sweater with sparkles	
1	3/8	00:20	4	INT	Dawn	Coffee Shop	Rosie, Petunia, Clerk	Rosie greets clerk and orders her regular.	Rosie's name on cup	Baby blue sweater with sparkles	
1	5/8	00:30	A4	INT	Dawn	Back Room	Stan, Lou	Stan and Lou unpack boxes. Lou tells Stan about his mom.	Boxes piled high		
1	1/8	00:10	6	INT	Day	YMCA	Lou	Lou is working out	200# weights	Very sweaty gym clothes	
7	2 1/8	02:00									

Fig. 3.5 Spreadsheet sorted with data for interior/exterior.

- The total scenes, pages, and run times are bold with a uniquely colored background to set that row apart from the rest.

- The boxed-in areas in the *Match* column group together consecutive scenes, showing that this group, scenes 1–5, are in tight continuity. Although scenes A4 and 6 share a character, the boxes make it clear that these two scenes are not in tight continuity.

A data bank that is clear and easy to navigate can give you new insight into the structure of your project. It also saves time when you need to look up information on set. A quick answer in a tense moment can make you a hero (or, at least, a competent professional).

> We add graphic elements to our data set in order to make it easier to read and navigate. **Good visual information can also clarify relationships within the data.**

Each Application Is Unique

Every digital application combines elements of data bank and graphic information differently. When you understand the way data banks and graphic functions work together, you will be able to recognize how various programs operate, and put together a digital workflow that will fit your personal work preferences and the particular project you are supervising.

Here is a short overview of the basic software choices available as I write this (in early 2022). Don't hold me to the specifics of any application. They will have shifted by the time you read this. I am including these specifics only as examples to illustrate how you might approach building your own personal workflow.

OFFICE SUITES

Office suites are bundles of general purpose paperwork and productivity software. They include applications for word processing, spreadsheets, note-taking, and slideshows, among various other applications. Common examples are Microsoft Office (Word, Excel, OneNote, PowerPoint), Apple iWork (Pages, Numbers, Keynote), Google Workspace (Docs, Sheets, Keep, Slides).

These general applications are the most flexible, least automated choices for us. If you are looking for a handcrafted workflow, they are a great choice. Here is a gorgeous spreadsheet designed by Sharon Watt for *Mr. Robot*.

WRAP BREAKDOWN | **MR ROBOT #403 // Dir: Sam Esmail** | **Script: DOUBLE WHITE 7/23/19**

SCRIPT DAYS: FBD1-FBD2 / D5 — This episode takes place the day after #402 : Xmas Eve, December 24th, 2015 [Sunrise 7:17am // Sunset 4:33pm], with flashbacks to 1982

SHOT ON	PAGE COUNT	PAGES SHOT	CREDIT TIMING	SCRIPT TIMING	Sc Shot	Tot Sc	SC	Script Day	TOD	DESCRIPTION		LOCATION	ADD'L CHARACTERS	HMU / WARDROBE	CONTINUITY
13-May	1 4/8	1 4/8	1:25	1:18	1	1	1	FBD1	TUES Apr 20 1982	YOUNG ZHANG flirts with translator CHEN PENG as he finalizes business partnership in Asia with unsuspecting IBM execs, paving the way to own the company's intellectual property	I	IBM CONFERENCE ROOM	CHEN PENG, MR GRAY, IBM execs	C: watch	IBM PC on pedestal
PINK							2-4			~~Zhang and Chen go clubbing; Zhang takes in the crowd's exuberance, then abruptly leaves~~					
3-May	4 1/8	4 1/8	7:15	5:43	1	1	A5	FBN1	Dusk 7:37p	Chen divines Zhang's fortune, predicts he will be named US ambassador and they can escape together; Chen explains he keeps to a schedule so that they have the time to be who they are	I	NYC HOTEL / HOTEL ROOM	Chen	C: watch, naked in blanket, Z: robe	Empty champagne bottle, bucket of ice, notepad, pen
3-May	2/8	2/8	0:40	0:30	1	1	B5	FBN1	Dusk to night	Chen leaves to have drinks with business executives; timelapse as sunlight fades to night - Chen returns, a little more relaxed	I	NYC HOTEL / HALLWAY	Chen	C: watch, rtns top button undone, tie loosened, hair less slick	
3-May	1 4/8	1 4/8	2:25	1:56	1	1	5	FBN1	9:25p	Chen enters a dark room, Zhang says there's a difference between controlling time and being a slave to it; Zhang reveals his true self - a young Whiterose; Chen is enamored, they kiss	I	NYC HOTEL / HOTEL ROOM	Chen	C: watch, Z: young Whiterose	Lamp turned ON for reveal
21-Jul	1 7/8	1 7/8	2:10	2:18	1	1	6	D5	WED Dec 24 9:11a	Zhang intends to wear the 1982 dress the day the project is shipped; Freddy's suicide and Price's resignation - Wang Shu suspects Elliot's involvement, requests patience to investigate	I	WHITEROSE'S NYC BROWNSTONE / PARLOR	Wang Shu	Z: watch	Match cut beg & end // 1982 dress, cigs, lighter
2-May	5/8	5/8	0:55	0:51	1	1	7	FBD2	1982	Zhang masks his jealousy as Chen's Bride-To-Be lights cigarettes for the male guests; she confides to him that Chen hasn't come out from his dressing room; Zhang slips away	I	BANQUET HALL - CHINA	Chen's Bride, wedding guests	Z: tux	Pre-wedding celebrations // Dish of cigs, matches, rice wine
3-May	3 3/8	3 3/8	5:05	4:17	1	1	8	FBD2	Cont.	Forced into a sham marriage, Chen is devastated they won't be able to escape to US as Zhang will be China's Minister of State Security; Zhang begs for patience but Chen commits suicide	I	BANQUET HALL / DRESSING ROOM - CHINA	Chen	Z: tux, C: watch, wedding tux, undone tie, tears	Knife, cheese plate, bottle of champagne, bouquet of white roses - bloodied
										MR ROBOT					
21-Jul	2	2	2:35	2:30	1	1	9	D5	Cont. from 6 9:14a	Zhang is officially out of patience; he orders a Deus meeting for tomorrow and instructs Wang Shu to promise Tyrell Wellick they will help retrieve his son if he takes over as E Corp CEO	I	WHITEROSE'S NYC BROWNSTONE / PARLOR	Wang Shu	Z: watch	As Sc. 6
										ACT 2					
6-Apr	2	2	2:05	2:13	1	1	10	D5	12:38p	VO: Russian Roulette, sooner or later Vera's coming // Elliot bumps into KRISTA and new BF; sternly she warns him they cannot be in contact, doesn't feel safe; DJ lurks and observes	E	NYC STREETS	JASON, DJ		E/backpack, DJ/phone [take photos!]
10-May	4 1/8	4 1/8	5:15	4:11	1	1	11	D5 Dusk	4:38p	Hacking Cyprus Bank's Olivia Cortez requires physical access; Elliot stops Darlene from coming with, the brutal truth - they were never a team; hurt, she backs off; Robot is concerned	I	ALLSAFE			E/backpack, E/laptop [Olivia Cortez], D/laptop, D/backpack, cigs, lighter
13-Jun	1	1	3:40	1:10	1	1	12	D5 Twilight	4:56p	VO: What do you call someone who's lost everyone? If you block everyone, what's the point? // Elliot and Robot search Olivia's apt, Robot finds her date's profile on her personal machine	I	OLIVIA'S APT / LIVING ROOM			Xmas stockings, Xmas tree and decs // E/backpack, lock picks, O/MacBook [Evan OKCupid], candy canes
13-Jun	1/8	1/8	0:00	0:14	1	1	13	D5 Twilight	Cont.	Elliot searches the bathroom, finds some Oxy	I	OLIVIA'S APT / BATHROOM			E/backpack, bottle of OxyCotin
13-Jun	2/8	2/8	0:00	0:12	1	1	14	D5 Twilight	Cont.	Fascinated, Robot reads all about Evan; Elliot re-enters, continues to bedroom	I	OLIVIA'S APT / LIVING ROOM			As Sc.12 // E/backpack
13-Jun	1 4/8	1 4/8	0:00	1:54	1	1	15	D5 Twilight	Cont. 4:58p	Elliot finds Olivia's work laptop and easily gains access but realizes the bank needs RSA authentication; he and Robot brainstorm how to get her security fob; Elliot has an idea	I	OLIVIA'S APT / BEDROOM			E/backpack, lock picks, E/laptop [Cyprus Bank, O/work laptop [login, PW manager], O/MacBook [Evan OKCupid]
										ACT 3					
2-Apr	2 7/8	2 7/8	2:25	2:30	1	1	16	N5	5:19p	Elliot and Robot observe that OLIVIA's been stood up; Elliot approaches, ready to blackmail a supposed reformed addict; Robot takes over, lays on the charm; Olivia says yes to a drink	I	NYC BAR	Waiter	O: watch, coat off	LED countdown clock w/sign, Xmas decs // O/phone [QR], Coke, purse, key chain w/fob, drink check, E/backpack
3-Jun	1/8	1/8	0:30	0:20	1	1	17	N5	5:34p	Close on the painting from #106: reveal a familiar restaurant; ISAAC enters and nervously heads towards the back	I	ADALINA'S RESTAURANTE	ISAAC		
3-Jun	4 7/8	4 7/8	5:15	5:54	1	1	18	N5	Cont.	VERA passes out drug stuffed Xmas chickens to the local kids, spreading fear and love; DJ brings photos of Elliot and Krista but not much else, Vera needs someone more detail oriented	I	ADALINA'S RESTAURANTE / KITCHEN	Isaac, JUANITO, MANNY, MIGUEL, JAVI, DJ	V: wrist scars, plastic gloves, blood splatter, DJ: shot in gut	Report cards, chickens, butcher paper, report cards, baggies of drugs, wiping rag, DJ/phone [Krista & Elliot], V/gun

Prepared by SHARON WATT, Script Supervisor // July 26th, 2019 — MR ROBOT S.4 — 1 of 2

Fig. 3.6 Gorgeous spreadsheet breakdown designed by Sharon Watt for *Mr. Robot*.

When I was working, office suites were all the digital software I needed. I usually worked on dense, multi-layered feature films. Non-automated prep and production gave me the best chance to study, analyze, and absorb my scripts. I was given enough time to do this and it worked very well.

SCRIPT SUPERVISING PLATFORMS

There are a handful of digital systems that are designed specifically for the work we do. The most popular at the time of writing are ScriptE, Peter Skarratt, and MovieSlate 8. Some tech-savvy script supervisors are building systems for themselves using FileMaker Pro. Each system is a bit different.

ScriptE is the most automated platform for script supervising at this moment. When importing a script formatted with categories (like Final Draft), ScriptE will recognize its data bank and transfer that data into your ScriptE documents. Categories in a digital script are recognized by the page formatting. For instance, ScriptE will recognize that certain words on the script page are formatted as speaking characters and populate its character list with the words (names) that are written in that formatting category. It will do the same for *Slug Lines, Location, Page Length,* etc.[4] See Fig. 3.7 for an example of the "General" form, auto-filled by ScriptE from a script with categories.

Scene #	Revision	INT/EXT	Set	Day/Ni...	Act	Day	Pages	Credited	Remaini...	Day Credited	Est. Time	Act. Time	Variance
10	PRODUCTI...	EXT	PI'S PRIMARY...	DAY			5/8	0/8	5/8		0:38	0:00	0:00
11	PRODUCTI...	I/E	SCHOOLYAR...				1/8	0/8	1/8		0:08	0:00	0:00
12	PRODUCTI...	INT	SCIENCE CLA...	DAY			1 3/8	0/8	1 3/8		1:22	0:00	0:00
14	PRODUCTI...	INT	FRENCH CLA...	DAY			2/8	0/8	2/8		0:15	0:00	0:00
15	PRODUCTI...	EXT	GEOGRAPHY...	DAY			2/8	0/8	2/8		0:15	0:00	0:00
16	PRODUCTI...	INT	SCHOOL HAL...	DAY			1/8	0/8	1/8		0:08	0:00	0:00
17	PRODUCTI...	INT	MATH CLASS...	CONTI...			3/8	0/8	3/8		0:23	0:00	0:00
19	PRODUCTI...	EXT	PONDICHERR...	DAY			2/8	0/8	2/8		0:15	0:00	0:00
20	PRODUCTI...	EXT	ASHRAM STR...	DAY			1/8	0/8	1/8		0:08	0:00	0:00
21	PRODUCTI...	EXT	PONDICHERR...	DAY			2/8	0/8	2/8		0:15	0:00	0:00
18	PRODUCTI...	INT	PI'S HOME	CONTI...			1/8	0/8	1/8		0:08	0:00	0:00
25	PRODUCTI...	EXT	ZOO ENTRAN...	DAY			2/8	0/8	2/8		0:15	0:00	0:00
26	PRODUCTI...	EXT	THE NURSERY	CONTI...			2/8	0/8	2/8		0:15	0:00	0:00
27	PRODUCTI...	INT	PI'S HOME, O...	DAY			5/8	0/8	5/8		0:38	0:00	0:00
28	PRODUCTI...	EXT	OUTSIDE THE...	NIGHT			2/8	0/8	2/8		0:15	0:00	0:00
29	PRODUCTI...	INT	PI'S BEDROO...	NIGHT			4/8	0/8	4/8		0:30	0:00	0:00
30	PRODUCTI...						1/8	0/8	1/8		0:08	0:00	0:00
34	PRODUCTI...						7/8	0/8	7/8		0:53	0:00	0:00
36	PRODUCTI...	EXT	MUNNAR TEA...	DAY			3/8	0/8	3/8		0:23	0:00	0:00
37	PRODUCTI...	INT	CATHOLIC C...	DAY			5/8	0/8	5/8		0:38	0:00	0:00
38	PRODUCTI...	INT	PI'S DINING R...	INTER...			1/8	0/8	1/8		0:08	0:00	0:00
39	PRODUCTI...	EXT	PLANTATION...	DAY			1/8	0/8	1/8		0:08	0:00	0:00
41	PRODUCTI...	INT	CATHOLIC C...	DAY	41		3/8	0/8	3/8		0:23	0:00	0:00
42	PRODUCTI...	INT	PI'S BEDROO...	DAY			2/8	0/8	2/8		0:15	0:00	0:00
43	PRODUCTI...	EXT	MUSLIM QUA...	DAY			2/8	0/8	2/8		0:15	0:00	0:00

Scenes	111	Scripted Pages	72 3/8	Total Est. Time	72:44
Credited	2	Credited Pages	2 5/8	Total Act. Time	2:38
Remaining	109	Remaining	69 6/8	Running Time	70:06	Projected 72:44

Title LIFE OF PI — *Episode* 1 — Timecode Started: 5/26/22 10:58:52

Fig. 3.7 ScriptE general form. Auto-filled from a script with categories (from Tony Pettine).

Of course, you have to check these breakdowns. There are elements that an automated data transfer will not catch. For example, non-speaking characters, which are formatted differently from speaking characters, will not be recognized. You will have to add these by hand. Still, the preliminary automation can save hours of prep work. See Fig. 3.8 for a detailed form with additional information added by hand. In ScriptE's shooting mode, there is a third input page to enter data collected during production. Some of it is automated (like timecode) and some of it is entered by hand (like director's comments). See Fig. 3.9 for an example of a shooting mode input page.

People who supervise episodic series with lots of last-minute rewrites love this system. If a new draft comes in on the day it will be shot, there is no time to make new breakdowns by hand. The limited, module design makes it easy to coordinate notes with other script supervisors, if they also are using ScriptE.

The trade-off with ScriptE is that it is quite rigid. You fill in category fields and the values populate various reports. The system's graphic elements are less flexible. But its bare-bones nature is what makes it so fast. This may have changed by the time you read this. The system is getting updated in wonderful ways all the time, so check it out yourself. If you are looking for a super-efficient system, this might be a good choice.

Peter Skarratt is what script supervisors call an unnamed application developed by Peter Skarratt, an assistant editor from New Zealand. He has

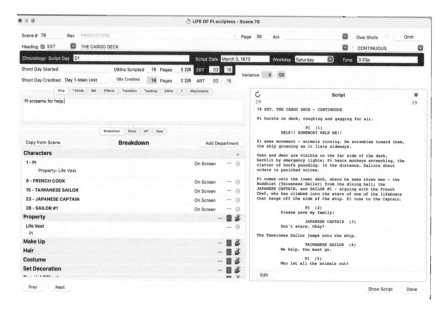

Fig. 3.8 ScriptE detailed form. Auto-filled with additional information added by hand (from Tony Pettine).

a FileMaker Pro-based system that can import data from digital scripts as well. It is a bit less automated than ScriptE and a bit more flexible. It makes better use of available graphic elements as described earlier in this chapter. I find the holistic layout of Peter's forms to be easier to grasp, imagine, and work with than the pop-up boxes of the ScriptE and MovieSlate 8 systems.

This is a great system for working on feature films and series that give you enough time to do a proper prep. It automates the bookkeeping aspects of the work in production without isolating data in pop-up cells.

MovieSlate 8 is a system designed to be used across multiple departments: camera, sound, and video playback. There is a division of software for script supervisors that interfaces nicely within the larger system. It is a great choice for projects like live/live-to-tape shoots where the entire crew works with the script supervisor's notes. It also has great shortcuts for entering notes, making it the number one choice for non-scripted shows and documentary-style commercials.

This system moves us farther away from data banks and closer to graphic systems. You must log information from your scripts by hand, even the

⏱ LIFE OF PI - Shoot Days

Shoot Days   Day 1   Unit: Main Unit   Date: 5/23/22

Report Group 1
Day 1 - 5/23/22
Main Unit

Slates | Scenes Shot Today | Setups | Wild Tracks | Weather | On Set Notes | Editor Notes | Production

Settings	Slate	Camera	Take #	Scene(s)	VFX	VFX Notes	Shot Look	Photos	Shot Description	CR
Modify	78	A	1	78	✓	#00082	wide	None	Crane - wide shot - PI runs to side of lower deck - WIDE PI runs from stern to rail. Camera swings over railing and ocean. *** VFX #00082 ***	A11
Modify		C	1	78	✓	#00082	mcu	None	CLOSER -- med/wide into mcu PI - (runs for takes 1-2, 6&7)	C11
Modify		A	2	78	✓	#00082	wide	None	Crane - wide shot - PI runs to side of lower deck - WIDE PI runs from stern to rail. Camera swings over railing and ocean. *** VFX #00082 ***	A11
Modify		C	2	78	✓	#00082	mcu	None	CLOSER -- med/wide into mcu PI - (runs for takes 1-2, 6&7)	C11
Modify		A	3	78	✓	#00082	wide	None	Crane - wide shot - PI runs to side of lower deck - WIDE PI runs from stern to rail. Camera swings over railing and ocean. *** VFX #00082 ***	A11
Modify		C	3	78	✓	#00082	mcu	None	CLOSER -- med/wide into mcu PI - (runs for takes 1-2, 6&7)	C11
Modify		A	4	78	✓	#00082	wide	None	Crane - wide shot - PI runs to side of lower deck - WIDE PI runs from stern to rail. Camera swings over railing and ocean. *** VFX #00082 ***	A11
Modify		C	4	78	✓	#00082	mcu	None	CLOSER -- med/wide into mcu PI - (runs for takes 1-2, 6&7)	C11
Modify		A	5	78	✓	#00082	wide	None	Crane - wide shot - PI runs to side of lower deck - WIDE PI runs from stern to rail. Camera swings over railing and ocean. *** VFX #00082 ***	A11
Modify		C	5	78	✓	#00082	mcu	None	CLOSER -- med/wide into mcu PI - (runs for takes 1-2, 6&7)	C11
Modify		A	6	78	✓	#00082	wide	None	Crane - wide shot - PI runs to side of lower deck - WIDE PI runs from stern to rail. Camera swings over railing and ocean. *** VFX #00082 ***	A11
Modify		C	6	78	✓	#00082	mcu	None	CLOSER -- med/wide into mcu PI - (runs for takes 1-2, 6&7)	C11
Modify		A	7	78	✓	#00082	wide	None	Crane - wide shot - PI runs to side of lower deck - WIDE PI runs from stern to rail. Camera swings over railing and ocean. *** VFX #00082 ***	A11
Modify		C	7	78	✓	#00082	mcu	None	CLOSER -- med/wide into mcu PI - (runs for takes 1-2, 6&7)	C11
Modify		A	8	78	✓	#00082	wide	None	Crane - wide shot - PI runs to side of lower deck - WIDE PI runs from stern to rail. Camera swings over railing and ocean. *** VFX #00082 ***	A11
Modify		C	8	78	✓	#00082	mcu	None	CLOSER -- med/wide into mcu PI - (runs for takes 1-2, 6&7)	C11
Modify	78A	A	1	78		#00082	cu	None	Crane M/W to cu - PI steps out on lower deck *vfx remove wire for door closing (focus best starting at take #6)	A11
Modify		A	2	78	✓		cu	✓	Crane M/W to cu - PI steps out on lower deck *vfx remove wire for door closing	A11

Delete Selected Slate   Add New Slate

Delete   On   Add   Total Slates: 4   Total Clips: 32

Fig. 3.9 ScriptE shooting mode input page (from Tony Pettine).

Fig. 3.10 Peter Skarratt uses a facing page layout for data input (from Lori Grabowski).

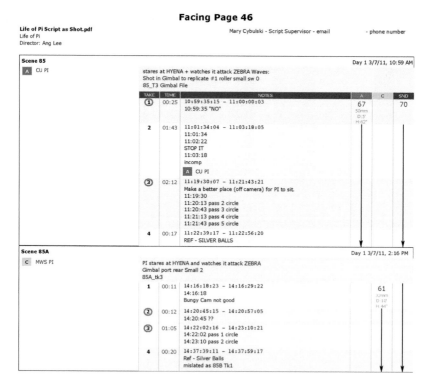

Fig. 3.11 MovieSlate 8 facing page (from Sean Pollock).

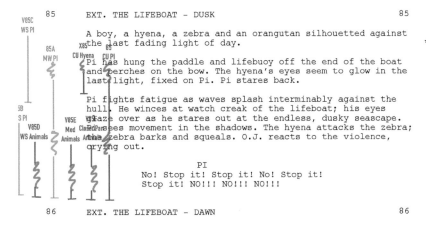

85   EXT. THE LIFEBOAT - DUSK   85

A boy, a hyena, a zebra and an orangutan silhouetted against
the last fading light of day.   *

Pi has hung the paddle and lifebuoy off the end of the boat
and perches on the bow. The hyena's eyes seem to glow in the
last light, fixed on Pi. Pi stares back.

Pi fights fatigue as waves splash interminably against the
hull. He winces at watch creak of the lifeboat; his eyes
glaze over as he stares out at the endless, dusky seascape.
He sees movement in the shadows. The hyena attacks the zebra;
the zebra barks and squeals. O.J. reacts to the violence,
crying out.

                    PI
          No! Stop it! Stop it! No! Stop it!
          Stop it! NO!!! NO!!! NO!!!

86   EXT. THE LIFEBOAT - DAWN   86

Silence. Morning. Hazy. Pi slumps over the oar, eyes half
open, glazed. He has stayed up a second night for fear of
being attacked, and now he slowly nods sideways, giving in to
exhaustion despite himself, and tumbles into the water.

Pi gasps in shock as the water slaps him into full
consciousness. He climbs back onto the life ring - coughing,
tired, wet, sad and fearful.

The lifeboat rolls and growls beneath Pi's feet as he stares -
and then he notices O.J. The poor orang is sitting on a side
bench half-hidden by the tarp, and horribly seasick. Her
tongue lolls out of her mouth and she's visibly panting.

                    PI
          I'm sorry, O.J.; I don't have any
          seasickness medicine for you -

And then it strikes him.

                    PI (CONT'D)
          Supplies! Ah, supplies!

Pi pulls up the edge of the tarp nearest the bow. A row of
benches with hinged lids curve around the bow. Pi opens the
rearmost bench and finds a "LIFEBOAT MANUAL AND NAVIGATIONAL
GUIDE" in a plastic bag along with a pencil lying on top of
bags of supplies. He pulls out the manual and flips through
it - an illustration shows that the boat is lined with
compartments. He opens the next bench - it's stuffed with
life jackets.

Fig. 3.12 MovieSlate 8 lined script page (from Sean Pollock).

name of the project and the scene numbers. That said, entering information
by hand is fast. MovieSlate has a feature called "snippets," which completes
reoccurring words from just a few typed letters. The system for lining pages
is more flexible, with the ability to continue set-up lines as the action resets.

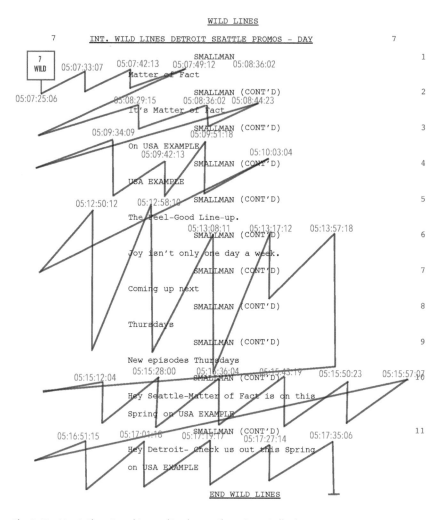

Fig. 3.13 MovieSlate 8 multi-cam lined page (from Sean Pollock).

And it is super easy to tag timecode throughout a long take. All these functions are elemental for live/live-to-tape recording.

Although this MovieSlate lined script records wild track, the basic form of the line is the same as a multi-cam shoot. There is one line for everything captured, showing restarts with timecode. See explanation of multi-cam shooting in Chapter 2 on pages 9–10.

APPLICATIONS FOR DIGITAL NOTATION

Certain tasks are best done by hand: roughing in a frame's composition, working out a floor plan for coverage, making notes that grab immediate attention. Digital notation applications bring handwriting and drawing into the digital workflow. They are important tools for people (like me) who benefit from brainstorming on paper. With a digital notation application and a stylus, you can make whatever freehand marks you like on your digital script page. I wish this had been available when I was working.

Lining a script is very intuitive with this sort of application. Unlike data-based applications, where each set-up line is built from a series of predetermined blocks (sections of straight lines, squiggles, and a few pre-programmed notations), you can draw a line exactly the way you want, with whatever personalized notations you like to use. The downside is that the information on that line will not automatically go to your facing page or daily report. You must enter it manually.

There are lots of good digital notating applications. General note-taking applications like Goodnotes and Notability, developed for the classroom, are a good place to start.[5] Most have a keyboard option and the ability to embed photos, videos, and sound recordings within your document.

The industry powerhouse for digital notation at this time is *Scriptation*. It is designed specifically for film production and has a number of robust features for coordinating revisions and transferring notes from draft to draft. If you are working on a project with constant revisions, it is a game changer.

DESIGNING YOUR PERSONAL SYSTEM

The options available for digital work might seem overwhelming at first. Here are some things to consider when building your personal system:

Complexity and Schedule

Think about what sort of projects you usually work on and what sort of projects you want to do in the future.

Projects that depend on complex layers of dramatic tension and surprise require a thorough prep and analysis. This sort of complex material benefits from a hand prep and production workflow.

Situational comedies with fast script revisions or lots of ad libs demand the ability to incorporate new material in real time. If you like the freshness and excitement that comes with this kind of production, look for applications that are light on their feet.

An episode of a long-running series will (usually) be built from recurring, predictable story elements. Applications using heavily automated data bank systems can rough in these elements in a flash, making it possible to work a long season without becoming exhausted.

Keyboard vs. Hand Thinking

If you grew up in a digital world, you may think as well with a keyboard as a pen. Personally, I depend on drawing to help me absorb visual information. Both are fine. Know yourself. The point is to learn your script and captured material well enough that you don't have to look up too many notes when under time pressure.

Make It Your Own

You can mix and match applications, selecting the best one for each task within a project. Script supervisors often use a spreadsheet for breakdowns, a digital notation application to mark up their scripts, and a data bank system for the facing pages, editor's report, and daily report.

Connecting the Pieces

Our most important contribution to our filmmaking team is the ability to see all the little details and understand how they relate to the larger story. A good graphic presentation makes information accessible. An excellent graphic presentation can connect bits of information that give you new insight.

NOTES

1   Using digital applications during prep is less risky. There is less time pressure and it is easy to back up your work.

2   There are programs like Photoshop that sort images by defined graphic categories, but that ability does not relate to the uses we will be talking about in this book.

3   Graphic elements have more impact when you are able to use color. In this case, blue for an exterior scene, yellow for an interior scene would be instantly understood.

4   Typical page formatting categories in a digital script are: *Draft/Revision, Act Number, Scene Number, Interior/Exterior, Time of Day, Location, Character, Dialog, Action, Transition, Scene Length, Page Breaks*.

5   Some office suites include a note-taking application.

Chapter 4

Preproduction

Breaking Down the Script

MAKING BREAKDOWNS USING DIGITAL APPLICATIONS

If you haven't read "Chapter 3: A Note about Digital Workflow," please read it now.

About Automated Digital Breakdowns

There are a number of computer programs that break down scripts automatically.[1] If you use this technology, remember that an auto-generated breakdown is a first pass, not a finished product. That said, using them can save you a lot of time.

Automated applications use the data embedded in a digital script to categorize and format the script's elements. Its accuracy depends upon how the elements of the script were categorized before it came to you. There may be mistakes and there will certainly be omissions. Go through your script as you would for any breakdown and check it against the automated document, adjusting whenever and however it helps you do your best work.

You want a breakdown that holds all the useful information and is easy to navigate. It should be formatted to help you relate bits of information to each other. If your digital program has a flexible format, you can tailor it to the way you like to work. If your system displays the breakdown on scene cards instead of a grid, consider using the information in those cards to make your own spreadsheet, so that you are able to see the flow of information from scene to scene. More about that later in this chapter.

Too Little Prep Time

Sometimes script supervisors are not given enough preproduction time to do proper breakdowns. If you find yourself in this position, do your best to get a full prep schedule: at least one week of ten-hour days for a feature, two or three days for each hour-long episode in a series.

DOI: 10.4324/9780367823665-4

If that is impossible, a data bank program with automated breakdowns can help you cut corners. Consider the challenges of your particular project and cut the corners that will make the least trouble. Usually, the production tallies are the safest to use as auto-generated. The time and day breakdowns are usually the most important to spend your prep on.

If you depend on auto tallies, make sure everyone in production, including the director, is aware that you are doing this, why you are doing it, and that you are not responsible for whatever the tallies are. If it is important to production to get exact numbers here, they will pay you to do it. It is not your responsibility to donate your time to production.

OVERVIEW

This chapter will focus on breakdowns for feature films. Breakdowns for single-camera episodic series are very similar, with the added considerations of coordination between episodes. Multi-camera sitcoms, live shows, and commercials have very different methods and will be mentioned briefly.[2]

In order to supervise the script, you need to know the script really well, better than anyone else on the crew. But here you are, your first day on a feature film. Other people have been working with the script for months, sometimes years. How do you catch up? You read the script again and again, analyzing every element that you think is important. This is called breaking down the script.

No matter what breakdown I am working on, I always keep a sheet of paper on my desk or a document open on my laptop where I can jot down any questions that come up. Most of these questions get answered in the process of doing my breakdowns. Some can't, and I will ask the director for clarification in our next meeting.

> Keep a sheet of paper or an open document to jot down **questions that come up**

Breakdowns for Every Movie

Here are the breakdowns I do for every feature film. I change the format a bit from project to project but the basic form and information remain the same.

- Scene/Page/Time Tally
- Master Breakdown
- Story Beat Breakdown
- Day Breakdown

Special Breakdowns

I make other, special breakdowns for almost every feature script. These are documents that chart a concern that is unique to the project, anything I see that could become problematic if it is not analyzed and understood. They are tailor-made, usually a one-off, and designed to best address whatever the concern is. This will be discussed in detail later in this chapter (see page 77).

> Design a unique breakdown for anything that could become **problematic** if it is not understood.

Prep Time

Prep time for script supervisors varies from job to job. On the East Coast, the minimum for a union, full budget feature is one week of ten-hour days. We use this time to do our breakdowns. For anything else—rehearsals, production meetings, tech scouts—you should be given additional prep days. I've had as little as a week and as much as four weeks for feature films. On the West Coast, the union minimum is two weeks and does not include a script timing. Low-budget union features (Tiers 1–4) allow for only three days of prep. Episodic series have a minimum two days for an hour-long episode, one day for a half-hour show. Multi-camera shoots prep all week long, and commercials are prepped the morning of shooting.

When working on a project with a short prep schedule, like a series or low-budget feature, you will want to consolidate the four breakdowns mentioned above. Your Scene/Page/Time breakdown can be folded into the master breakdown. Choose just one of the time breakdowns: either day or story beat, whichever tracks the story's time the best. I recommend adding a special breakdown for anything that you feel is going to be a problem during production.

Some production supervisors don't realize that the quality of our work on set depends on a thorough prep period. If you feel that you have not been given enough time to do what is required, speak to your supervisor and let them know how much time you will need. Keep a record of your prep hours and what you were working on during those hours. This can be useful if you need to ask for more time to complete a proper prep.[3]

Working for Free

When I was new to the craft, I jumped in on small projects. I was often in over my head, made a lot of mistakes, and figured out how to do the job. To compensate for my lack of skill, I put in a lot of unpaid hours, mostly in prep. This seemed like a fair deal to me. I was learning a lot and happy about it.

At some point you will be good at your job and should not do unpaid work. If you are competent and do not have enough prep time, despite asking for more, do what seems like the most important work and tell production why you haven't finished the prep. At that point, it is their problem, not yours.

What follows is my method of breaking down a major feature film. Feel free to tailor your prep to your situation and the time allotted to you.

YOUR SCRIPT

Your Working Script Is a Trusted Assistant

Your final script (the one you turn in) is a product for the editor—but your working script (the one you carry on set) is for you. It is your best and most trusted assistant.

Rereading, making breakdowns, and marking up your script transforms a standard issue document into a personalized secret weapon. This is true whether you use paper and pencil or a graphic application and digital pages.[4] By the end of production, you will have pulled the script apart and put it back together again dozens of times. You will add notes for the director, for the editor, for production, for yourself. Your working script becomes the container you fill with all the help you will need to do your job well.

Every script supervisor's working script is unique, because it is crafted to each script supervisor's personality, methodology, and the project at hand.

- A **final script** is the document you turn in to production.
- A **working script** is the document you carry on set.

A Typical Page Format for Feature Films

Here is a page from a typical feature film script, with its elements labeled (Fig. 4.1). Narrative movies of all lengths follow this format. It is the default format in digital scriptwriting applications.

Formats for Episodic, Live/Live-to-Tape, and Commercials

Script formats for smaller projects vary from project to project. There are no hard rules, but parent companies tend to have a consistent format for

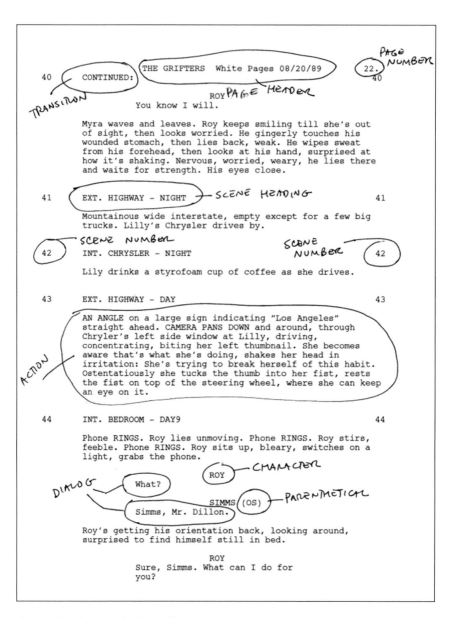

Fig. 4.1 The elements of a feature film script. From *The Grifters*.

all their projects. Here are some formatting variations you are most likely to see. The major digital screenwriting applications have templates for these formats as well.

EPISODIC

The elements in single-camera episodic scripts are pretty much the same as features. A typical episodic script is shorter and divided into acts. The running time of each act is important for a series that breaks for commercials. The start and end of acts are notated as underlined titles, centered on the page. There may also be a teaser at the start and a tag at the end, noted the same way. Episodic scripts that do not have to break for commercials can be formatted like feature scripts without notated act divisions. Each script is numbered to indicate its season and episode. The first season's scripts are numbered 101, 102, 103, etc. The second season's scripts are numbered 201, 202, 203, etc.

MULTI-CAMERA SITCOMS

Do not confuse multi-camera shoots with "single-camera" shoots that have multiple cameras. Multi-camera situational comedies are recorded on a sound stage with three or four cameras that adjust their positions in real time as the action continues, like the action in a play. Multi-camera sitcoms such as *Seinfeld* and *The Big Bang Theory* have notated acts with precise timing, refined during rehearsals. The scenes are lettered, not numbered, starting with *Scene A*. The participating characters are listed at the start of each scene, in parentheses. The layout is a little bit different: the action is capitalized, the dialog has more space between lines.

LIVE/LIVE-TO-TAPE

Live and live-to-tape projects, such as game, news, and talk shows, are usually multi-camera shoots, similar in shooting style to multi-camera sitcoms. Typically, the scripts are presented in an AV format, a grid with three columns: one that describes what will be seen (the video), one that describes what will be heard (the audio), plus a column for scene numbers or running times. The audio column might include dialog, music, and effects. These elements may be broken into separate columns. If the show is comprised

entirely of talking heads the script may include the dialog only, usually jus-
tified to the left side of the page.[5]

COMMERCIALS

Commercials come in every style of filmmaking: testimonial, documentary,
dramatic story, to name a few. Traditionally, commercials use an AV format.
Storyboard drawings may be included in the video column or as a separate
document. Typically, each shoot will provide material for several spots as
multiple parts of a single campaign. There will be a separate script for each
spot (for example, 60-, 30-, and 15-second versions), even when they use
the same set-ups for multiple versions. There may be similar versions at the
same length with alternate audio or video elements. Commercials have an
Ad-ID number that will be assigned before your shoot. This is important to
note, as it is used to track all the spots from agency through broadcast.

STARTING THE BREAKDOWNS

Defining the Scenes

I start my feature breakdowns with an activity that helps me quickly survey
the whole of the story: go through the script front to back and draw lines
across the page at each scene break. Do this for all the scenes in the script,
including the ones that start at the top of the page or end at the bottom.
This can be done on paper with pencil or on a tablet with a graphic-based
application.[6]

Scenes are the basic building blocks of the script. The dividing lines make
it easier to see each scene as a separate unit, which helps to make your logical thinking more elegant. It is also useful for checking that the scene divisions embedded in your digital script are correct.

PAGE/TIME/SCENE TALLY

This is the first breakdown I do because it requires the least understanding
of the script. It is the best breakdown to automate for the same reason.

Overview of the Breakdown

This breakdown will list all the scenes in the script and measure them for
page length and screen time. We will tally these measurements to get a total
number of scenes, running time, and pages for the entire script. This will

```
                         THE GRIFTERS  White Pages 08/20/89      22.
 40       CONTINUED:                                             40

                                  ROY
                        You know I will.

                 Myra waves and leaves. Roy keeps smiling till she's out
                 of sight, then looks worried. He gingerly touches his
                 wounded stomach, then lies back, weak. He wipes sweat
                 from his forehead, then looks at his hand, surprised at
                 how it's shaking. Nervous, worried, weary, he lies there
                 and waits for strength. His eyes close.

 41       EXT. HIGHWAY - NIGHT                                   41

                 Mountainous wide interstate, empty except for a few big
                 trucks. Lilly's Chrysler drives by.

 42       INT. CHRYSLER - NIGHT                                  42

                 Lily drinks a styrofoam cup of coffee as she drives.

 43       EXT. HIGHWAY - DAY                                     43

                 AN ANGLE on a large sign indicating "Los Angeles"
                 straight ahead. CAMERA PANS DOWN and around, through
                 Chryler's left side window at Lilly, driving,
                 concentrating, biting her left thumbnail. She becomes
                 aware that's what she's doing, shakes her head in
                 irritation: She's trying to break herself of this habit.
                 Ostentatiously she tucks the thumb into her fist, rests
                 the fist on top of the steering wheel, where she can keep
                 an eye on it.

 44       INT. BEDROOM - DAY9k                                   44

                 Phone RINGS. Roy lies unmoving. Phone RINGS. Roy stirs,
                 feeble. Phone RINGS. Roy sits up, bleary, switches on a
                 light, grabs the phone.

                                  ROY
                        What?

                                SIMMS (OS)
                        Simms, Mr. Dillon.

                 Roy's getting his orientation back, looking around,
                 surprised to find himself still in bed.

                                  ROY
                        Sure, Simms. What can I do for
                        you?
```

Fig. 4.2 Dividing the script into scenes. From *The Grifters*.

help us track our progress while shooting. When there is rewriting during production, this breakdown will help us know how much longer or shorter we are making the movie with each revision.

> **We track our progress during production by:**
> 1. Scene count
> 2. Time count
> 3. Page count

Some script supervisors like to include this breakdown as part of their master breakdown. This can be especially helpful for episodic cross-boarding, when the number of breakdowns would otherwise become overwhelming. Either way, the concepts and analysis are the same.

Using a Spreadsheet

I recommend using a spreadsheet for this tally. A spreadsheet can total the counts and make adjustments to the totals when rewrites change the length of the script. There are a million spreadsheets available.[7] Select whichever suits you and your project best.

Figure 4.3 is a tally I made for *Syriana*. It has a lot of detail because the shoot was complicated. There were a dozen storylines and a few dozen characters. We shot in many cities on three continents. There were constant rewrites. I spent the time in prep to design a detailed breakdown that was flexible and would double-check the math for me. There is a super-scaled-down version of this tally later in this chapter on page 57.

At the time, we were dependent on photocopies for distribution, so I was limited to using black and white documents. If I were to do this break-down now, I might add some thoughtful color coding, by continents maybe, making it easy to check that we weren't getting on an airplane with missing scenes or shots.

The Basic Idea

This form is designed to not only track our progress during production, but to constantly compare the script "Totals" to the combined work "To Do" and the work "Done." If the totals do not match, I know there is a problem with my math and I can solve it right away. The "Date Completed" column is a quick guide when you need to look up the daily reports related to a certain scene.

Mary Cybulski
6/24/04

SYRIANA
Time and Page Tally

page 1
From white script

Scene #	Action	Total			Date	To Do			Done		
		Pages	Time	Scene	Comp	Pages	Time	Scene	Pages	Time	Scene
1											
2											
3											
4											
5											
6											
7											
8											
9											
10											
11											
12											
13											
14											
15											
16											
17											
18											
19											
20											
21											
22											
22A											
23											
24											
25											
26											
27											
28											
29											
30											
31											
32											
33											
34											
35											
36											
37											
38											
39											
40											
41											
42											
43											
44											
45											
46											
47											
48											
49											
50											
51											
52											

Fig. 4.3 A blank Page/Time/Scene Tally form. From *Syriana*.

The Format

There is one line for each scene. Reading across, left to right, each line will show:

- The scene number.
- A brief description of the scene's action.
- A "Total" block of three columns that show the page and time count for the scene, plus a "1" in the scene column. This block will track the number of pages, time, and scenes in the total script. It will change as the script is rewritten.
- A cell to fill in with the date as each scene is officially completed.
- Two blocks, with three columns each, that will track how much of each scene is yet to be shot and how much has been completed.

Before the first day of shooting, the "To Do" block will look exactly like the "Total" block. The counts will shift bit by bit from the "To Do" block to the "Done" block as each scene's work is completed. At the end of the job the "Done" block will look exactly like the "Total" block. See Figs 4.5a and 4.5b for examples of this.

Making the Breakdown

If you have never used a spreadsheet before, watch a tutorial online to get the specifics of the application you are using. Any spreadsheet should be able to do the following.

Open a new spreadsheet template and fill it in as in the example above. Add enough rows so there is a row for each scene, plus a few more at the top and a few more at the bottom. The header should include the name of the project, the name of the breakdown, which draft of the script the data comes from, a page number, the date, and your name. There is usually an option to set the header so that it repeats at the top of each page.

ADDING SCENE NUMBERS

The first column on the left is for the scene numbers. List them top to bottom. There may be some scenes with the same number and different letters: 5, 5A, 5B, etc. Each one will get its own row.

There will be a more detailed discussion about how to label scene numbers containing letters in Chapter 6, "Production Overview: Keeping the Notes," pages 194–201. Should it be 5A or A5? Movie-specific software will be able to sort scenes with a letter before the number. General-use applications, like these spreadsheets, will sort the scene numbers in alphabetical order, so here the letters must follow the numbers to maintain proper sequence.

WAIT TO DESCRIBE THE ACTION

I wait to fill in the scene description until after I have completed the "Action" section in my master breakdown. I will know the story better then, and be able to describe the scenes more specifically and more economically. I will copy and paste the descriptions from the master breakdown into the "Action" column of this form, saving time. The master breakdown is explained in the next section of this chapter.

FORMATTING AND FUNCTIONS

Spreadsheets can be set up as data banks. We can input values and choose how those values are expressed. We will set the scene count to be expressed in whole numbers, the page count in eighths, and the screen time in hours, minutes, and seconds. We can also embed mathematical formulas into the spreadsheet that will total our tallies and compare one total to another.

SCENE COUNT

Format the cells in the scene count column (at the right of the "Total" block) for plain numbers. This option is found in the *Data Format* menu or as part of the cell description. It is a standard option for all spreadsheets. If this choice is not apparent, search the *Help* menu for *Data Formatting*. Choose the option: *Number*. This will prevent the program from turning your whole numbers into dates, decimals, etc. Add a "1" in the scene column for each scene.

Use the SUM function to tally this column. Look for the *Function* or *Formula* menu in your application. It may be in your *Standard* toolbar or a pull-down menu called something like *Insert*. If it is not apparent, search *Help* for "insert formula" or "insert function." Highlight the cell where you want the total to be displayed, choose *SUM*, and select the column of cells that you would like to add together. Each application is a bit different, but this function is standard for all. The total will be displayed in that first cell you chose. A new total is generated automatically when scene values change and when whole scenes are added or deleted from the form.

WHAT IS A SCENE?

A scene is all the action that is continuous in time and place. If the location changes, that's a new scene. If there is a time jump, that's a new scene.[8] If actors enter and leave, that is *not* a new scene. If your screenwriter, AD, or production people are inexperienced, your script may have scene headings in odd places throwing off the scene divisions. This makes the organizing of the story and the physical production confusing.

Sometimes a writer will write an action like: *CU: THE BOOK IS ON FIRE* formatted as a Scene Heading element. This will be read by applications that make automated breakdowns as the start of a new scene, but it is not. It is an insert shot, a part of the scene that comes before and after it. If you see badly formatted action in the script, throwing off the automated scene tally like this, bring it to the attention of the first AD and decide together what's to be done about it. If it is early in preproduc-tion, the non-scene should be combined to make more sense.

> A **scene** is all the action that is continuous in time and place.

PAGE BREAKDOWN

The "Pages" column lists the page length of each scene and adds them together to get a total page count for the entire script. We measure page length in whole pages and fractions. The fraction we always use is the eighth of a page. We never call a half page 1/2 page. We call it 4/8 of a page. One and a fourth of a page is 1 2/8 page. Format the pages column for fractions, using eighths. Again, this is found by using the *Formatting* function. Look for the *Fractions* option. You may have to go down another layer to choose eighths.

WHAT IS AN EIGHTH OF A PAGE?

Some pages of your script are probably longer than others. If a locked script has been revised, there are probably some A Pages, which are mostly blank.[9] Flip through your script and find a page that you think is an average length for a full page. Lay your ruler vertically and measure from the top of the text (not counting the page header) to the bottom of the text (not counting the transitional notations). If that length is eight inches, then each inch of the script is 1/8 of a page, no matter how much text is on a particular page.

If the average page length is something less tidy than exactly eight inches, I use a graphic designer's trick and measure the length with my ruler slanted across the page. Here is how to do that: if the page is more than eight inches tall, I mark off eight sections on my ruler that are each 1 1/2 inches long. Then I slant my ruler from one corner on the top to the opposite corner on the bottom, diagonally. The 12 inches of the ruler start at the top of the text and end at the bottom. The 1 1/2″ sections are equidistant; there are eight of them. That makes each section 1/8 of the page (see Fig. 4.4).

Measure each scene and write its length in the bottom right corner above the dividing line. If a scene carries over to the next page, mark the page length on each page in parentheses and the scene total without parentheses (see Fig. 4.4).

Scene divisions rarely fall exactly on the 1/8 mark. Use your best judgment. Some scenes will be rounded up, some rounded down. It can't always be exact. Try to make each full page add up to 8/8. Here's the exception: if the page has 12 short scenes, each scene should be given 1/8 of a page, for a total of 12/8 on that particular page.

The ADs will have a page count by the time you are hired, but if the production wants you to do a count, yours will be the official tally. The AD's count is generated by whatever software they are using. It will be approximate. It may or may not match a hand count or the count of the application you are using.

Some ADs make their page count based on daily production concerns, not total script length. For instance, if we have a 6/8 page telephone conversation, some ADs will give 6/8 pages to both sides of the conversation. We do have to shoot 6/8 pages twice, once on each side of the conversation, but I prefer to give each half of the conversation 3/8 pages. This way my total page count will match the total page count in the physical script, which makes the progress report more accurate. This system also gives a more meaningful relationship between the page count and the screen time.

> Try to make each full page add up to **8/8**.

ADDING THE PAGE COUNT

Enter the page count for each scene in the "Pages" column of the "Total" block. Assign the *SUM* function to the column, as you did for the scene count, and your total page count will be added automatically. This will show up at the bottom of the page column as whole pages with the remainders in eighths. When you add new scenes or adjust any scene's length, this document will give you a new total (see Fig. 4.5).

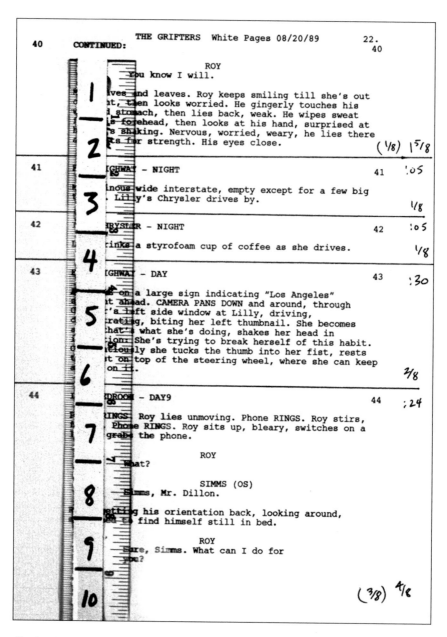

Fig. 4.4 Measuring 1/8 pages; first in inches, then in eighths of a page. From *The Grifters*.

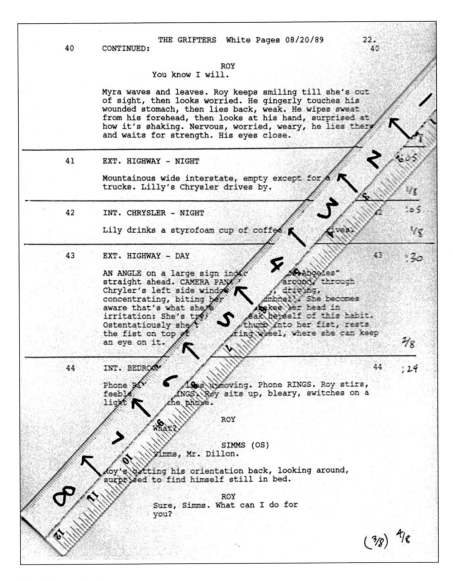

```
                         THE GRIFTERS  White Pages 08/20/89           22.
      40        CONTINUED:                                            40

                                        ROY
                              You know I will.

                 Myra waves and leaves. Roy keeps smiling till she's out
                 of sight, then looks worried. He gingerly touches his
                 wounded stomach, then lies back, weak. He wipes sweat
                 from his forehead, then looks at his hand, surprised at
                 how it's shaking. Nervous, worried, weary, he lies there
                 and waits for strength. His eyes close.


      41         EXT. HIGHWAY - NIGHT

                 Mountainous wide interstate, empty except for
                 trucks. Lilly's Chrysler drives by.


      42         INT. CHRYSLER - NIGHT

                 Lily drinks a styrofoam cup of coffee


      43         EXT. HIGHWAY - DAY                                   43

                 AN ANGLE on a large sign in
                 straight ahead. CAMERA PAN               around  through
                 Chryler's left side window             , driving,
                 concentrating, biting                      She becomes
                 aware that's what she                  her head in
                 irritation: She's tr              ak herself of this habit.
                 Ostentatiously she             thumb into her fist, rests
                 the fist on top                 ring wheel, where she can keep
                 an eye on it.


      44         INT. BEDROOM                                         44

                 Phone                 moving. Phone RINGS. Roy stirs,
                 feebl               INGS. Roy sits up, bleary, switches on a
                 lig               the phone.

                                        ROY
                           What?

                                        SIMMS (OS)
                           Simms, Mr. Dillon.

                 Roy's getting his orientation back, looking around,
                 surprised to find himself still in bed.

                                        ROY
                              Sure, Simms. What can I do for
                              you?
```

Fig. 4.4 *continued.*

SCRIPT TIMING

Along with the scene and page count, we track our progress during production using screen time. One of our tasks in preproduction is to estimate what the screen time of the finished film might be, scene by scene and for the script in total.

For the timing, you will need a quiet, private place; a stopwatch; a pencil or stylus; and the same hard or digital copy of your script. Start at the beginning of the script and read the dialog out loud. Imagine all the action. Get up and walk around the room if it helps. See what the camera sees as it pans across a vista; notice when you get bored during transitional action so you know how much shoe leather to cut out.[10] Act out the entire movie, scene by scene, trying to imagine how the director and editor will use the screenplay. For consistent pacing, try to time the entire script in as close to one sitting as you can. Don't drink too much coffee. No wine or beer!

Start the timing at the beginning of each scene and stop it when you feel it is time to cut to the next scene. Those bold dividing lines you added between scenes will help you keep your attention in the story without missing the exact moment to turn off your watch.

Write that scene's time on the page, in the top right corner, just below the dividing line (see Fig. 4.4). Do this for all the scenes in script. Don't add them to your breakdown yet. The extra step will bog you down and may affect the tempo of your reading.

After you have timed all the scenes to your satisfaction and written them on the page, it is time to enter them in the breakdown. Format the cells in the "Time" column of the "Total" block using hours, minutes, and seconds. Spreadsheets have lots of different variations for this value. You may have an option of *Time* under the numbers menu. You may have a choice of *Date and Time*, in which you can isolate the time by selecting *None* for the date. There may be something called *Duration* that will have a variety of formatting options. If it is not clear what your spreadsheet has to offer, look it up in the *Help* menu. Add the *SUM* function to this column as before. Enter each scene's running time, scene by scene. Again, once your form is set up, changing any scene's running time will automatically give you a new total time for the whole script (see Fig. 4.5).

Ideally, you will have had a conversation with the director about pace. If not, schedule one. It should only take a few minutes. They might tell you some films you can watch as a reference before you start your timing. If your story is a period film, chances are the pace of the dialog will reflect the speaking habits of the time: rapid fire in the 1920s, laid-back in the 1960s, etc. Scenes without dialog are harder to nail down ("Atlanta burns!"). If the movie has a lot of action in it, ask if there are storyboards. These can help you imagine non-dialog scenes with more precision.

Some script supervisors time a script two or three times and use an average. Still, it's a guess. Any director or editor will tell you that the length of a film keeps changing until the picture is locked. All you can do is use your best, informed imagination.

Studios and producers will often use our pre-timing to judge if a script is too long or short. This is important on low-budget films, which are always short on shooting days; also on big action projects, where every shot is really expensive. It's a good thing to think about even on dramatic, character-driven films. If the running time is too long, subplots and characters may have to be trimmed or dropped in the edit.

When script timing is needed very early in preproduction, a script supervisor may be hired just for a day or two to do a cold timing of a script. Some projects are predictable enough to use a pre-timing this way. If the project is a genre film, if its star is a known comedian or character actor, if the director has a signature dramatic style—you can get pretty close. An established episodic TV show is pretty easy to get right with a little research.

If your director is new or trying something very different, if the production style is fluid or has an unusual tone, the pre-timing is only a general guess. Even then, if the pre-timing is consistent and carefully done, it can be a good reference for tracking the accumulating screen time of any production.

I always give my pre-timings, scene by scene, to the editors. Sometime around the second or third week of production, they have enough consecutive scenes to start comparing my guess timing with the timing of their rough cut. If there is a big difference between the two, it is really good to know. If, in my pre-timing, the total running time is an ideal length (whatever that is for the production) but the rough cut is coming in much longer, the director may decide to tighten up the pace, cut down the ad-libs, or drop some scenes.

> **Things that make a cold script timing more accurate:**
> 1. The project is a genre film
> 2. Its star is a known comedian or character actor
> 3. The director has a signature dramatic style

Once, I was on a film with a director who wanted to make changes to the shooting script, but didn't want to fight about it with the studio. The dialog changed a lot during production. After the third week, our running times were 25 percent shorter than my pre-timing. If we kept going that way, we were not going to have enough screen time for a feature.

> When the editors have a few minutes of scenes cut together, it is helpful to **compare the rough-cut timing to your pre-timing**.

Once the director was aware of this, she started making some scenes longer by adding more non-scripted dialog, something she wanted to do anyway, and we had a nice movie at a good length.

When spending a long day painstakingly timing a script, my husband, who was a picture editor, would often walk by and say, "A minute a page and go to the beach!" I never did, but this is basically how running times are generated in automated breakdowns. And they can be pretty close. Again, if production cares, they will pay you to do a timing. If not, the accuracy of the running time is not your problem. Spend your prep time on more important things, things that will help you do a good job on set, like developing a deep understanding of the story.

FILLING IN THE "TO DO" AND "DONE" BLOCKS

After the information for each scene has been added to the "Total" block, and you have checked to see that the *SUM* functions are working, the entire block may be copied en masse and pasted into the "To Do" block (see Fig. 4.5a). The *SUM* formulas should migrate with the scene values and totals. Change a few numbers as a test in the "To Do" block to make sure they are all working correctly. Don't forget to change them back!

Add the *SUM* function to the columns in the "Done" block, just as you did in the "Total" block, even though there are no counts entered yet.

During production, as each scene is completed, cut and paste the page, time, and scene count for that scene from the "To Do" block to the "Done" block. This will give you running totals of the work completed and the work still to be done. Note the date when each scene was completed in the "Date Comp" column. At the end of the job, the "To Do" block will be empty and the "Done" block will be full (see Fig. 4.5b).

You can add an additional formula that double checks your work by combining the "To Do" and "Done" block totals and comparing them to the "Total" block. If the combined numbers don't match the "Total" block, you have a mistake that needs to be found and corrected.

To add this check, select a range of empty cells below the "Total" block, enter a *SUM* formula for each category. Select the column totals from the "To Do" and "Done" blocks as the values to be added together.

If this last step is too much programming for you, you can add the "To Do" and "Done" totals by hand at the end of each shooting day. You can also set up your Daily Production Report to do this for you. More about this in the section on "Digital Daily Production Reports" in Chapter 6, page 149.

Mary Cybulski
6/30/04
SYRIANA
Time and Page Tally
page 7
From white script

Scene #	Action	Total Pages	Total Time	Total Scene	Date Comp	To Do Pages	To Do Time	To Do Scene	Done Pages	Done Time	Done Scene
184	Bennett gives Syd to Farish	2	0:02:03	1		2	0:02:03	1			
185	CIA - Target acquisition	4/8	0:00:33	1		4/8	0:00:33	1			
186	Bryan changes places with Nasir's wife	2/8	0:00:18	1		2/8	0:00:18	1			
187	The convoy passes through the sheep	1/8	0:00:09	1		1/8	0:00:09	1			
188	Bob runs into sheep herd	1/8	0:00:11	1		1/8	0:00:11	1			
189	Bob in sheep herd sees convoy ahead	2/8	0:00:12	1		2/8	0:00:12	1			
190	Bob backs out of sheep herd	1/8	0:00:11	1		1/8	0:00:11	1			
191	Predator flies in desert	1/8	0:00:07	1		1/8	0:00:07	1			
192	Bob drives away from sheep herd	2/8	0:00:16	1		2/8	0:00:16	1			
193	The predator's bay opens	1/8	0:00:09	1		1/8	0:00:09	1			
196	The predator drops a bomb	2/8	0:00:06	1		2/8	0:00:06	1			
197	The convoy seen from inside Bob's Taurus	1/8	0:00:07	1		1/8	0:00:07	1			
198	Wasim pulls out the stinger with the smiley face	3/8	0:00:19	1		3/8	0:00:19	1			
199	Bob honks & flashes at the convoy	1/8	0:00:07	1		1/8	0:00:07	1			
200	CIA - Franks worries that there is no hit yet	4/8	0:00:19	1		4/8	0:00:19	1			
201	Bryan sees Bob's Taurus coming closer	1/8	0:00:07	1		1/8	0:00:07	1			
202	Nasir's kids quiet down	2/8	0:00:10	1		2/8	0:00:10	1			
203	Bob & Nasir make eye contact & the bomb hits	1/8	0:00:07	1		1/8	0:00:07	1			
204	CIA - sees the hit	4/8	0:00:15	1		4/8	0:00:15	1			
205	Janus thanks his co-workers	3/8	0:00:20	1		3/8	0:00:20	1			
206	Bryan walks by crater & child's doll	2/8	0:00:19	1		2/8	0:00:19	1			
207	Janus thanks his international friends	5/8	0:00:25	1		5/8	0:00:25	1			
A207	Bennett comes home. His dad is waiting	1/8	0:00:10	1		1/8	0:00:10	1			
AA207	Oil Creeps discuse the viability of Suriana	1/8	0:00:40	1		1/8	0:00:40	1			
208	Bob upside down in Taurus	1/8	0:00:05	1		1/8	0:00:05	1			
209	Bob gets out & helps Bryan to his feet.	5/8	0:01:00	1		5/8	0:01:00	1			
210	Farooq sends the dhow into the tanker	5/8	0:00:35	1		5/8	0:00:35	1			
211	Wasim's martyr video tape.	3/8	0:00:35	1		3/8	0:00:35	1			
	TOTALS	100 2/8	1:45:48	231		100 2/8	1:45:48	231	0	0	0

Fig. 4.5a A Page/Time/Scene Tally form at the start of a job. From *Syriana*.

Mary Cybulski   SYRIANA   page 6
12/3/04   Time and Page Tally   From green script:11/10/04

Scene #	Action	Pages	Time	Scene	Comp	Pages	Time	Scene	Pages	Time	Scene
188	Bob runs into sheep herd	1/8	0:00:15	1	11/2				1/8	0:00:15	1
189	Bob in sheep herd sees convoy ahead	2/8	0:00:12	1	11/2				2/8	0:00:12	1
190	Bob backs out of sheep herd	1/8	0:00:11	1	11/2				1/8	0:00:11	1
191	Predator flies in desert	1/8	0:00:07	1	11/20				1/8	0:00:07	1
192	Bob drives away from sheep herd	2/8	0:00:07	1	11/2				2/8	0:00:07	1
193	The predator's bay opens	1/8	0:00:07	1	11/20				1/8	0:00:07	1
194	Nasir's family in car. The kids need attention.	2/8	0:00:11	1	11/2				2/8	0:00:11	1
194A	Mary Alice dances for Reza	1/8	0:00:12	1	8/18				1/8	0:00:12	1
195	Janus awarded Oilman of the Year	1 3/8	0:01:29	1	8/19				1 3/8	0:01:29	1
196	The predator drops a bomb	2/8	0:00:06	1	11/20				2/8	0:00:06	1
197	The convoy seen from inside Bob's Taurus	1/8	0:00:07	1	11/2				1/8	0:00:07	1
198	Wasim pulls out the stinger with the smiley face	3/8	0:00:16	1	11/15				3/8	0:00:16	1
199	Bob honks & flashes at the convoy	1/8	0:00:07	1	11/2				1/8	0:00:07	1
200	CIA - Franks worries that there is no hit yet	4/8	0:00:19	1	11/20				4/8	0:00:19	1
201	Bryan sees Bob's Taurus coming closer	1/8	0:00:07	1	11/2				1/8	0:00:07	1
202	Nasir's kids quiet down	2/8	0:00:10	1	11/2				2/8	0:00:10	1
203	Bob & Nasir make eye contact & the bomb hits	1/8	0:00:07	1	11/2				1/8	0:00:07	1
204	CIA - sees the hit	4/8	0:00:15	1	11/20				4/8	0:00:15	1
205	Janus thanks his co-workers	3/8	0:00:20	1	8/19				3/8	0:00:20	1
206	Bryan walks by crater & child's doll	2/8	0:00:15	1	11/3				2/8	0:00:15	1
207	Janus thanks his international friends	5/8	0:00:20	1	8/19				5/8	0:00:20	1
A207	Bennett comes home. His dad is waiting	1/8	0:00:10	1	8/18				1/8	0:00:10	1
AA207	Oil Creeps discuss the viability of Suriana	1/8	0:00:40	1	9/7				1/8	0:00:40	1
208	Bob upside down in Taurus	1/8	0:00:05	1	11/3				1/8	0:00:05	1
209	Bryan walks away from the crash	5/8	0:01:00	1	11/3				5/8	0:01:00	1
210	Farooq sends the dhow into the tanker	5/8	0:00:36	1	11/15				5/8	0:00:36	1
211	Wasim's martyr video tape.	3/8	0:00:35	1	11/1				3/8	0:00:35	1
	Totals	144 1/8	1:48:49	231		0	0:00:00	0	144 1/8	1:48:49	231

Fig. 4.5b At the end of a job.

209	Bryan walks away from the crash	5/8	0:01:00	1	11/3					5/8	0:01:00	1
210	Farooq sends the dhow into the tanker	5/8	0:00:36	1	11/15					5/8	0:00:36	1
211	Wasim's martyr video tape	3/8	0:00:35	1	11/1	3/8	0:00:35	1				
	Totals	144 1/8	1:48:49	231		44 1/8	0:48:49	31		100	1:00:00	200
	Check	144 1/8	1:48:49	231								

Fig. 4.5c Mid-shoot: A section of the Page/Time/Scene Tally with an added math check.

THE MINIMUM TALLY

If you are working on a non-professional, micro production, a shoot that has no production report—maybe no production department—it will not be appropriate to make a detailed Scene/Page/Time tally like in the example above. You can still do something. At the very least, make a simple scene check-off tally. It is surprisingly easy to finish a shoot without getting all the planned shots.

Make a grid, note all your scene numbers, and leave a space for the date each scene is completed. If a scene is partially completed, make a note (as in Figure 4.6 for scene 20), but do not cross a scene off until every last piece of the scene is in the can.

MASTER BREAKDOWN

Overview

The master breakdown is where the real work of getting to know your script starts. This breakdown will help you track all the production details indicated or implied in the script.

When you are finished making a master breakdown, you will have a powerful document that can be referenced quickly to answer hundreds of questions during production. Even better, all sorts of details will reveal themselves to you as you do the work. Pay close attention while you are doing this breakdown, or you will miss its most valuable benefit.

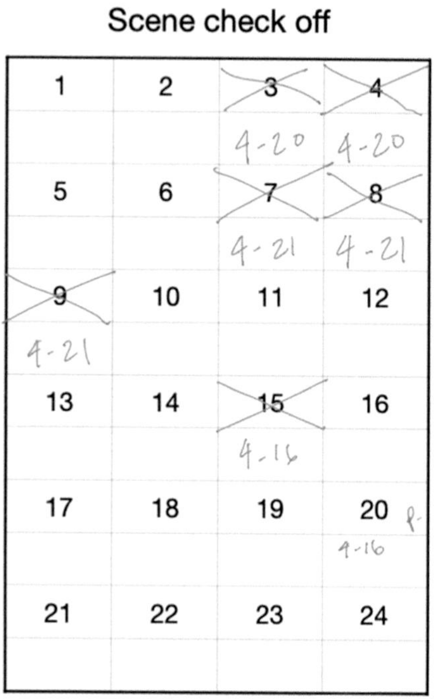

Scene check off

Fig. 4.6 Simple scene check-off tally.

As I said earlier, an auto-generated breakdown is not a finished product. Use that document as a first pass and work into it as you would any master breakdown. Any story worth its salt will have important elements that are not apparent in a superficial reading.

The most **valuable** benefit of the master breakdown is the study needed to make it.

To prepare for a master breakdown, read the script again, noting all the production elements indicated on the page. Many script supervisors use translucent markers to highlight each element. This can be done on paper or tablet. If you do this, use a different color for each category of element. I found these mark-ups to be too distracting and unnecessary, but it could be a good way to make sure nothing is overlooked.[11] Either way, log the elements you identify into your master breakdown template. Look for the mention of location, time of day, characters, specific props, wardrobe, makeup, voice-overs, pre-lapsed dialog, playback, weather, visual effects, TV dialog—anything that is essential for each scene.

An automated breakdown will save you the logging work. You still have to do the reading and thinking work.

Setting Up a Master Breakdown Form

I used an Excel workbook for my master breakdowns because it could handle a large amount of information without crashing. Do a little research to determine which spreadsheet fits the way you like to work. For example, at this writing, a Google Sheet is great for instant online distribution and collaboration. Apple Numbers has the best technical integration with Apple iPads. The market changes every day but all spreadsheets can accommodate a master breakdown.

To make a standard form for a master breakdown, open a spreadsheet and add a header that identifies your project, which draft of the script you are working from, the date the breakdown is made, and your name. Label the first ten columns, left to right (see Fig. 4.7):

1. "Sc" (Scene number)
2. "I/E" (Interior or Exterior location)
3. "D/N" (Day or Night—or a more exact time of day)
4. "Loc" (Location)
5. "Action" (or "Description")
6. "Characters" (who is in this scene)
7. "Ward/MU/H" (Wardrobe, Makeup, Hair)
8. "Props/Art" (Property, which is any object the actors handle; and Art Department, which is any object important to the scene, which the actors do not handle)
9. "PB/VO" (PB is "playback," sound and/or picture that is recorded in some other place or time and played during the shooting of the current scene; VO is voice-over, dialog that is recorded either before or after the scene is shot; it will run with this scene in the final cut but will not originate from the scene you are shooting; "VFX," visual effects, might go in this column, if you have any)
10. "Match" (a column for notes that will remind you of an important continuity moment or transition in the story)

Feel free to change these columns depending on the needs of your particular script. Makeup may need a column of its own if characters will age or if there are a lot of injuries. You may want to add a column for weather or light, as I did for my breakdown of *The Ice Storm*. *Eat Pray Love*, the film that the breakdown in Fig. 4.7 was made for, takes place on four continents. I added a special column on the far left to identify the action by one of these four places.

Go through the script, using the highlighted production elements if you have them. Fill in the cells with as much information as you can for each scene before moving on to the next. If you do not highlight the elements, use that read-through to fill in this form. If you need to adjust the format, this is usually the pass where it will become apparent.

As you log, pay attention to the details, and also to how the details work together to tell the whole unified story. Keep a page nearby so that you can note anything that is not clear, any questions you have, or something you may want to research later.

SCENE NUMBERS

List the scene numbers in the first column. You may want to copy and paste the whole column of scene numbers from your Page/Time/Scene breakdown all at once to save time. Check that no numbers have been skipped or repeated.

INTERIOR/EXTERIOR

Each scene heading will indicate if the action takes place inside or outside. Mark either "I" or "E" in the next column as per the scene heading.

DAY/NIGHT

Each scene heading will indicate if the action takes place in the daytime or night. Mark either "D" or "N" in the third column. If the scene heading in the script is more specific, be more specific in your breakdown; "Dwn" for dawn, "Ev" for evening, "Aft" for afternoon, etc. When you find a night scene that is followed by a day scene, add a blank row between them. This space will indicate the beginning of a new story day. Don't number the days yet. There may be other day breaks that cut from day

	Sc	I/E	D/N	Loc	Action	Characters	Ward/MU/H	Props/Art	PB/VO	Match
	DAY	1			(2002 Winter)					
	1	E	D	Mountain Road	Liz rides along mountain Road	Liz		Bike, Backpack??	Liz VO:	
	2	E	D	Ketut Compound	Liz meets Ketut	Liz, Ketut, Nyomo		Bike, Backpack??	Liz VO:	
	3	E	D	Ketut Porch	Ketut studies Liz's palm, tells her that she will come back.	Liz, Ketut, (Nyomo)		Mats, Backpack??		
BALI	4	E	D	Ketut Compound	Ketut gives Liz the drawing.	Liz, Ketut, (Nyomo)		Bike, drawing, Backpack??		
	DAY	2			(2002 Spring/Early Summer)					
	5	E/I	D	Liz's Upstate NY	Liz's POV of family picnic.	Liz, Stephen, Lynn (mom) Peter (dad) Katherine (sis) Graham (bil) 2 kids, dog.		BBQ	Titles up: EPL, One Month Later. Picnic voices	
	6	E	D	Liz's Upstate NY	Liz shows up and adds to joke.	^^		BBQ		
	7	I	D	Kitchen	Liz & her mom talk about kitchens & husbands	Liz, Mom		Corn, chardonnay		
	DAY	3			2002 Summer					
	8	I	N?	Bathroom	Liz tries to make up her red eyes	Liz	Crying		Knocking	
	9	I	N?	Bedroom	Stephen says 'Worth the wait'	Liz, Stephen	Crying			
	10	I	N	Delia's apt	CU Jack, Stephen holds Baby Jack at a distance.	Liz, Stephen, Baby Jack, Delia (other guests, Andy?)	Old crying?			
NEW YORK	11	I	N	Delia's apt	Jump cut, party swirl. Liz meets Walter. Stephen gives Baby Jack back. Stephen has changed his job.	Liz, Stephen, Baby Jack, Delia (other guests, Andy?) Walter				
	12	I	N	Delia's bedroom	Jack is changed. Delia talks about wanting a baby.	Liz, Delia, Baby Jack		Diapers changed. Box of baby clothes.		
	13	I	N	Car	Liz talks about Aruba, Stephen talks about going back to school.	Liz, Stephen				
	A14	I	N	Foyer	Liz drops keys onto the table	Liz		Keys		Renumber
	14	I	N	Bedroom	Liz stares at ceiling, Stephen sleeps	Liz, Stephen	Old crying? Nightgown	Nightgown		
	15	I	N	Hallway Kitchen	Liz as a ghost, passes photos of herself. Liz as a ghost	Liz	Nightgown Nightgown			
	16	I	N	Bathroom	Liz prays on the bathroom floor.	Liz	Nightgown			
	17	I	N	Bedroom	Liz looks at Stephen sleeping and gets into bed.	Liz, Stephen	After crying? Nightgown	same?		Between 18 & 19?
	18	I	N	Bathroom	Liz's voice tells her to go back to bed.	Liz	Nightgown			

Fig. 4.7 Master breakdown (page 1). From *Eat Pray Love.*

to day or night to night. We will add those later, and then number all the story days.

LOCATION

This will also be named in the scene header in the script. Fill in the appropriate cell. Watch out for general location names in the scene header that may mean different actual places: for example, two locations called "Kitchen" that may be in different houses. Include the added distinction when necessary.

ACTION (OR DESCRIPTION)

This is a short one-line description. Its purpose is to identify the scene, not to name everything important about it. The ADs will have a one-line description for each scene already. If you like what they have, you can just use that. It is less confusing if everyone's one-line descriptions are the same, especially for complex scenes. If the AD's descriptions are not meaningful to you, you are perfectly free to make your own.

After you have the descriptions filled in, you can copy and paste those notes into your Page/Time/Scene breakdown. Check to make sure the descriptions are lining up to the correct scene numbers.

CHARACTERS

List all the characters mentioned in the dialog or action as well as any that are implied but not written on the page. Discovering and notating these implied elements is called "matching back." This is a very important part of our job.

Say you have three guys robbing a bank and some cops coming after them. These (basically) two scenes cut back and forth. Each time we cut from one to another we will have a new scene number, so technically a new scene.[12] One of these scenes might only mention one robber and his action of drilling into the safe. If none of the robbers have left the room, you can assume that they all are there and all should be included in your breakdown for each bank robbing scene. You may distinguish implied characters by putting their names in (parentheses).

If you have a big sprawling scene, like in a courtroom, wedding, or battle scene, there may be days of shooting where one side of the action is not seen and the actors there are not needed. If you think this may be the case, make a note to ask the first AD if there are any whole scenes (or breakout sub-scenes) that will not require all the characters to be on set. If there are, include the missing characters on your breakdown but put them in [brackets]. This will indicate that they are theoretically in the scene but not on set.

If a character appears at very different ages, include their current age after the character name.

Include all principal characters, whether they speak or not. Also list bit players or background artists that impact the action. Don't include general atmosphere background players.

Important animal characters can go here or under props.

If we will hear a character but not see them, indicate that in the VO/PB/VFX column. There is more about this later in this chapter (see page 65).

THE IMPORTANCE OF MATCHING BACK

Sometimes script supervisors are called the Logic Department. I like that. By digging deep into the logic of the story we come up with details that make the story's world more unified, and often more resonant. The master breakdown really helps this by making it easy to match back. Here's an example.

I was working on a film called *People I Know*, which stars Al Pacino. In that film, Al's brother's widow, played by Kim Basinger, meets him in a restaurant. She offers to return a book that was meaningful to both brothers. This is the only time the book is mentioned in the script. The script doesn't indicate whether Al's character takes it or not. When I did the master breakdown for that movie, I noted the book as a prop in the restaurant scene. I also matched back to see, if he did take the book, where else we might see it. I wrote the note "Book?" in the prop column in the master breakdown for those scenes and on the appropriate script pages.

Al's character takes a long moody walk around the city after that meeting. We shot the first little bit of his walk before we filmed the restaurant scene. At that point no one, including the director, Al, or myself, was thinking about the book. But because I had matched back in prep and made notes in my script and master breakdown, I could ask Al, "Do you think your guy takes the book? You haven't been home or to your office yet. Do you want to have it in this scene?" Al thought about it and said, "Yeah, that's great!" In the final cut, Al holds the book closely all during that walk, which really helps deliver the emotional impact of his wandering around the city, which was the point of the sequence. This logical thinking, this understanding of how to deliver a story, is what script supervisors do and what automated breakdowns cannot do.

- **Check** with the prop master to make sure the prop is ready before talking to the director.
- **Check** with the director before talking to the actor.

Before I spoke to Al, I checked with the prop master to make sure he had the book ready, and then to the director to see if he liked the idea. Don't ambush your prop master. They will look bad if an actor or director wants something that is not made yet. It would have been much, much better if I had asked the director about the book in preproduction! But better late than never.

You can see in Fig. 4.7, in scenes 1–4, I have made a note to check if Liz will be carrying her backpack.

PROPS/ART/WARDROBE/MAKEUP/SPECIAL EFFECTS

This is my most flexible column. It may be one, two, or three separate columns, depending on the needs of the story.

Props

"Props" is short for property. Any prop mentioned in the script should be entered in your breakdown. For each mentioned prop, think about where else it might show up. If an actor is carrying a briefcase in an afternoon scene, he probably has it when we see him leaving for work that morning. Does the prop change during the story? Scraps of paper get more crumpled as they are handled. Lost things may get dusty or discolored.

> Feel free to formulate the columns in this breakdown to **best serve your story**.

Art

Think about what happens on each set that might affect the continuity of set dressing. There may be evidence of a fight or a meal. If a character is distracted, their apartment may be untidy. If a scene takes place in the middle of a snowstorm or a heat wave, there may be heavy coats hung by the door or a fan in motion.

Wardrobe

Think about what happens to the character while wearing each costume. Do they get in a fight? Get caught in the rain? Dance all night? Mark down significant events in the "Match" column and match back and forward to make sure the costume looks right, even when the action is filmed out of order.

Any mention of a specific item of clothing should be noted and checked for matching back. Forty pages after the wardrobe is set, there may be a line that says, "He takes the gun out of his jacket pocket." That character should have a jacket with a pocket that has been established in a natural manner.

Makeup

Think about what happens to each character that may affect the makeup. Do they get their nose broken? Does the character's health change? Are they sweaty from running in the last scene? Have they been crying or drinking for hours? Make a note and match back (see Fig. 4.8).

If a character ages, there may be special makeup for the different stages of the story. If so, note the character's age in all scenes and try to find the points that allow for elegant shifts between looks.

If the makeup changes are complicated, you will make a special breakdown, in partnership with the makeup department, showing those details. Abbreviate that breakdown to the master breakdown. Make a note of the character's makeup whenever that look is important for the story.

Special Effects[13]

If the script says that it is snowing in a particular scene, it should be snowing in continuous scenes before or after. Match back and mark it as such, even if the adjacent scene is an interior. We may see a window or someone coming in from outside. If the scene before is not continuous, you have some leeway. Make a note on your side page to find out what the director, DP, and production designer are thinking. The AD is a good person to ask about this as they have been to dozens of meetings before you were hired. If it has been settled, the AD will tell you what is planned. If it hasn't come up yet, they will say, "Thank you!"

VOICE-OVER/VIDEO AND AUDIO PLAYBACK/VISUAL EFFECTS/TV AND AIRPLANE DIALOG

This column will change with the needs of your project. Not all movies have all these production elements. Include only what is relevant to your script.

As you go through your scenes, note any mention of video or audio playback, voice-over, off-camera dialog, and visual effects. If you need to record alternate dialog for TV or airplane edits, note them here. Alternate dialog is explained a bit later in this chapter and in the section on "TV and Airplane Dialog" in Chapter 9, page 302.

Voice-Over (and Off-Camera) Dialog[14]

Often voice-over dialog will start or end on camera. When this is the case, the entire dialog, both on- and off-camera, will be recorded when you shoot the on-camera lines. Treat all the lines that run together as one piece, no matter how many scenes they cover. Mark it well so that you don't forget any stray pieces. Also mark your script for dialog that crosses scene breaks. It is easier to forget than you might think.

Even when none of the voice-over is on camera, look for lines that are meant to play together. The pieces could be scattered through the script or play as bookends at the beginning and end of the movie. As long as they are meant to feel like one piece, it is better to record them at the same time, in the same place. Make a list that includes every little bit. It is our job to make sure none are left out.

Playback

Note any mention of video or audio playback. If you are not sure whether a scene has some, make a note on your side sheet: "Is the TV on in sc. 58? Is there a chance we might see it?"

If the TV is on, but we won't see it, it becomes sound only, which can be added in post-production. This is still important to note, even if we don't hear it on set as we are shooting. The actors will want to know what playback will sound like in the finished scene. They may want to react to it emotionally. If it is loud they may have to change their performance to sound like they are shouting over the noise.

Visual Effects

If your project has some visual effects, you need to keep track of all the elements that will be needed for each composite shot.[15] If there are just a few simple effects, I track them in my master breakdown. I make a row for each composite shot, with rows under that for each element. If it is a very complicated VFX shoot, I work from the VFX department's breakdown. There will be more about this later in this chapter (see pages 77–79) and in Chapter 6.

EAT, PRAY, LOVE — Mary Cybulski — MASTER BREAKDOWN — White Script — page 5 of 15 — 8/5/09

Sc	I/E	D/N	Loc	Action	Characters	Ward/ MU/H	Props/Art	PB/VO	Match
67	E	D	Piazza	Liz translates a newspaper story	Liz		Newspaper: Obeita bambini, v.very worn dictionary. Espresso, biscotti, fountain like drawing, drawing		
68	I	D	Gelato store	Liz returns for gelato	Liz, clerks		Gelato		
69	E	D	Street, church	Liz eats gelato, passes a couple making out.	Liz make out couple 2		Gelato		same as sc 68
70	I	D	Church	Liz eats gelato in church.	Liz, nun		Gelato	VO Liz	same as 68
DAY	27-29								
71	I	D	Barber Shop	Luca tells Liz that Americans don't know pleasure, Bel far niente. The barber talk about gestures	Liz, Sofi, Giovanni, Luca, 2 barbers	Shaving	Sofi's pastry, dictionary?	Italian song	Liz in Rome 3 weeks
72	E	D?	street, Café	Gesture Montage: Woman tells the waiter that her meal was good.	Waiter, woman				
73	E	D?	Campo de Fiori	Gesture Montage: Ancient woman bites her knuckles. He replies	Ancient woman, vendor				
74	E	D?	Street	Gesture Montage: Man slaps Sofi's butt. She tells him to buzz off.	Liz, Sofi, butt slap man				
75				Omit					
76	E	D	Street	Gesture Montage: Taxi almost hits them, all 4 say buzz off.	Liz, Sofi + 2 (Luca & Giovanni?)		Wild Taxi		
DAY	30								
77	E	D	Restaurant	Liz orders a complicated meal in Italian. Montage of CU food being eaten. See Roman woman. What is Liz's word?	Liz, Sofi, Giovanni, Maria, Guilio +1? (Luca?)	Roman woman	Leaves turn & fall. CU Lots of food being eaten.		Leaves are turning
DAY	31								
78	I	Mrn	Liz's Flat	Liz looks at her Yoga matt and invites Sofi to Naples.	Liz		Espresso, Dusty Yoga mat	Dial tone. VO Liz	
79	E	D	Naples	Liz & Sofi cross a wild street in Naples.	Liz, Sofi, 7 year old girl		Wind, drying clothes. Dirty.		
80				Omit					
81	I	D	Pizzeria da Michele	Liz & Sofi eat lots of pizza	Liz, Sofi	Sofi & Liz have gained weight	Great pies.		weight gain
DAY	32			Is it still - The next day					
82	I	N	Bar	Liz & friends watch football game	Liz, Giovanni, Old man who swears.			Football on TV	
85	I	N	Bar	Cont.	Cont			Football on TV	Out of order
87	I	N	Bar	Cont	Cont			Football on TV	

(left margin labels: ROME, NAPLES, ROME)

Fig. 4.8 Master breakdown (page 5) from *Eat Pray Love*.

TV and Airplane Dialog

If a script's dialog contains profanity, the studio may require alternate dialog that can be used for PG versions of the final film. This material could be recorded in an additional take as you shoot the scene, or it could be wild track recorded either on set or in post-production. Your producer can tell you what the policy is on your project. If your production needs to get alternative material on set, it is your responsibility to remind everyone.

Taking time to record PG dialog in the rush of a production day can be challenging. Actors and directors are often hesitant to participate in the deliberate watering down of a strong performance. A weak producer may tell you to make sure to get alternate dialog, then conveniently leave set, assuming you will act as an enforcer. Don't fall for it. It is not your job to tell the director what to do. Your job is to remind the director that alternate dialog is owed.

That said, PG dialog can be a contractual obligation, even when it doesn't make sense. Talk to your producer to find out how they want to play this. My favorite story about navigating this nonsensical situation comes from David Mamet's movie *Homicide*. David's movies have very specific language. The profanities are no exception. The producers agreed with him that it was ridiculous to replace a certain car crash of expletives with something softer. When the cops break into a sweet but fierce lady's apartment, looking for her grandson, she tells them, "Get out of my M-F apartment." They fulfilled their contractual obligation by recording the alternate dialog as, "Get out of my freshly vacuumed apartment."

MATCHING

This is a wild card column for any continuity issue that I want to flag for matching back during my breakdown or for finding quickly on set. It could include a major event that changes the mood or the physical world of the story. Something like, "Jared & Josh are shot" or "Erica gets her ring back."

ADDING COLOR

If you generate and distribute your breakdowns digitally, color can be a huge help in presenting a format that helps you understand and work efficiently with your breakdown. Let's look closer at the beautiful master breakdown that Sharon Watt made for *Mr. Robot*. I wish I could reproduce it in color for the print version of this publication. I will walk you through what she did and maybe you will be able to imagine it well enough to be inspired when you use color in your own breakdowns.

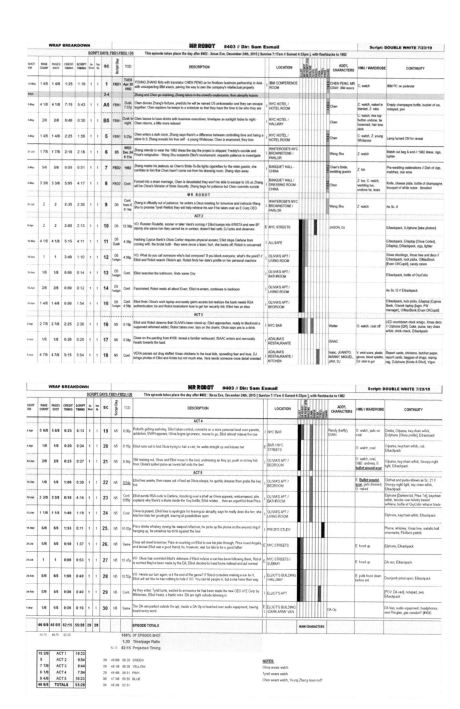

Fig. 4.9 Sharon Watt's master breakdown for *Mr. Robot.*

Here are a few of the many things I admire about this breakdown:

1. The color stripe for tracking characters. Each character has their own bright color, making it incredibly easy to get an overview of how the characters populate the script. Sharon invented this. Genius.

2. *Mr. Robot* is an episodic series. When cross-boarding (capturing media for more than one episode at a time), multiple breakdowns can make your workflow cumbersome. Sharon has incorporated the Scene/Page/Time breakdown into the master breakdown to cut down on how many breakdowns she has to reference, making her workflow more efficient. The danger of including too much information on one page is that the breakdown can become muddled and difficult to read. Sharon solves this by putting the scene/page/time information to the left and using a visually strong scene column, bold type, and a muted fill color to separate them. This breakdown reads like two breakdowns on one page.

3. The strong scene numbers make them easy to use as a spine. You can quickly find your place in the story and jump off from there.

4. The font is very simple, which makes it readable even when small. She can fit an amazing amount of information on one page. This is important when cross-boarding.

5. Using a soft but distinct background color in the cells that divide the acts lets you see the divisions but holds the episode together.

6. Giving a slightly more eye-catching fill to the flashback scenes makes them perfectly present. A less vibrant color makes the omitted scenes fade back, away from your attention.

7. This story has a lot of voice-over from Mr. Robot. Sharon gives the voice-over its own character stripe. Unorthodox but perfect for this situation. The VO has the same color as Mr. Robot but paler. This is an elegant expression of elegant thinking.

Sharon has revised her master breakdown format over the years, and has arrived at what I think is a perfect episodic breakdown. It is a graphic representation of her strategy—which is exactly the goal of the task.

TIME BREAKDOWNS

I usually make two different time breakdowns for every feature film: the day breakdown and the story beat breakdown. They are as important and informative as the master breakdown.

The Different Uses of Time Breakdowns

Day breakdowns are more condensed than story beat breakdowns. Their purpose is to quickly show what actions take place on the same story day, and how much time passes between those days. The information in them should be brief in order to see the entire story in an overview.

Much of the crew will organize their creative work based on the start and end of each story day. Because day breakdowns are the easiest to read for day breaks, this is my time breakdown that other crew members will usually use. The costume, set dressing, prop, makeup, hair, and AD departments will want to see this breakdown as soon as you have it ready.

> Day breakdowns are more **condensed** than story beat breakdowns.

A story beat breakdown is more detailed. In this breakdown, each scene in the movie has its own entry, which includes a mention of all major and medium story points. Usually there is a time of day for each scene. This breakdown is valuable for locating a particular event in the time frame of the story. It is also good for seeing the progress within each story day.

> Which time breakdown is most important **depends** on the time frame of the film's story.

I depend on both these breakdowns, but sometimes the time frame of a story makes one much more valuable than the other. The film I mentioned above, *People I Know*, takes place over 36 hours, as did the major part of M. Night Shyamalan's *The Happening*. These stories develop minute to minute. For them, the more detailed story beat breakdown had almost everything I needed. *Syriana*, *Eternal Sunshine of the Spotless Mind*, and *Synecdoche, New York* were just the opposite. These films have dense action with lots of players and subplots. Most often a single scene, or just a few closely related scenes, will define one story day. Here, even the condensed day breakdown has plenty of information, and the story beat breakdown is so complicated that it was hard for anyone but me to use. Still, I always do both, and make both available to all departments.

I work out the more complicated story beat breakdown first, because the process unearths more information. By selecting and writing down every story beat that I think is important, little bits of information that I had missed before come into view. Often, that new information changes how I see some part of the story. When the story beat breakdown is complete, I condense its information into the day breakdown.

Story Beat Breakdown

I use a word processing program for my time breakdowns but you could also use a spreadsheet.

SETTING UP THE BREAKDOWN

Start by listing your scene numbers and one-line descriptions. I usually copy and paste them from a completed master or Page/Time/Scene breakdown. Set another column between them. This will be for time of day. Label the columns and add a header (see Fig. 4.10a).

Read through the script again one scene at a time. Replace the one-line description for each scene with all its important story points. Be brief and clear. By this time, you will have a very good idea about what is important to the progress of the story and will be able to get to the heart of each story point precisely. Don't make a note for everything that happens, just what you think is important.

In the "Time" column, note the most exact time of day you have. The script might mention the time on a clock, that the characters are eating lunch, that high school is getting out, the sun is rising, that it is three hours later, it is the next day, or that the fire has burnt out. If you can find nothing else, just add the indication from the scene header: "DAY" or "LATER," etc.

Make story day divisions between any night scene that is followed by a day scene. If the script has some information about how much time has passed between these days, either directly or implied, make a note of that here.

Logic and Guessing

There are always things about time progression that are clear even though they are not stated in the script. I enter these, too. If a character opens a door in one scene and comes out the other side in the next, the scenes are joined by continuous action. If an exterior shot of a new location is used to introduce the action inside, it is assumed that the time of day is the same for both scenes. I keep *assumed* and *known* times of day distinct by noting information that comes straight out of the script in bold type, and implied information in plain type. If I have a guess that I need to talk to the director about, I put it in (parentheses). That way I can progress in my logic without being fooled by mistaking a guess for fact (see Fig. 4.10a).

> Use a system of notating story times that will keep you from **mistaking a guess for fact**.

```
MICHAEL CLAYTON      STORY BEATS                    Page 1 of 8
Mary C.                                                 1/18/06
                         NOT APPROVED
Sc   Time      Action              Sunrise: 7am; Sunset: 5:15pm.

DAY 5 FEBRUARY 6-7, 2006
MONDAY NIGHT - EARLY TUESDAY MORNING

1    2am       VO as: Intro KB&L. Empty, half lit. Size & power.
2    (same)    VO as: Xerox machine printing letterhead.
3    (same)    VO as: Huge empty bullpen.
4    (same)    VO as: Long dark corridor, cleaning crew.
5    (same)    as: Document area. 3 stack paperwork onto trolley.
6    (same)    VO as: Guard smokes in senior partner's office.
7    (same)    VO as: 12 lines blinking on the phone.
8    (same)    VO as: Document trolley past an empty kitchen.
9    (same)    VO as: Maintenance worker vacuums in reception.
10   (same)    VO as: 20 temp workers at word processors.
11   (same)    VO as: Trolley exits elevator at reception.
12   (same)    VO as: Empty hallway. Left over catering.
13   (same)    VO as: Trolley goes through big doors.
14   (same)    The conference room is jumping. 40 people. Marty takes
                 a call from reporter. Barry listens.
15   (same)    U/North logo in Ladies room.
15A  (same)    VO as: Karen Shuler fights off panic on the toilet.
16   (same)    CU ID card. Chinatown casino. Michael weary. He plays
                 cards with the dealer, a Dominican, a plumber & a
                 Chinese landlord. He's out. Talk about the restaurant
                 as his beeper & phone ring.
17   + :04     Michael in elevator, tries to read his pager.
18   + :10     Michael on the phone, walks to the car.
                 Someone is in trouble.
19             West Side highway. Mercedes speeds north.
20             INT. Mercedes, Michael gives up on the GPS system.
21             Mercedes speeds to the Geo Washington Bridge.
22   + :45?    Mercedes pulls up to a Westchester mansion.
23   + :01     In Garage: Michael looks at damage on Jaguar.
24   + :10     Mansion kitchen. Mr. Greer is not happy about finding
                 a trial lawyer. We see what Michael does.
25 sc 24 +1 hr Driveway. Jerry takes over the case,
                 asks for a favor.
26   +:05      Driveway: Mercedes speeds away from the mansion.
27   Pre-dawn  Mercedes comes out of the mansion driveway.
28   Pre-dawn  INT Mercedes, Headlights over Michael.
29   Pre-dawn  Mercedes turns onto a small country road.
30   Pre-dawn  Mercedes. Windows open. Fast. 3 pieces.
30A  Pre-dawn  EXT. Mercedes drive-bys. 3 pieces.
31   Pre-dawn  Michael's POV trestle.
32   Pre-dawn  INT. Mercedes stops.
33   Pre-dawn  Michael gets out, goes to the field. His car
                 explodes. He throws all his IDs into the burning car.
```

Fig. 4.10a An early version of a story beat breakdown, as I was working it out. From *Michael Clayton*.

```
MICHAEL CLAYTON    STORY BEATS              Page 1 of 8
Mary C.
Sc   Time       Action              Sunrise: 7am; Sunset: 5:15pm.

DAY 5 FEBRUARY 6-7, 2006
MONDAY NIGHT - EARLY TUESDAY MORNING

1    2am        VO as: Intro KB&L. Empty, half lit. Size & power.
2    2:01a      VO as: Xerox machine printing letterhead.
3    2:01a      VO as: Huge empty bullpen.
4    2:01a      VO as: Long dark corridor, cleaning crew.
5    2:01a      VO as: Document area. 3 stack paperwork onto trolley.
6    2:02a      VO as: Guard smokes in senior partner's office.
7    2:02a      VO as: 12 lines blinking on the phone.
8    2:03a      VO as: Document trolley past an empty kitchen.
9    2:03a      VO as: Maintenance worker vacuums in reception.
10   2:03a      VO as: 20 temp workers at word processors.
11   2:03a      VO as: Trolley exits elevator at reception.
12   2:03a      VO as: Empty hallway. Left over catering.
13   2:04a      VO as: Trolley goes through big doors.
14   2:04a      The conference room is jumping. 40 people. Marty takes
                a call from reporter. Barry listens.
15   2:05a      U/North logo in Ladies room.
15A  2:05a      VO as: Karen Shuler fights off panic on the toilet.
16   2:06am     CU ID card. Chinatown casino. Michael weary. He plays
                cards with the dealer, a Dominican, a plumber & a
                Chinese landlord. He's out. Talk about the restaurant
                as his beeper & phone ring.
17   2:10a      Michael in elevator, tries to read his pager.
18   2:14a      Michael on the phone, walks to the car.
                Someone is in trouble.
19   2:30a      West Side highway. Mercedes speeds north.
20   2:30a      INT. Mercedes, Michael gives up on the GPS system.
21   2:45am     Mercedes speeds to the Geo Washington Bridge.
22   3am        Mercedes pulls up to a Westchester mansion.
23   3:02a      In Garage: Michael looks at damage on Jaguar.
24   3:10a      Mansion kitchen. Mr. Greer is not happy about finding
                a trial lawyer. We see what Michael does.
25   6:25a      Driveway. Jerry takes over the case,
                asks for a favor.
26   6:30a      Driveway: Mercedes speeds away from the mansion.
27   6:31a      [Predwn/Mhr] Mercedes comes out of the mansion
                driveway.
28   6:32a      [M Hr] INT Mercedes, Headlights over Michael.
29   6:40a      [M Hr] Mercedes turns onto a small country road.
30   6:50a      [M Hr] INT Mercedes. Windows open. Fast. 3 pieces.
30A  6:50a      [M Hr] EXT. Mercedes drive-bys. 3 pieces.
31   6:55a      [M Hr] Michael's POV trestle.
32   6:57a      [M Hr] INT. Mercedes stops.
33   6:58a      [M Hr] Michael gets out, goes to the field. His car
                explodes. He throws all his IDs into the burning car.
```

Fig. 4.10b A completed version of the story beat breakdown. From *Michael Clayton*.

Find out what time the sun rises and sets in your story place at your story time of year. This will help you fit the time of day into the day/night frame of your story.

After you have combed through the script once, take a good look at the breakdown. See what other guesses you can make based on what you know. Add these into the "Time" column, in the appropriate type style. Note the wild guesses with a question mark. Write notes on your side sheet either explaining your guesses or asking the question you need answered before you can move on to the next level of logic. "Scene 65 feels like a new day. Is it?" and "In scene 19, Michael drives to Westchester. I figure, it's late, no traffic, it takes about 45 minutes. Is that right?" These will be some of the things you will ask the director during your next meeting.

You will probably need a few meetings with the director to get the time breakdown right. There will be some big questions that need to be answered in order to work out the details. If you are organized, these meetings can (and should) be short: 15 or 20 minutes each. Ask for a meeting when you can't go forward without some input. When your guess times have all been approved, drop the font variations, and write all the times of day in plain text (see Fig. 4.10b).

DAY BREAKS

The day breaks are the most important elements in your time breakdown. When you have found all of your day breaks, give each new day a heading: Day 1, Day 2, etc., according to their sequence

> **Day breaks** are the most important element in your time breakdown.

in the story. The second story day is called Day 2 even if years have passed since Day 1. A flashback will have an earlier story day than the scene that comes before it in the script.

Give each story day a date, including the year. This will be essential to the prop and set dressing departments when they fabricate newspapers, magazines, legal documents, calendars, and the like for use in the scene.

Generally the day breaks are set at midnight. Each calendar day is a new story day. If your film has a lot of night scenes, as our example does, it may make more sense to break the days at dawn. That way you avoid having a new story day that starts in the middle of continuous or closely associated action.

REPRESENTING THE DIRECTOR'S IDEAS

Here's something you should never lose sight of: even though script supervisors make the time breakdowns, the breakdowns must represent the director's concept of the story's time passing. We help the director by doing lots of research, working out the logic puzzle as much as we can on our own, then coming to them when there is a creative choice. I often recommend a choice to the director and explain my reasoning, as this saves them valuable time, but a time plot is worthless if it is just what I think. It must be a record of what the director is imagining.

> A time plot must be a record of **what the director is imagining**.

THE POWER OF TIME BREAKDOWNS

Once we have a tight time breakdown, the creative departments will use it to make the world of the movie more specific. Say there's a scene that takes place in midtown Manhattan. If it is at noon, the ADs will have the extras sitting in the background and the prop department will have lunches for them. If the scene is at 5:30, the ADs will stage background actors running to the trains and props will bring briefcases. If it is on the same story day as a rainy scene, the background actors will have umbrellas, even if they are not open. These decisions get made thousands of times on every movie. There may be nothing in the dialog that says it is noon, or it is 5:30, but if the scene is placed correctly with appropriate production details, the audience will feel a reality and unity to the story day that is passing.

> A good time breakdown **adds reality and unity** to the story.

HOW TO THINK ABOUT TIME

If all the time references in the script can logically be true, use them. If not, talk to the director/showrunner about which should be adjusted. Everything else has to be figured out. Here are some things to think about as you work out the way time passes in your story.

What time of year is it? All else being equal, I try to match the time of year that we will be in production, especially when shooting in places where the seasons are extreme and apparent on camera. This cuts down on work for the art department and lets the actors be more comfortable in their wardrobe.

If your story takes place over several times or places, you will need a different sunrise/set chart for each sequence. You may have an international phone call with one character in day and the other in night.

Find the distances between places that the characters travel. Give them enough time to get there.

It may seem overly fussy to nail down the exact time of day for each scene, but this really comes in handy when the set dresser needs to set a clock in a hurry. It also makes the time passage between scenes very clear for all departments. This is especially important to the hair and makeup department and the actors. It should be decided and known well before shooting the scene.

```
MICHAEL CLAYTON            STORY DAYS            Page 1 of 3
Mary C.
                           Sunrise: 7am; Sunset: 5:15pm.
Sc         Time       Action

DAY 5 FEBRUARY 6-7, 2006
MONDAY NIGHT - EARLY TUESDAY MORNING

1-13       2:15am     Temp workers turnout stacks of paperwork.
14         2:15am     Full Conference room. Marty takes a call.
15-15A     2:15am     Karen fights off panic on the toilet.
16-24      2:15-3am   Michael plays cards in Chinatown. He gets called
                      to Westchester, sets up Mr. Greer with Jerry.
25-33      6:50-7am   Michael talks to Jerry in the driveway. He drives
                      away fast. He gets out, walks to a field, his car
                      blows up. He throws his stuff into the burning
                      car.


              FOUR DAYS EARLIER


DAY 1 FEBRUARY 2-3, 2006
THURSDAY DAY & NIGHT — INTO EARLY FRIDAY MORNING
()= Central time, 1 hour earlier. All others are NY time.

34-38      8:30am     Michael drives Henry to school.
39-41      9:30am     Auction at Tim's.
42-43      10:30      Law firm. Intro Michael at work.
44-45      11a-12p    Michael takes phone calls.
45-55      (7-7:45am) Nebraska. Karen practices for an in-house promo.
           (11am)     She tapes it with Don. It is interrupted.
56-57      12:30-1:21p Michael leaves for Milwaukee.
58         (3pm)      Karen arrives at Milwaukee hotel.
59         (4pm)      Michael visits Arthur in jail.
60-66      (7pm)      Karen reviews video of Arthur, gets bio of
                      Michael as:
           (8-10p)    Michael gets Arthur out of jail.
67         (11pm)     Michael debriefs 4 deposition lawyers.
68-71      12mn       Henry talks to Arthur on the phone.
           (11pm)     Arthur on phone, central time.
72-72A     (11:10pm)  Michael & Karen in the bar.
                      Karen tells what happened in the parking lot.
73-74      (11:45pm)  Michael pays Elston for watching Arthur.
                      Arthur asks Michael if this is what he wanted.
75         (12:45am)  Karen has Arthur's briefcase and Memo #229.
                      She calls Mr. Vern, gives him a code from Don.
```

Fig. 4.11 Day breakdown. From *Michael Clayton*.

Often I discover something while working on my time breakdown that makes me go back to the master breakdown and finesse some matching back notes.

CHEATING TIME

All this logic and puzzle solving is background to help the director make choices. If the director wants to stretch time a bit, it is almost always fine. No one will be examining the time passage like you

> If the director wants to **stretch time** a bit, it is almost always fine.

are. If you think it will be an obvious mistake, you can argue for the logic, but always imagine how time will feel to the audience, not how it looks on your breakdown.

Day Breakdown

When you have all the times and day breaks worked out in your story beat breakdown, condense the action to only the most major beats. Group them as tightly as you can into story days and publish that as your day breakdown. Get it down to the shortest it can be and still tell the story (see Fig. 4.11). Notice how the shape of the flash-forward (Day 5, at the top of the page) stands out when the story is condensed like this. Also take a look at the dual times of day in Story Day 1. This is because some continuous action takes place in New York City and some in Nebraska.

If there are a lot of flashbacks or any other sort of complicated time structure, I will logic out the time progression in chronological order. This helps make the time flow visible. Once that is done, I make a separate breakdown in script order. For more about this, see the breakdowns for *Eternal Sunshine of the Spotless Mind*, Figs 4.19–4.21.

SPECIAL BREAKDOWNS

If there is something in the story that I think may be difficult and important to track, I make a special breakdown just for that arc. It could be anything. Here's some examples of special breakdowns I've done.

Visual Effects (VFX)

VFX shots are a combination of original live action set-ups and/or computer-generated images (CGI). For instance, the combination of 1) an actor in front of a studio green screen, 2) a mountain vista photographed

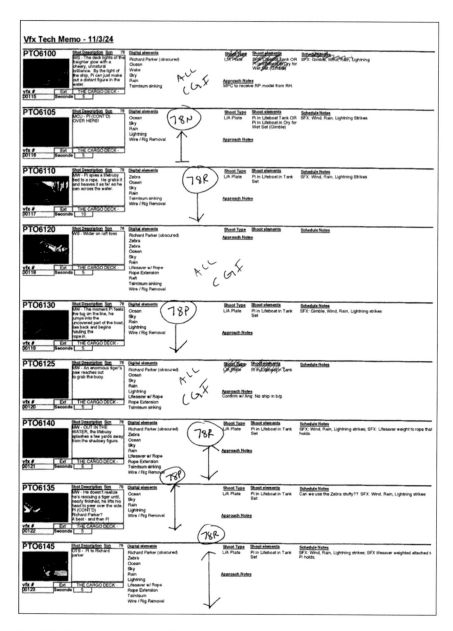

Fig. 4.12 VFX breakdown. From *Life of Pi*.

on location, and 3) computer-generated falling snow may be combined to make a final shot of an actor in front of a mountain vista in a snowfall. We call the three, original, individual images "elements" and the finished combination shot a "composite."

If you have composite shots in your movie, break down each one to show its original elements. That way, you can make sure you've recorded all the pieces that the visual effects crew will need. This breakdown also gives you and the editors a good reference for tracking which elements go together. You can do this work as part of the master breakdown, as explained earlier in this chapter or, if there is a lot of complicated VFX work, you can make a dedicated VFX breakdown.

Some films have so many composite shots that it is better to start from the breakdown that the visual effects department generates. We did this in the film *Life of Pi* (see Fig. 4.12).[16] On this project, we had so much material to keep track of (an hour and a half of VFX shots) and most of them looked kind of similar: a boy in a boat in a wave tank! Because I lined the VFX crew's own breakdown with the set-up numbers from set, it was very clear to them which live action shot was made for which composite shot. It also made clear which set-ups still needed to be shot. This is harder than it seems; some composites have two elements, some have half a dozen, and some are entirely computer generated.

Composite shots will have their own VFX shot number, designed by the visual effects team and shown here as three letters and four numbers. Live action elements will keep the set-up number they were assigned when shot.

This lined breakdown goes to the VFX department, the edit room, and the production office. Live action elements are labeled here with their set-up numbers ("78P," for example) and a line drawn over the VFX composites where they belong.

Many Parallel Story Lines

The action of *Syriana* had so many story lines and jumped around the world so often that I made a set of two master breakdowns: one in script order and the other grouped by continent.

Change in a Character

I worked on a film called *Thousand Pieces of Gold* in which the lead actress, Rosalind Chao, starts as a young girl in China speaking only Mandarin. She is sent to the American West, where we follow

Whenever I have an element that needs **special tracking**, I design a breakdown that lets me see the development of that element.

her for many years. By the end of the story, she is speaking fluent English. I worked with Rosalind and our dialect coach to make a Chinese to English transition breakdown. We had six variations within the transition with specific traits of each stage: very round vowels, dropped adjectives, things like that. My job was to find the best breaks between stages. The dialect coach designed and defined the stages. This was incredibly helpful; we shot out of order and Rosalind and I could check in easily before each scene and know which stage of language she should have and which traits we had to keep in mind.

Weather and the Natural World

An important element of *The Ice Storm* was a brooding feeling of the storm moving in, hitting, and then dawn breaking. I made a weather breakdown that included a minute-by-minute sunrise progression.

Injuries

The makeup, hair, costume, prop, and set dressing departments will all make their own breakdowns based on the time breakdowns you give them. Still, if there is a special continuity concern with one of them, I will work with that department and we will make an additional breakdown that is based on the script's story points. Here are a couple of examples that track injuries.

I worked on a cowboy movie, *The Hi-Lo Country*, in which the cowboys were always fighting. I made an injury breakdown that tracked who was hurt, how, and when, as well as how and when they healed. This involved a three-way dialog with the director, the makeup designer, and me (see Fig. 4.13). You can see that this breakdown was not made to track the details of the injury makeup, but as an overview, so that the makeup could be designed with the story's time frame in mind.

In *People I Know*, Al Pacino's character spends the 36 hours of the film drinking and taking drugs. I made a breakdown for him that he loved. It was one page, 36 lines: one line for every hour of story time. It listed every mood altering substance he took and when.

The evolution of this breakdown is a good example of the importance of organization and presentation. The first chart I made for this breakdown, Fig. 4.14 (two pages), has the information I pulled from the script. It's good, has a lot of details, but the simplicity in my next breakdown, Fig. 4.15, is better. Because the later breakdown has the information hung on a spine of uniformly progressing time, one hour per line, you can pick any scene in the movie and feel immediately where Eli is in the flow of his chemical influence.

```
Hi Lo Country  Injuries                                  p. 2

sc. 55 Big Boy gets out of jail.

He was in a fight the night before and hurt. He has some injuries
     like dried blood on his lip that he can clean up at Levi's and
     be done with.
We see it in sc. 56, at Levi's getting cleaned up.

sc. 68 Coyote hunting. Pete, Big Boy & Uncle Bob jump from
the truck.

Pete limps.
We see him limp in sc. 69, walking back. Make-up will be decided when
     we see the truck roll.
Next see Pete 2 days later in sc. 70-73, Big Boy wins at cards.
Next see Pete 3 days later in sc. 74, bringing groceries to Ma.
Next see Pete 1 month later in sc. 75, driving cattle from hills.

We will decide Big Boy's injuries when we see the truck roll.

Uncle Bob will also be decided when we see the truck roll.
Only seen that day in sc. 69, walking back.

sc. 77: Changing a tire on Hoovers truck.

Big Boy gets hit in the face by a pry bar. It bleeds.
Big Boy next seen that night in sc. 80, Mona has bottom
Big Boy next seen 3 weeks later at the rodeo

sc. 84: Little Boy s rodeo ride.

Little Boy starts to get mauled. We will decide how hurt he gets
     after we see the stunt.
Little Boy next seen that night in sc. 86, at dance.

Big Boy is hooked by bull.
He has a hole in his thigh. He has no stitches.
Next seen that night in sc. 85-92, from the big fight to Meesa.

sc. 86: The Big Fight at the dance.

Big Boy's rodeo injury opens up & bleeds. It will not bleed enough to
     leave a trail of blood on the floor. He has some facial injuries
     and some teeth that have loosened.
Next seen that night in sc. 87-92, continuous to Meesa.
Big Boy next seen 1 month later for blizzard sequence.

Does Pete get hurt? BRUISE on CHEEK

Les is beaten badly. He is not seen again.
```

Fig. 4.13 Injuries breakdown. From *The Hi-Lo Country*.

Complicated Hair and Makeup

The hair color breakdown for Kate Winslet in *Eternal Sunshine of the Spotless Mind* was hilarious. We figured it out in a chronological breakdown, then put it back into the script order, including notes about how far her roots had grown out for each scene (see Fig. 4.21).

The Big Boards

The background action in Ang Lee's *Taking Woodstock* was very important to the story. The movie is about a family living in upstate New York when

"PEOPLE I KNOW"   Mary C.   1/31/01

Eli's Chemical Damage Breakdown   page 1 of 2
From Original white pages 1-16-01 draft

Scene	Time	Action	Condition	Damage
1	9:05p	Eli tries to pee at theater	sweating/ Bay Rum	
3	10:54p	Eli asks Ross for some percocet & gin		Asks for gin & Percocet
4	11:45p	At Joe Allen's		cigarettes
6	1:45a	At home		a joint
9	1:45a	At home		a pill
16	1:50a	In Cary's car		cigarettes
20	2:40a	Eli & Jilli in town car		Xanax, scotch
23	2:54a	Eli & Jilli in WTC elevator	sweating	cigarettes
24B	2:56a	WTC party		opium
37A	3:27a	In Jilli's hotel bathroom	Looks ghastly, heart racing	Ambien (no more Xanax) 2 pills from pill case
38	7 am	Eli wakes up	Impossibly disheveled In shock	
41	9 am	At home in bed, Regis on TV		Large Starbucks
44	9:15a	Sandy at Eli's apartment		B12 shot
45	11:55a	Intro Eli's office	sweating & disheveled	
53	12:13p	Rev. Blunt's church	drenched with sweat	
54	1:25p	Four Seasons	Eli looks good.	Whiskey sours talked about

Fig. 4.14 Chemical damage breakdown, first try. From *People I Know*.

"PEOPLE I KNOW"   Mary C.   1/31/01

Eli'S Chemical Damage Breakdown   page 2 of 2
From Original white pages 1-16-01 draft

Scene	Time	Action	Condition	Damage
55	1:40p	Vicky's hotel room		scotch Xanax cigarettes
62	2:09p	At payphone		coffee
64	2:30p	In Sandy's office	Shaking, ashen	cigarettes. a pill to relax him.
65	3:05p	At the med lab	flushed, red	Demoral drip
66	3:55p	Central Park	Limping a little	
67	4:28p	Eli puts Wormly out	Drained	
69	4:28p	Cary is waiting in Eli's office	looks awful	
83	4:35p	Eli has been fired		whiskey
86	4:37p	Eli loses it in the elevator	Drained, disheveled bloodshot	
94	5:40p	Eli calls Cary on a payphone	shaking	Xanax
95	6pm	Eli in shower with drink		whiskey?
97	6:50p	The Palm bar		bourbon
98	7:41p	Eli lying on the floor		same bourbon?
104	7:45p	Eli negotiates in kitchen		Lots of shrimp
107	8:30p	In Palm bathroom	vomits	3 Xanax, whiskey
113	11pm	Eli is 'bumped' at the news stand		Eli is shot
114	11:20p	Eli pisses blood		
115	11:30p	Eli limps over to TV		bourbon cigarettes

Fig. 4.14 *continued.*

the Woodstock music festival comes to town. The festival had to be a full-bodied character, arriving like a tidal wave that destroys everything in its path. David Silver, our historian and expert hippy, did months of research to come up with hundreds of little stories, each full of period details: characters, action, props, set dressing, and attitudes that would make the flood

"PEOPLE I KNOW"

Time Line of Eli's Drug Taking
Based on Original White Pages 1-16-01 draft
M. Cybulski   1/31/01

Time	Scenes	Location	Drugs
9pm			
10pm			
11pm	3	EXT Theater	Asks for gin & Percocet
12mdnt	4	Joe Allen's	cigarettes
1am			
2am	6, 9, 16	At home	a joint, a pill, cigarettes
3am	20, 23, 24B	Party w Jilli	xanax, scotch, cigarettes, opium
4am	37A	Jilli's hotel	Ambian, 2 pills from case
5am			
6am			
7am			
8am			
9am	41	At home	Large Starbuck's, B12 shot
10am			
11am			
12noon			
1pm	54	Four Seasons	Whiskey sour, scotch, xanax, cigs
2pm	62	At payphone	Coffee
3pm	64	Sandy's office	cigarettes, pill to relax, demoral drip
4pm			
5pm	83	Eli's office	whiskey
6pm	94	phone, shower	xanax, drink (whiskey?)
7pm	97, 98	The Palm	bourbon
8pm	104, 107	The Palm	Lots of shrimp, 3 xanax, whiskey
9pm			
10pm			
11pm	113, 115	Street & home	Shot, (sleeping pill) bourbon, cigs
12mdnt			
1am			
2am			
3am			
4am			
5am			
6am			
7am			
8am			
9am	121	Home	Found dead

Fig. 4.15 Chemical damage breakdown, final version. From *People I Know*.

of the festival feel real. I led a team of four that worked for weeks organizing and plotting the details on what we called "the Big Board," an 8′ by 30′ grid that helped Ang plot the physical and dramatic arcs of the festival. It was insane and really worked (see Fig. 4.16).

Each scene has its own column on the big board. Blue vertical lines divide the story days. Each row is a category: sometimes physical, like traffic flow or level of filth in the pool; sometimes atmospheric, like the level of peace and harmony. The post-its are production notes: either details showing, for instance, what is in the dumpster, or a synopsis of a little story that is happening in the background of the scripted action. At the bottom of each scene's column are reference photographs that relate to that scene. We could walk up and down the board, following one or a number of related themes, and feel how each dramatic arc would play over the length of the story and how each arc affected the others.

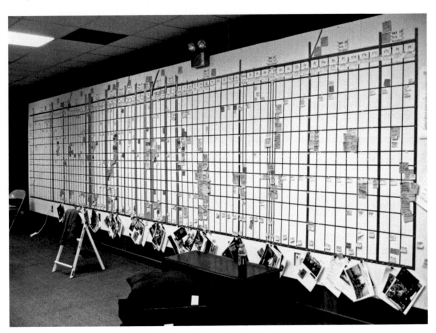

Fig. 4.16 The Big Board for *Taking Woodstock*.

We couldn't have the Big Board on set. We tried to make a spreadsheet that replicated the board, but its information was too cramped. In the end, we made up supplementary handouts for each story day and attached them to the call sheet. The handouts filled in the part of the movie that wasn't in the script (see Fig. 4.17). They had so much additional information that the

DAY 18 **July 28** Monday   **PEOPLE COME**

58-60   Sonia parks van in the swamp.
         People want tickets. Gangsters get beat up by the
Teichbergs
61-62   Mike opens a bank account

> Traffic: 3 lanes — 2(west)/1 — 2 west are slow and
>   heavy
> Crowd: Mostly hippies, 15-20% College students
> Parking lot: Full
> Dumpster: trash filled to top
> Ticket line: 30 people. The line goes toward Elliot's
>   bungalow. Dialog & (in another scene) Vilma.
> Pool: A few pieces of found furniture:
>   2 stools & a milk crate?
> Landing area: Circle of rocks, no peace sign
> Pay Phone: small line, 8-10, dialog.

Vignettes:

Sc 58. Bus parks in swamp: There will be 6 hippies in the bus,
looking out the back window. (Cast from family next door to location)

A leader type, who is not the driver, will pay Sonia so we don't have
to see the front of the bus. Maybe a woman.
Ask David what kind of hippies they should be (what haven't we seen?)
and what do they use for a purse to keep their common money in? We
see the money come out of that. A cookie box?

Shtupping in bushes , MEDITATOR ADDED ON PATH.

Sc 58-60 Gangster scene.
 START LITEN · OH GROUND.
Breakaway glass, side view mirror

16mm crew

All the tribal leaders will be here by this point. 60

Pool family is arriving (sc 58B?). Puts out awning (sc 60?).
Photo #55 Painted hippy bus
Photo #25 Painted Pool Family
Photo #53 Painted Pool Family
Photo #107 Painted Pool Family
Photo #108 Painted Pool Family
Photo #109 Painted Pool Family

See Willow people carrying sofa from back, wire spool from dumpster,
someone else digging in dumpster.

Fig. 4.17 Additional action handout. From the information worked out on *Taking Woodstock*'s Big Board.

```
8/21/08  8:15 PM        Woodstock Progress                  p. 8 of 28
Other Willows unload something from truck. Boxes of food? Something
to build their life.
They are Native American in theme. One plays a wooden flute. One has
a baby in a papoose that is on her back or leaned against a wall.

We see 2 musicians through the office window.

Sc 60
Place short people around Vilma in ticket line to make her look
really tall.

Sc 61
Looking out WV office window.

We see the littlest bit of action, almost nothing. Some Willow
action?

Sc 62
See out bank window

People coming to town. Mostly by car & foot.

Group of Sharon Tate hippies. Maybe hanging around a truck where
watermelons are being sold off the back.

Other selling stands.

(skip 2 days)
```

Fig. 4.17 *continued.*

ADs made a second call sheet just for the background action.

You can see by the different formats of the Big Board and the handouts that the Big Board is designed to help us figure out which elements should be in each scene, while the handouts are designed to help us deliver those elements. This is why I believe that scene breakdowns formatted as cards are fine for ADs but not for script supervisors. The ability to walk up and down the board and experience the flow of the entire story is incredibly helpful in understanding story progression and selecting meaningful production elements.

> Our **Big Board** helped us to see and adjust the flow of information. Once that was set, we could condense that information to a form that was easier to execute on set.

We made a similar board for *Life of Pi*, which included the state of the weather, ocean surface, light, decay of the boat, Pi's weight loss, sunburn, emotional state, his acquired skills, how much he became like a tiger himself, among other details (see Fig. 4.18).

Non-Continuous Time

When I work on a film with a lot of non-continuous time, I make two sets of time breakdowns, one set in script order and one set in chronological, story time order. This was essential for *Eternal Sunshine of the Spotless Mind* (see Figs 4.19 and 4.20). I went back and forth between the two day breakdowns and the two story beat breakdowns for every scene. I did the same for *Michael Clayton*, which helped to make sure the bookend action held solidly.

Notice that the breakdown in script order, Fig. 4.19, starts with Day 23.

Fig. 4.21 shows a day breakdown for the same movie. You can see how both the chronological and compressed time is really useful in mapping Clementine's hair color. To get an idea of how impossible it would be to track this story's chronological continuity by scene order, read the scene numbers from the top of the page down.

Post-Modern Time and Place

Synecdoche, New York takes place over 50 years during which different characters age at different rates. This could get really confusing, so I made a year breakdown similar to "Eli's Chemical Damage," using one line per year (as experienced by the main character, Caden) and a column for all the main characters listing their age during each year they were alive.

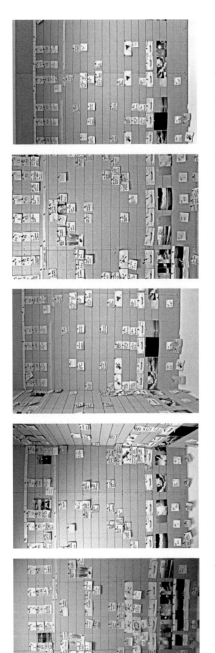

Fig. 4.18 Five sections of the big board for *Life of Pi*, midway through prep. By the end of the shoot, it was jam-packed with information.

```
"ETERNAL SUNSHINE OF THE SPOTLESS MIND"    Mary Cybulski      page  1
SCENE BREAKDOWN                                      1/19/03
From Yellow pages, with production notes

Scene Time        Action
_____

DAY 23 Feb 14,2003

DAY
1     7:58am      Joel changes platforms & gets on empty train.
                  1 — On platform & in train.
                  1pt — Joel in parking lot.
                  X1 — 2nd unit in parking lot.
A1    8:30am      Joel riding on the train, away from the city.
                  XA1 — POV out window.
                  (Shoot some for sc 11 & some at dusk for sc 12, too)
                  (Some running shots from X11 may be used here.)
2     11:30am     Joel calls in sick from Montauk.
3     11:45am     Joel nods to an old man on the beach.
4     12 noon     Joel looks out at the ocean.
5     12:30am     Joel writes & draws in a notebook, we get some
                  history. He sees Clementine on the beach.
6     1pm         Joel peaks into empty beach house.
7     1:15pm      Joel digs in the sand with a stick.
8     2pm         Joel is eating in a diner, Clementine comes in,
                  takes a nip and orders what he is having.
9     3:30pm      Joel & Clem both stare at the ocean.
10    4:45pm      Clem waves at Joel on the platform. He writes.
11    4:55pm      Clem enters the train car where Joel is.
                   She is friendly, he is shy.
                  11 — Finish scene
                  11ptA — Start scene
                  X11 — 2nd unit, Ext. Running train, afternoon.
                   (Also can use some of XA1 POV out window)
12    5:35pm      DUSK. On the train, Clem sits closer & watches Joel.
                  X12 - 2nd unit, Ext. Running train, evening.
                   (Also can use some of XA1 POV out window)
NIGHT
13    7pm         Dark outside, Clem sits closer still. Some women
                   have valentines.
14    7:45pm      Joel exits train & goes to his car, sees dent.
15    7:50pm      Joel asks Clem if she wants a ride.
      7:55pm      She asks him inside.
                  15 — In Mt. Vernon
                  15ptA — In Williamsburg
                  X15 - Ext. Joel's car: POV from car & Drive-bys.
16    8:05pm      Joel and Clem have drinks and get to know each
                   other.
                  16 - On stage (Int. Apartment.)
                  16ptA - In Williamsburg (stairway, hall, Ext.)
_____
```

Fig. 4.19 Script order story beat breakdown. From *Eternal Sunshine of the Spotless Mind*.

```
"ETERNAL SUNSHINE OF THE SPOTLESS MIND"          1/7/03              page   1
Scenes in Chronological Order                    Mary Cybulski

Scene   Time      Action
```

JOEL IS A KID

R+C
PLANE + VIDEO TAPE

DAY 1 - 1969   MEMORY Joel is 1 years old.
95   4pm   Baby Joel & Clem in sink.

DAY 1A - 1972   MEMORY Joel is 4 years old.
88   5:30pm   Joel hides under the table. Clem is a
                  neighbor lady who gets under the table with Joel.
92   5:35pm   Under the table, Joel & Clem have sex.
                  His mom pats him on the head & he tells Clem that
                  Pat is copying him.

DAY 2 - 1973   MEMORY Joel is 5 years old.
105   Day   Joel smashes a bird with a hammer.
                  Clem smothers him & disappears.

DAY 3 - 1978   MEMORY Joel is 10 years old.
114pt. 1pm   Joel draws Clem. His dad is fishing
                  outside the window, drunk & surly.

DAY 4 - 1981   MEMORY Joel is 13 years old. (in Jr. High)
101   9pm   Joel masturbates. His mother comes in.

DAY 4A — 1991   MEMORY Joel has grown up & gone off to college.
art 114A   Joel's dad's boat, half sunk & rotting. *OMIT*
```

**JOEL & CLEMENTINE MEET** Clementine has GREEN hair.

```
DAY 5 — Sept 29, 2000   MEMORY   Two years ago.

133 (½ BEAM)      Joel gets ready to go to the beach party,
136   4:30pm      Joel, Rob & Carrie get out of the car at the beach.
137   4:31pm      Joel, Rob & Carrie walk to the beach.
138   4:32pm      Joel, Rob & Carrie arrive at the beach party.
139   5-7pm       Joel sits alone. Clem comes to talk to
                  him. She eats his food and they hang out for hours.
140   7:30pm      Joel & Clem walk near the beach houses.
141   7:33pm      Joel & Clem break into the beach house.
                  (They say goodbye.)
141A              Replay Clem's shirt in surf.
142   7:36pm      Joel runs past the bon fire.
143   8pm         Joel, Rob & Carrie drive home from the party. Out
                  the window he sees faded scenes.
130   11:30pm     Rob & Carrie drop off Joel after the beach.
```

Fig. 4.20 Chronological order story beat breakdown. From *Eternal Sunshine of the Spotless Mind*.
```

```
"ETERNAL SUNSHINE OF THE SPOTLESS MIND"     1/7/03        page  1
Story Days in Chronological Order              Mary Cybulski
```
                                            Low Beard -

JOEL IS A KID

DAYS	DATES	SCENES	ACTION
1-4A	1969- 1981	95, 88, 92,105, 101,114.	Joel is 1, 4, & 5 years old. Joel is 10 & 13 years old.

JOEL & CLEMENTINE MEET & HAVE THEIR FIRST DATE.

DAYS	DATES	SCENES	ACTION
5	Sept 29 2000	136-143 130-131	The beach party. After the party.
6&7	Sept 30 & Oct 1,2000	128-129	Joel breaks up with Naomi & asks out Clementine.
8	Oct 2 2000	115,117 119-121	Joel & Clem's first date.

GREEN AT END of COLOR

RED Now

RED NEW

JOEL & CLEMENTINE WERE HAPPY   *RED*

DAYS	DATES	SCENES	ACTION
9-11	Winter 2000	118,104 103,108	Clem models button dress They play pillow game, see the beach house & react to horn.
12	Spring 2001	96,68, 98B,98D	Joel & Clem at drive-in
13	''	114,86	Joel draws Clem. They read on sofa.
14	''	85	Joel & Clem hiking.
15	Winter	77,79,81	Joel & Clem on the Charles (#1)
16	2002	70,71	Clem models her orange shirt & tells Velveteen Rabbit story.

PARKA

ORANGE NEW

JOEL & CLEMENTINE FALL APART   *ORANGE*

DAYS	DATES	SCENES	ACTION
17	Spring 2002	65-66, 68	Chinese restaurant, drinking tea in bed.
18	Fall 2002	61, 63 123	Flea market. Clem flirts at bar. Mary's affair w. Howard remembered.
19	Jan 2003	53-56, 58-60	Clem leaves as Joel watches TV. She comes back drunk. Joel follows her to scary street.

Fig. 4.21 Day breakdown, chronological order. From *Eternal Sunshine of the Spotless Mind*.

This was really helpful to the makeup department, both in designing the different stages of makeup and in deciding when to transition into the next look. We based our detailed makeup continuity on that information (see Fig. 4.22).

YEARS				Caden		Hazel		Claire		Others	
				Hair	MU	Hair	MU	Hair	MU	Hair	MU
YR	DATE	SC #	ACTION	Wig / Adds / Appli / Adjust	Adjust	Wig / Adds / Appli / Adjust		Wig / Adds / Appli / Adjust		Wig / Adds / Appli	
1	2005	A1-10	Olive has green poop. Caden gets hit with faucet & goes to hospital.	Caden 40s wig SC A1-82	No Appliance SC A1-102	10 lens		No Appliance SC A1-102			
2	2006	11-44	'Death of a Salesman.' Hazel buys her house. Adele goes to Berlin.			14 lens 44 leg lumps	27-447 arm lumps			41 Maddy feet blister, band aid.	
3	2007	45-48	Caden meets Hazel at the bar, goes home with her and has sex.								
4	2008	49-57	Caden takes a taxi to the hospital. His autonomics are going haywire.				56-57, 67 mouth swell bleed				
6	2010	67-75	He meets Claire at the bar. They get married.							61 Maddy foot prosth	
7	2011	76-82	Claire plays Hazel. Claire & Caden have a baby.					79 Back			
	2012		Skip 2012 - 2014								
	2013		Caden's age jumps (46-50)								
	2014		after art gallery			83-84 Red eyes, face					
11	2015	83-88	Caden sees Maria in café. He looks at the warehouse to rent.	wig 83-A114							
12	2016	89-91	The warehouse floor is divided into 'apartments'. Caden & Claire have separated.								
13	2017	92-95	Caden meets Hazel in NYC. Olive loves Maria more than him.	en's 50s wig							

Hair Make-Up Tally #1 / Mary C — Synecdoche, NY / April 27, 2007 Blue draft — 5/15/07 page 1

Fig. 4.22 Hair and Makeup breakdown for characters that age at different rates. From *Synecdoche, New York.*

The time progression was so complicated in this story that I made up a second master breakdown, just to show the time passing (see Fig. 4.23). Notice that in 2018, Caden is 53 and Ariel is 4, and in 2022, Caden is 57 and Ariel is still 4.

The Warehouse

In *Synecdoche, New York*, Caden, played by Philip Seymour Hoffman, is a theater director who builds a set of New York City inside a warehouse in New York City. On this set is a replica of his warehouse. Wanting to make the set as real as possible, Philip's character builds another set of New York City inside the warehouse set, and another inside that, and another inside that.

Scene Continuity #1 Synecdoche, NY 5/18/07
Mary C May 18, 2007 draft. Pink. page 5

YEAR	SC #	ACTION	I/E	D/N	Location	Character
	95	Caden reads Olive's diary. She loves Maria more than him.	I	N	C&A Bedroom	Caden 52
		DAY 29				
2018	96	Caden asks to come back to Claire. He has a cane.	I	N	Claire's NYC hallway	Caden 53, Claire 32, Ariel 4
	97	Caden & Claire have sex. Caden's father died.	I	N	Claire's NYC bedroom	Caden 53, Claire 32, Ariel 4, Sammy
		DAY 30				
	98	At Caden's dad's burial.	E	D	Cemetery	Caden 53, Claire 32, Ariel 4, Caden's mom
	99	Caden leaves Claire at his mother's wake to call Hazel.	I	D	Caden's mother's house	Caden 53, Claire 32, Ariel 4, Caden's mom, fat lady
	100	Caden calls Hazel.	E	D	Caden's mom's	Caden 53
	A 100	Hazel on the phone with Caden at his mother's funeral.	I	D	Burning House	Hazel 47
2019	101	Omitted				
	102	Omitted				
		Day 31				
2020	103	Caden walk up scaffold sets with cane.	I	D	Warehouse - City set - scaffolds.	Caden 55, Michael, other acotrs.
		Day 32				
2021	104	Caden reads that Olive is a woman.	I	Lt N	Claire's NYC kitchen	Caden 56
		Day 33				
2022	105	Caden sees poster of 'Flower	E	D	Berlin St	Caden 57
	106	Caden waits in line to see 'Flower Girl'.	I	N	Lobby	Caden 57, bunch of men.
	107	He sees Olive's dancing naked and gets beat up.	I	N	Small dark Room	Caden 57, Olive 21, bouncer
		Day 34				
	108	Caden is depressed. He is bruised from getting beat up.	I	Mn	Claire's NYC bedroom	Caden 57, Claire 36, Ariel 4.
2023	109	Caden drives to Hazel's house and asks her what he should do.	E	D	Burning House	Caden 58, Hazel 53, Derek 57
		Day 35				
	110	Caden tells the actors he will give them scraps of paper with his notes. He has cane. He	I	D	Warehouse - City set - scaffolds.	Caden 58, Claire 37, actors.
		Day 36				
	111	Omitted				
	112	Caden passes a dying Santa.	E	D	NYC department Store.	Caden 58, Dying Santa
		Day 37				
2024	113	Hazel calls Caden from her job She got fired, wants to work for	E	D	Mall 'Lens Shapers'	Hazel 54
	A11 4	Caden on phone in his office.	I	D	Warehouse Office	Caden 59
		Day 38				
2025	114	Sammy is cast as Caden.	I	D	Warehouse, audition corner.	Caden 60, Hazel, 55, Sammy, 5 Caden look alikes. Actors living on set.

Fig. 4.23 Time detail. From *Synecdoche, New York*.

The story had one real and three fake warehouses and one real and three fake cities, one inside another.

We used the same physical locations for all the different layers of sets. Each level of warehouse was in a different state of construction (as per the story), so had slightly different set dressing as well as different action, different costumes, and Philip usually made-up to be a different age. Sometimes there were different characters within the story "playing" Caden. All the locations were shot using some camera angles at the stage and some out in the real streets of New York City, making it impossible to shoot a whole scene at once.

As is usual in film production, we shot out all versions of each physical location before moving on. That means we would arrive at a location that was to be used as five different sets, shoot all the camera angles with the right production elements for one "level" before moving on to the next level for that location. Of course we had the usual scramble, racing to finish the work before the sun goes down. It was very tricky, as many of the details were almost the same in each level of warehouse and based on dream logic. The chance of getting confused in the rush of production was really high.

I made up my all-time favorite breakdown to help me keep this mind-twister straight (see Fig. 4.24). It fits on one page and let me know instantly, by scene number, what level of theater set we should be in.

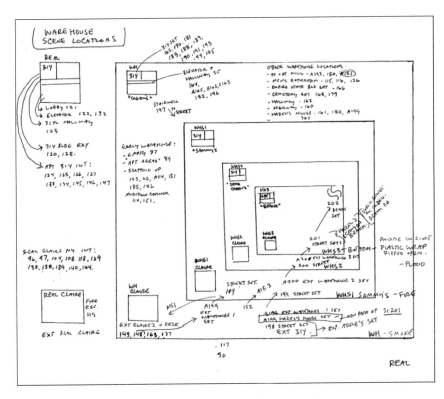

Fig. 4.24 The warehouse breakdown. From *Synecdoche, New York*.

WHAT I DON'T DO

Some script supervisor books I've read tell you to make a separate wardrobe breakdown. I've never found this to be helpful. Even small movies have an on-set dresser whose job it is to track only that. I feel it is more useful to supply the costume department with good time breakdowns, make sure to notate the wardrobe mentioned in the script on the master breakdown, and then track what comes to set with photographs and notes about special items. I have found that anything more is duplicating work and keeps me from things that only I am tracking.

NOTES

1 ScriptE, Peter Skarratt, MovieSlate, to name a few.

2 For excellent, detailed information about script supervising live/live-to-tape shows, look up Roe Moore and Patti Mustari on the internet.

3 I recently learned about this helpful practice from Sharon Watt, one of the best script supervisors we have. I wish I had done this when I was working!

4 Graphic applications include systems such as PDF Expert, Scriptation, and Notability.

5 A "talking head" is a close-up or medium close-up shot of a person talking.

6 Such as Scriptation or Notability.

7 At this writing, some of the most popular are Numbers (free, but limited to Apple devices), Excel (powerful but costly), and Sheets (great for using online but glitchy on iPads).

8 There are a few exceptions to this definition: a montage scene is made of many tiny scenes; a telephone conversation may or may not get a new scene number every time we cut back and forth between the speakers.

9 There is more about this later under "Rewrites," in Chapter 5, pages 99–103.

10 "Shoe leather" is action that does not further the story.

11 A digital application which uses layers, such as Scriptation, can accommodate permanent highlighting which can be made visible or invisible, which would have solved my complaint.

12 As noted, a scene is an action that is continuous in time and place. If you change place or jump ahead in time, this starts a new scene.

13 These are physical effects. They are mechanical and applied on set. Don't confuse them with visual effects, which are optical or digital and applied in post-production.

14 Voice-over is dialog from a character that is not present in the current scene. Off-camera dialog is from a person who is present, but not in any picture for those lines; for instance, they may be calling from the next room.

15 An element is one piece of visual information that will be combined with others to make a finished, composite shot.

16 In this breakdown, you can see the digital elements listed as well as the shoot elements we need ("L/A," in this breakdown, stands for live action).

Chapter 5

Preproduction
Non-Breakdown Preproduction

This chapter will focus on preproduction for feature films. Prep for a single-camera episodic TV show is similar, with variations depending on how the scripts are released—by season or by episode. Prep for multi-camera studio shoots, like sitcoms and live/live-to-tape, are a cross between this and theater, and usually repeated in weekly cycles.[1]

REHEARSALS

Even in feature films, the process of rehearsing in preproduction varies from director to director and project to project. Depending on the process, script supervisors may or may not be asked to attend. When I worked with Stephen Frears, he was very concerned with keeping the performances fresh for shooting. His "rehearsals" were long, private conversations with the actors. M. Night Shyamalan workshopped the script for weeks and wanted the script supervisor to be there. The most specific rehearsals I've taken part in were for *The Crucible*. We taped off a rehearsal room floor, matching the layout of the sets that were being built. All the major blocking decisions for these scenes were made during these rehearsals.

If you are asked to be at rehearsals, you will be expected to note all the changes in dialog and action, as well as any creative or production ideas that come up. You will be responsible for understanding and recording the details of whatever is discussed, distributing that information to production for the record, and to the specific departments for action.

You may be asked to read dialog if all the actors are not present. Try to be as unobtrusive as you can and still hear everything that is going on.

I like to run a watch during rehearsals and note the running times on the side of my scene. It is not an exact timing of the script, but can be informative.

Listen for clues about how the director is thinking about pacing and about the project in general; what do they feel is important, what sort of tone do they want on set, do they like to work from the general towards the details, or the other way around?

DOI: 10.4324/9780367823665-5

As I said earlier, you should be paid for attending rehearsals. For a union project, this is in addition to your time to do the breakdowns.

REWRITES

The script is usually updated as it goes through preproduction. Changes may come from rehearsals, tech scouts, notes from the studio, executive producers, or actors they are courting. A fully funded episodic series will have a script

> **In rehearsals:**
> 1. Note the changes in dialog and action
> 2. Note creative or production ideas
> 3. Record and distribute notes to production and specific department heads
> 4. Read dialog if requested
> 5. Run a watch
> 6. Be unobtrusive
> 7. Deepen your understanding of the director's approach

coordinator who is responsible for updating the official scripts and justifying an episode's changes within the larger story. On features, a director's, writer's, or producer's assistant will usually be in charge of keeping the master script and publishing updated drafts. If you are on a small movie, there might not be such a position and you may be in charge of this.

Flagging Changes in the Script

When an updated version of the script is published, every line that has a change will be flagged with an asterisk (*) on the far right side of the page. This is a great help as it saves everyone the time of combing through new pages looking for the changes. If the script is being rewritten with an application like Final Draft, this will happen automatically when the settings are correct. If you are on a very small, non-union project and are put in charge of script changes, the production should supply you with a Final Draft subscription. Check to make sure you are doing your rewrites in "Revision Mode" and that the changes are automatically producing asterisks.

Changes in Scene Numbers

Typically, a script doesn't have scene numbers until the production team needs to start cataloging the elements of production. When that time comes, the script is "locked," and the first AD will number the scenes. Now, all departments can organize and coordinate their ideas and material using common, permanent scene numbers as a reference.

Of course, rewriting usually continues after a script is locked. Some scenes are added and others are dropped. It would be very confusing to renumber the scenes after the crew has been using the original numbers. To avoid this, we keep the numbered scenes as they are and name the new scenes with a combination of numbers and letters. For example, if we originally had the scenes 1, 2, 3, 4, and 5, dropped scene 2 and added a new scene between 4 and 5, our new script is numbered like this: 1, 3, 4, 4A, and 5. If later, we add a new scene between 4A and 5, we call it 4B. If a new scene is added between 4 and 4A, we call it 4aA. The new progression would look like this: 1, 3, 4, 4aA, 4A, 4B, and 5.

Whenever a scene is dropped, we keep the scene number in the script with a note saying "Omitted," so there is no confusion.

Scene numbers as the script changes

Early:
1. In development—no scene numbers
2. Locked script—scene numbers are assigned

Rewrites:

3. Added scenes are named using both numbers and letters
4. Omitted and added scenes do not change the following scene numbers

---

Renumbering scenes
1. Start with scenes **1, 2, 3, 4, 5**
2. Drop scene 2 and add a scene between 4 and 5
3. We have **1, 3, 4, 4A, 5**
4. Add a scene between 4A and 5
5. We have **1, 3, 4, 4A, 4B, 5**
6. Add a scene between 4 and 4A
7. We have **1, 3, 4, 4aA, 4A, 4B, 5**

Scene Number Formatting

Professional movie applications (such as Final Draft) usually can sort scene names with letters either in front or in back of the numbers. Most general purpose applications cannot. Since many crew members use non-movie-specific applications (such as spreadsheets), production companies usually like to name additional scene numbers with the letters after the numbers.

Scene names with letters after their numbers sort correctly, but must be changed when slating so that the letters come first. More about this in the section on "Slating Added Scenes" in Chapter 6, page 196.

> **How numbers sort on non-movie applications:**
> - Example 1 (**letters behind, sorted correctly**): 1, 3, 3A, 4, 4A, 4B, 5
> - Example 2 (**letters in front, sorted incorrectly**): 1, 3, 4, 5, A3, A4, B4

Changes in Page Numbers

We treat page numbers in a locked script the same way. Once the script is locked, omitted pages are left blank but for the page heading, page number, and the word "Omitted." If a number of sequential pages are omitted, the page numbers are combined in a range, named as "Pages 62–65 Omitted," on a single sheet of paper (or page in a document file).

If we add a new page between pages 7 and 8, it is named page 7A. A page added between 7A and 8 is called 7B.

If rewriting changes one page of the script into one and one eighth of a page, we add a new page that is one eighth text and seven eighths blank, give that page a new name (7A), and add "1/8" to our page count.

Color Pages

The first draft of a locked script is always printed on white paper. After that, new pages are printed on colored paper. This is an industry-wide convention to help the cast and crew double-check that they have the most current script in hand. The first revisions are traditionally on blue, the second on pink, the third on yellow, then green, etc. It's a really good system. If you are in a rehearsal and see that everyone else has green pages in their script and you don't, you know you have missed a round of rewrites. Revised digital pages may have a color background or just have the revision color noted in the page's header.

Kinds of Rewrites

As a movie is developed, shot, and edited the script will go through many stages.

"Working scripts" are used in development. Rewrites are expected. The scenes are not numbered.

A "shooting script" is the first draft that production uses to organize the shoot. Scene numbers are assigned for the first time. The text is printed on white paper. The scene and page numbers are locked.

"Color revisions" are published page by page, as needed, when changes are made to the shooting script. They are printed on colored paper in a traditional sequence of colors. These new pages will be inserted into the locked white pages without changing the page or scene numbers that follow. By the time shooting starts, it is not uncommon to have a script containing a rainbow of different colored pages.

"Script as shot" script pages are the updated pages made by the script supervisor during the shoot. They contain all the script changes that happen on set. This version is used for the lined script and sent to the editors and production office day by day, as the work is completed.

A "continuity script" is a transcription of the film in its final cut. It is helpful for making subtitles and translations.

> **Versions of scripts:**
> 1. **Working scripts** are used in development
> 2. **Shooting scripts** are used to organize the shoot
> 3. **Color revisions** are used when changes are made to the shooting script
> 4. **Script as shot** is updated by the script supervisor during the shoot
> 5. **Continuity script** is a transcription of the film in its final cut

A White Copy of Revised Pages

If you are working on paper, ask for a second copy of the shooting script. This will be the base of your final, lined script as shot. Let the office know you will need two sets of script pages whenever there are revisions: one on colored paper for your set book, and another on white paper for your final lined script.[2] Each new page should have a header that includes the date the page was published and a note to clarify which revised draft the page comes from.

Tracking Revisions in a Digital Format

If you are working digitally, you will need an application to help you organize script revisions and insert new pages into the existing script. There are a number of great graphics-based applications as of this writing and, no doubt, more by the time you are reading this. PDF Expert, Scriptation, and Notability are a few. All will allow you to tint the "paper" color, make notes on each page, and individually replace older pages with new, revised pages. Make sure the script file is locked before you import it into your device, so the page format does not shift. If you like, you can add blank pages between the script pages and use them for your private notes, as if they were the back of the preceding pages in a paper script. Scriptation allows you to save multiple drafts in layers, and can automatically transfer notes from older versions onto your new pages.

Most script supervising systems, like Peter Skarratt and ScriptE, have features that allow you to insert revised pages into an active script. They will highlight the changes and generate a report listing them. As of this writing, their notation capabilities are not as flexible or powerful as the graphics-based applications mentioned above. This may have changed by the time you are reading this.

THE READ-THROUGH

At some point during prep we get as many of our actors together as we can and read through the whole script, start to finish. The non-dialog description is condensed, and the cast and crew fill in for the actors who can't make it. I always run a watch on this reading, keeping a running tally, noting the lapsed time at the end of every scene. This will not be the exact running time of the script, but it can help you figure out what the running time should be.

Sometimes script supervisors are asked to condense the action. Sometimes we are asked to read that action. Other times the first AD will do that, or an actor is brought in especially for this. Once in a while, you will be asked to read a small character, or several small characters.

These read-throughs are usually very exciting, even after lots of rehearsals. It's the only time we get to hear the story out loud, start to finish, in one sitting, with many of the real actors taking part. Every other time we hear the story, it is in small, repeated fragments. This is a great chance to get a better understanding of the flow of the story. Pay attention to the big dramatic arcs. Notice how they develop over many scenes. Identify the essential bits of information and emotion needed to deliver them.

At the read-through:
1. Run a time tally
2. Listen for big arcs

TECH SCOUTS

If your movie is shot out in the real world, the technical crew will visit these locations before the shoot to talk about the logistics of production. Script supervisors are not usually in this group. The conversation is mostly about routing electrical cable, listening for sound problems, and the like. I have gone and found these trips useful when the production logistics and story structure are interwoven. This happened on *Eternal Sunshine of the Spotless Mind* and *Synecdoche, New York*. In both these cases, the stage sets and practical locations were interwoven in unusual and complicated ways. Seeing the locations and hearing how they were to be captured helped me immensely when sorting out issues of continuity.

THE PRODUCTION MEETING

In the week before shooting starts, the principal crew members get together and go through the entire shooting schedule. This is called the production meeting. It can last three hours or 12. Some movies have a smaller, weekly production meeting throughout prep.

What Happens at a Production Meeting

The meeting is run by the first AD, who hands out two essential breakdowns, the shooting schedule and the one liner. The shooting schedule will list all the production elements needed for each scene: actors, location, key props, wardrobe, equipment, special effects, etc. This is useful for us, as we track production details from scene to scene. The one liner is a condensed version of the shooting schedule. It is good for seeing what days the company is working and what work will be done each day.

We script supervisors don't usually have a lot to say at the production meeting, but we learn a lot, especially if we haven't been on the tech scouts. Listen for things that are planned but not on the script page: things like rain effects, special time-of-day lighting, specific wardrobe, and so forth. Add these to your master breakdown and match back. When you

> **At the production meeting:**
> 1. Bring time and master breakdowns
> 2. Listen for new production elements
> 3. Match back new elements
> 4. Check in with your crew members

hear new production elements or ideas mentioned in the meeting, check your time breakdowns, too. If rain has been added to a scene, check the AD's shooting schedule to see that all the scenes attached to it by your continuity also have rain. Speak up if you think an element is missing. Keep your ears open and take notes during the production meeting, and you will have fewer questions on set.

Side Conversations

There will be someone from every department at the production meeting: all producers, all department heads, and often their key assistants. This is a good chance to say hello and exchange vital information. I bring copies of my two time breakdowns, my master breakdown, and any special breakdowns to pass out. I check in with the on-set costumers, the set dressers, the prop department, hair and makeup, and the editor to ask them if they have any concerns. We schedule a side meeting if there is anything we need to figure out before we start shooting.

If you are using a digital workflow, touch base with the departments that will digitally interface with you: the POC about distributing your daily notes, the assistant editor about formatting your notes to work with their system, and the camera department about how they are outputting their video to set.

Build email address groups for various breakdowns and reports (updates of your breakdowns, the lunch report, daily production report, the editors' log, wrap notes, etc.) so your files can go to all the proper people with one click.

GETTING PHYSICALLY READY FOR THE SHOOT

Making movies is physically very hard. If you prepare yourself, the process will be less difficult.

The standard working day for a movie crew is 12 hours long. This does not include travel, a lunch break, homework, watching dailies, or prep for the next day. For a script supervisor, this means that a typical 12-hour day lasts 15 hours. Often, the days are much longer than that. Some productions, especially low-budget films, shoot six days a week. At best, this schedule leaves very little time for anything but work. At worst, it is dangerously exhausting.

Before you start shooting, make an effort to sleep more, spend time with your family and friends, pay the bills, and do the laundry.

WHAT'S IN YOUR KIT

A Mobile Office

Your kit contains all the equipment and supplies you will use to do your job. Think of it as a mobile office that will store easily and won't get damaged bouncing around in the back of a truck. You must be able to tote it from the truck to the set and have quick access to equipment and supplies.

Paper or Digital?

Because the physical equipment needed for paper and digital workflows are quite different, I have divided the tools you need according to the two systems. Keep in mind that our tasks are the same whether we use a paper or digital system, and that almost everyone's workflow is a combination of both.

SCRIPTS AND NOTES

Paper Workflow	Digital Workflow
Five notebooks containing:	A tablet and stylus or a laptop, the appropriate software, and files containing:
1. Your working script, including:	1. Your working script, including:
• The most up-to-date script pages	• The most up-to-date script pages
• Reference material for the day's work	• Reference material for the day's work
• The day's call sheet	• The day's call sheet
• Enough blank forms for two days' work: daily report, editors' log, and facing pages	• Templates for your daily report, editors' log, and facing pages
• Your breakdowns and tallies	• Your breakdowns and tallies
• A crew list with contact information	• A crew list with contact information
2. The editors' final script, which contains:	2. The editors' final script, which contains:
• Script as shot, lined with set-ups	• Script as shot, lined with set-ups
• Completed facing pages	

Paper Workflow	Digital Workflow

• Completed script supervisor's daily reports
• Completed editors' daily log
3. Blank pages
  • More blank forms, enough for a week or more
  • Blank sheets of paper
  • Extra page dividers
4. Script archives
  • All the older versions of the script
5. Backup notes
  • Notes and breakdowns from other departments
  • Continuity photos, if you print them
	• Completed facing pages
	• Completed script supervisor's daily reports
	• Completed editors' daily log
	3. Script archives
	  • All the older versions of the script
	4. Backup notes
	  • Notes and breakdowns from other departments
	  • Continuity photos
	5. Storage to back up your work as you go: an exterior drive, access to cloud storage, or better yet, both
	6. A backup notation system, either on paper or a second device with appropriate software, in case there is a problem with your electronics
	7. Extra batteries, stylus, and chargers
	8. A smartphone with appropriate applications can sometimes be used for tiny jobs instead of a tablet or laptop

I recommend starting with a mostly paper workflow and adding digital elements when you have a feel for the way you like to work and a clear idea about how each digital element will help you. Pen and paper is the most flexible and gives you fewer technology fails to deal with when you are on set, under the gun.

Making breakdowns on a digital spreadsheet is a great way to introduce digital elements into your workflow. On set, you will probably want to use a tablet for reference material (previous scripts, continuity photos, breakdowns from other departments) long before you are comfortable using it to write digital notes during a take.

Necessary Items

CASES

Paper Workflow	Digital Workflow
• Sturdy boxes with wheels and small compartments such as catalog cases and rolling file boxes work well for toting around a lot of heavy paper • Divide your notebooks between a case you will bring to set every day and other cases that can stay on the truck • Large pencil cases with adjustable compartments are great for organizing writing tools and other office supplies. You can find these in various sizes in the tool section of hardware stores	• A shockproof case for your phone and high impact cases and covers for your laptop and tablet are mandatory. All your cases should be waterproof • A case for your tablet with a strap on the back makes holding the tablet with one hand more secure and frees your second hand for writing • If you leave electronics on the truck overnight, they should be well protected against bumpy rides in a hard case with a foam interior

WATCHES AND TIME

Paper Workflow	Digital Workflow
• You will need a dependable source to tell you the exact and correct time of day. This is easily taken from your smartphone • You will need at least two stopwatches, with the beep silenced	• If you are using a digital script supervising system, it will include a function for capturing timecode, running time, and time of day. If not, you can download an application (or applications) that will provide those functions • A backup stopwatch of some sort

CAMERAS AND IMAGE CAPTURE

Paper Workflow	Digital Workflow
• You will need a still camera, nothing fancy, plus a backup. One of these can be your smartphone or tablet	• Many digital applications include a function to capture frames from the movie camera. To do this, you will need some sort of hardware to tap into that feed. There are many available

Paper Workflow	Digital Workflow
• Make sure to have extra memory cards and batteries. Keep a charger handy and your extra batteries charged • You will need a system to label and organize the pictures	• You should also have a camera that can capture non-feed pictures: wardrobe details, wide shots of sets, etc. Use a separate still camera or the camera on your phone or tablet

WORKING LIGHT

Paper Workflow	Digital Workflow
• Flashlight, headlamp or book light, and extra batteries	• Flashlight, headlamp or book light, and extra batteries

OFFICE SUPPLIES

Paper Workflow	Digital Workflow
• Extra binders • Pens, pencils, Sharpie markers, highlighters • Erasers, White-Out, and/or correction tape • Rulers, three or four, clear, the kind for graphic designers (one tied with a string to your set book) • Plastic envelopes to send forms to and from production (label them clearly with your name and position) • Pocket dictionary • Three-hole punch and hole re-enforcers • Large paperclips, for marking pages	• Thumb drives • A backup stylus • Extra nibs for your stylus • Batteries

OTHER USEFUL TOOLS

You may want a few of these, depending on your project.

Paper Workflow	Digital Workflow
• A device to access the internet	• A device to access the internet
• Foldable camp stool, as small as is comfortable	• Foldable camp stool, as small as is comfortable
• A music stand to hold your binder	• A music stand to hold your tablet
• Handheld TV monitor	• A Bluetooth keyboard
• Photo printer for continuity stills	• Handheld TV monitor
• Waterproof "Rite in the Rain" paper and pen	• Photo printer for continuity stills
• Area map or GPS if you will be driving to set	• Office printer for paperwork
• Bug spray	• External hard drives for storage
• Suntan lotion	• Software: Final Draft for rewrites
• A toiletry kit with toothbrush and paste	• Area map or GPS if you will be driving to set
	• Bug spray
	• Suntan lotion
	• Heating pad for your electronics if working in frigid temperatures
	• An electric fan for your electronics if working in very hot temperatures
	• A toiletry kit with toothbrush and paste

WEATHER GEAR

Pack a duffle bag to keep on the truck with any extra clothes you may need during the shoot. What is in your bag will change depending on your climate and time of year. Think about how cold or hot it could possibly get and provide for both extremes. Don't forget that you may be outside for 15 hours straight, and that it gets colder when the sun goes down. Also keep in mind that the shooting crew may be creating their own cold, heat, rain, and snow independently of the natural world. Here are my recommendations:

Rain Gear

Slicker, rain pants, rain hat, rain boots, dry socks. Rags for drying everything off. Waterproof tarps to cover your cases. Bonus points for a poncho with a piece of clear plastic at the torso. This will allow you to see your notebook or tablet through the poncho, on your lap, and keep working in the rain.

Cold Gear

Parka, snow pants, lined boots, warm hat, super warm hat, warm gloves, super warm gloves, scarf or face covering. Electric vests, gloves, socks, and heating blocks can be a huge help in extreme situations.

You need to be able to write or type in the cold. Rubberized fingertips may make it possible to keep your gloves on while writing. If it is not too cold, you can use gloves with exposed fingertips. Some have little mitten-like hoods that cover your fingertips when you are not writing. If it is frigid, use two pairs of gloves, one thin and one thick. You can take the thick pair off to write and leave the thin pair on. If you are using touchscreen electronics, get gloves that can transmit touch.

Hot Weather Gear

Shorts, tee or cotton shirt, hat with sun brim. Consider long-sleeve shirts and pants with UV protection if you will be exposed to bright sunlight for many hours a day.

Transitional Gear

Hooded sweatshirt, fleece vest, silk and/or wool long underwear (top and bottoms), thin gloves.

NOTES

1   See the section "What Sort of Projects Are Right for You?" Chapter 2, pages 8–10.

2   More about set scripts and final lined scripts in Chapter 9, "A Day on Set."

Chapter 6
Production Overview
Keeping the Notes

Motion pictures of all kinds are built from bits of picture and sound. A big part of the script supervisor's job is to organize and catalog these bits, so that the editors know what was shot and can find the media they need efficiently. This chapter will focus on keeping notes for feature films. Other types of motion pictures will be mentioned briefly.

WATCHING SET AND TAKING NOTES

There is inherent tension between watching set and taking notes. How can you write while looking at the scene at the same time? It's tricky, especially when the takes are long and the action is complicated.[1] Every script supervisor develops their own best way of working. The only constant is that watching the set takes priority over note-taking.

Your number one job, as a script supervisor, is to see and understand what is happening on set; how it relates to the story and to the storytelling craft of your particular production. Everything you do comes from that foundation. Your notes must be accurate (labeled completely and correctly) and insightful (having a clear hierarchy of importance and relevance). Typed, beautifully presented notes, delivered instantly at wrap, are great, but not if their content is sloppy or coverage is missing.

Too Much Information

In most cases, too much information is as bad as not enough. Editors tell me that when given notes that record everything that happens in a shot, with no indication of what is important or what is intended, they choose to not read the notes at all. Reading a swamp of notes takes them out of their editing mindset. It takes work to figure out what information is useful and what is noise. This is our job, not theirs. We were on set and know how the director was reacting to the material. We heard the conversations about how the material is meant to be used.

The only way we know what is important and what is intended is by watching set: the action in front of the camera; and also, the director, DP, and other crew members as they work.

DOI: 10.4324/9780367823665-6

Start with Pen (or Pencil) and Paper

When you start working, keep notes with pen and paper. It is the most direct, immediate, and flexible way to work. Once you have practice watching set and have developed a method that suits you, you can choose a digital workflow that allows you to watch the way you like and take notes in a manner that is best for the particular way you work.

INTRODUCTION TO THREE KINDS OF NOTES

Every Day, Every Movie

Here are the notes that script supervisors use every day, on every feature film:

- The lined script
- The facing page
- The editors' log
- The script supervisor's daily report

Some Days, Some Projects

Here are the notes we use on some days or on some projects:

- A wild track tally
- A wild picture tally
- An owed list tally
- A set of lined storyboards
- A set of lined visual effects storyboards

On-Set Matching Notes

We keep a third kind of note for our personal use on set to help us remember and match details of action and continuity. These matching notes are made as needed and tend to be less standardized. Here are some of the important things that most often get notated:

- The direction an actor is looking
- When an actor enters, exits, stands, sits, stops, and turns
- When an actor makes a dialog mistake or change
- How an actor handles props
- When an actor crosses camera, or a camera crosses an actor

- When a moving camera starts or stops
- A moment that the director likes
- A moment that is no good in an otherwise good take
- A section of action where the camera was running, but the media is not good to use in the conventional way

If these matching notations will be helpful to the editor, they will be included on the final lined script page. Most will not. There is more about matching notes starting on page 172 in this chapter, and examples, both personal and for the editor, starting on page 175 in this chapter.

NOTES USED EVERY DAY, ON EVERY MOVIE

Lined Script

We use the lined script to place each piece of picture and sound in the exact moment of the story for which it was intended. An editor, using the lined script, can read across any line of dialog, action, or description, and be able to know what material is intended for that story moment.

LINING THE SCRIPT

For movies and episodic series, each vertical line of the lined script represents one set-up.[2] There is an ID at the top of each line.[3] This is the set-up number. Whenever we talk about a particular set-up—in the lined script, on the slate, in the editors' log, etc.—we will use the same ID to name this set-up. Next to the set-up number there is a very brief description of the set-up.

Each line is drawn over the part of the script that its set-up covers, starting with the first dialog, action, or description on that piece of film or digital file and ending with the last. If a section of dialog or action is on-camera, the line is straight. If a section of dialog or action is off-camera, the line is wavy. In our example, Fig. 6.1, this is seen most clearly in scene 105.

> An editor can use the **lined script** to see what material is intended for each moment of the story.

If a set-up continues onto the next page, we put an arrow pointing down at the bottom of the page. This set-up will start on the next page with an arrow pointing up. When a set-up ends, we make a horizontal "stop" line there.

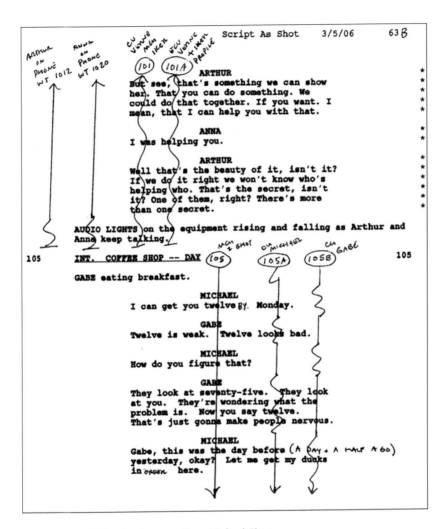

Fig. 6.1 A simple lined script page. From *Michael Clayton*.

HOW EDITORS READ THE LINED SCRIPT

When the editor, John Gilroy, got the lined script page shown in Fig. 6.1, he could see that there were three set-ups for the beginning of scene 105:

1. A medium close-up two-shot
2. A close-up of Michael
3. A close-up of Gabe

If he wanted to use a shot that shows Michael's dialog on camera, he had two choices: the two-shot and Michael's close-up. If he wanted to cut away from Michael during his dialog, which is often a very useful option, the only choice is Gabe's close-up.

Here's a more complicated lined script page from the same film (see Fig. 6.2).

This action has seven set-ups. Look at the action about a third of the way down the page that says, 'CLOSE-UP — THE BOOKMARK. It's a receipt. "COPY MASTER — YOUR ONE STOP FOR COPIES."' Reading across the page at that point, we see five wavy lines and two straight lines. The straight lines belong to set-ups that are inserts of the book. These set-ups were shot to show what the receipt says. The other five are shots of Michael that do not show the receipt's writing. The information is off-camera on these five wavy set-ups.

The line that starts a bit later, on the left of the page, is a notation for a wild track.

WILD TRACK

A wild track is a piece of recorded sound that has no corresponding picture. It is always noted on the far left side of the page, as shown in Figs 6.1 and 6.2, and labeled at the top.

Fig. 6.2 shows that the characters "VOICE" and "MALE VOICE" are never on camera. They exist only on the wild track. Read across the drawn lines at this dialog and you can see how this notation works. In Fig. 6.1, the two straight lines on the top half of the page are wild tracks of a telephone conversation that the characters Verne and Iker are listening to on camera.

If the wild track contains dialog, that dialog is marked by a solid line, as seen here. If the wild track is a sound effect intended to be used at a certain point in the scene, it should be noted at that point. If it contains a constant, atmospheric sound, it should be noted at the start of the scene only.

The wild track in Fig. 6.2 is a sleight of hand. Two police officers interrupt Michael's snooping, but their off-camera dialog is spoken not by the actors playing the cops, but by our two nasty hitmen, Verne and Iker. The audience is led to believe, for a moment, that the assassins have caught up with Michael. The audience is relieved when they see the police, even though Michael is caught breaking the law and will go to jail. This unusual switch is flagged for the editors with a note at the top of the wild track.

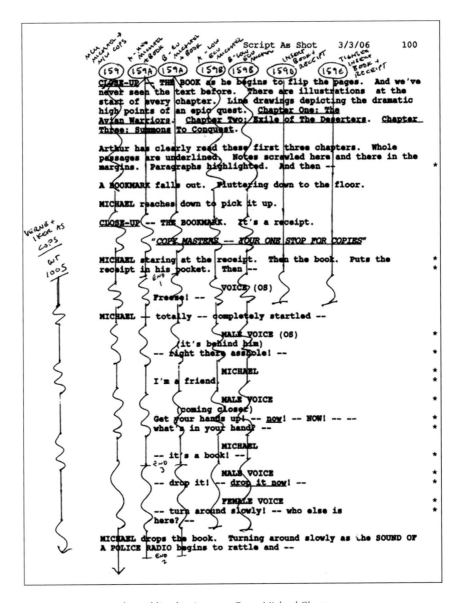

Fig. 6.2 A more complicated lined script page. From *Michael Clayton*.

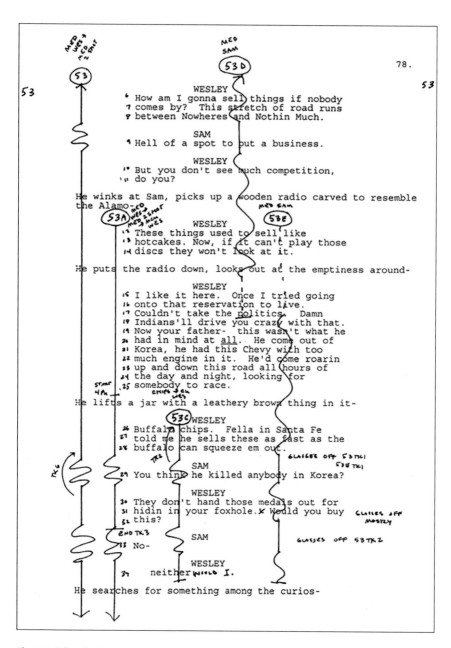

Fig. 6.3 A lined script page. From *Lone Star*.

NUMBERING DIALOG

When there is a lot of dialog, I sometimes number the blocks of dialog. If the dialog blocks are long, I might number each line of dialog (see Fig. 6.3). This makes it easy to refer to a specific dialog in shorthand in the facing pages.

LINING A DIGITAL PAGE

If you haven't read Chapter 3, "A Note about Digital Workflow," please read it now.

Digital script pages can be lined using either graphic-based or data-based applications. There are advantages to both.

The graphic-based methods are similar to using pen and paper. A tablet and digital stylus are used to make any mark you like, anywhere on the page. There is virtually no limit of colors, shapes, and placements available to you. This freedom gives you the greatest ability to design an expressive and informative graphic presentation. A well-designed lined script can direct the reader's attention, convey priority of information, and highlight special notes, just as thoughtful graphic design on a spreadsheet can.

Your graphic application may be able to transfer notes from one draft to another. At this writing, only a few applications can do this. I imagine by the time you are reading this book, other applications will have seen the value of this tool and have incorporated this function into their programs.

Data-based script lining works by setting up a series of fields (boxes or cells) for each line. Think back to our example of the fields in a digital address card to help you imagine how this works. The fields may be called *tubes*, *channels*, or *tramlines*, depending on which program you use, but they are all the same thing.

The advantage of this approach is that the data in the line's fields (like timecode or set-up number) may be automatically included when you generate a report, making the workflow faster. The disadvantage is the limited options of shapes, colors, and placement. And, if there is something off in your script's formatting, it can sabotage some functions of your application.

The following images (Figs 6.4a–c) are all examples of data-based set-up lines.

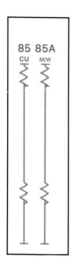

Fig. 6.4a Digital set-up line detail in ScriptE (from Tony Pettine).

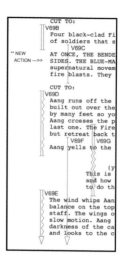

Fig. 6.4b Digital lined detail in Peter Skarratt (from Lori Grabowski).

Fig. 6.4c Some common lined script components in Peter Skarratt (from Lori Grabowski).

USING COLORED LINES

Traditional line colors:		Additional line colors:	
		Vista	Brown
Wide	Red	Med/Wide	Purple
Med	Blue	Med close-up	Turquoise
Close-up	Green	Extreme close-up	Orange

A long time ago, we used different colors to indicate the framing of each set-up: a red pen was used to draw a wide shot, blue for a medium, green for a close-up. Elegant. A glance at a page showed the editor the basic coverage plan. It was possible to thumb through a sequence of related scenes in the lined script and see the big shape of the sequence before getting to work on an individual scene. The practice of color-coding set-up lines stopped when we started using black-and-white photocopies to distribute our notes.

Digital notes, with their ability to be distributed in color, have brought back colored lines. But the return has come with a curious function. In most data-based programs, different colored lines are used to indicate different camera bodies: one color for the A camera, another for the B camera, etc. Why make this choice? Is information about camera bodies more valuable to editors than information about frame size? I don't think so.

I suspect that very few people remember the old use of color in lining a script.[4] My guess is that pairing colored lines with camera bodies is more convenience than thoughtful design. There was already a data category for camera body, so why not give it an indicator—like a colored line? This is a perfect example of our on-set practice being driven by program design, not what is best for our craft.

If I were still working, I would bring back color coding by frame size. This is very easy with a graphic-based program. Just use a different pen color. If three sizes are not enough, you could add intermediate colors for intermediate frame sizes.

If you agree, talk to your application designers. They are very responsive to what we want and could easily define a category called frame size and link it to the fields for set-up lines.

BACK UP YOUR NOTES

Whether you use a graphic or data-based system, make sure you back up your work as you go and have a paper fallback ready in case you have a digital system failure.

EXAMPLES OF LINED DIGITAL PAGES

Graphic digital applications like Scriptation and Notability are as flexible as pen and paper, and have additional features that integrate nicely into digital workflow.

85   EXT. THE LIFEBOAT - DUSK   85

         A boy, a hyena, a zebra and an orangutan silhouetted against
         the last fading light of day.

85 85A
CU   M/W
         Pi has hung the paddle and lifebuoy off the end of the boat
         and perches on the bow. The hyena's eyes seem to glow in the
         last light, fixed on Pi. Pi stares back.

         Pi fights fatigue as waves splash interminably against the
         hull. He winces at each creak of the lifeboat; his eyes glaze
         over as he stares out at the endless, dusky seascape.

         Pi sees movement in the shadows - the hyena attacks, the
         zebra barks and squeals. O.J. reacts to the violence, crying
         out.

                              PI (1)
                         NO! Stop it! STOP!

86   EXT. THE LIFEBOAT - DAWN   86

         Silence. Morning. Hazy. Pi slumps over the oar, eyes half
         open, glazed. He has stayed up a second night for fear of
         being attacked, and now he slowly nods sideways, giving in to
         exhaustion despite himself, and tumbles into the water.

         Pi gasps in shock as the water slaps him into full
         consciousness. He climbs back onto the life ring - coughing,
         tired, wet, sad and fearful.

         The lifeboat rolls and growls beneath Pi's feet as he stares
         - and then he notices O.J. The poor orang is sitting on a
         side bench half-hidden by the tarp, and horribly seasick. Her
         tongue lolls out of her mouth and she's visibly panting.

                              PI (1)
                         I'm sorry, O.J.; I don't have any
                         seasickness medicine for you -

         And then it strikes him.

                              PI (2)
                         Supplies! Ah, supplies!

         Pi pulls up the edge of the tarp nearest the bow. A row of
         benches with hinged lids curve around the bow. Pi opens the
         rearmost bench and finds a "LIFEBOAT MANUAL AND NAVIGATIONAL
         GUIDE" in a plastic bag along with a pencil lying on top of
         bags of supplies. He pulls out the manual and flips through
         it - an illustration shows that the boat is lined with
         compartments. He opens the next bench - it's stuffed with
         life jackets.

                         Camera Color Key: A -
                         LIFE OF PI - PRODUCTION

Fig. 6.5 Lined script page using ScriptE (from Tony Pettine).

"The Last Airbender"   Blue Rev. March 2, 2009   64

V69A

69   CONTINUED: 69

Aang finds himself in an area of the courtyard where
there are large conch shell like tubes on wooden bases.
Aang moves himself to the center of these giant shells.

There are markings on the ground of the courtyard — Aang
follows them with his feet and moves his hands
simultaneously towards one of the shells.

AIR EXPLODES OUT OF ONE OF THE SHELLS, CLEARING OUT ONE
SET OF SOLDIERS SURROUNDING AANG. Aang traces more of the
intricate circles on the ground with his feet. He swivels
his hands towards another shell. AIR BURSTS OUT AS THE
SHELL ITSELF TURNS — ANOTHER SET OF SOLDIERS ARE SENT
SKIDDING.

Aang lowers his hands.

WT1019

                         AANG
                      (saddened)
            ...This was their practice area.

CUT TO:

V69B

Four black-clad Fire Nation soldiers stand before a group
of soldiers that surround the blue-masked being.

                 V69C

** NEW   AT ONCE, THE BENDERS PULL FIRE FROM BURNING POTS FROM ALL
ACTION -->>   SIDES. THE BLUE-MASKED BEING turns and with the deft,
supernatural movements of his blades deflects all the
fire blasts. They come at him again.

CUT TO:

V69D

Aang runs off the courtyard onto wooden piers that are
built out over the bottomless canyon. They are separated
by many feet so you have to leap from one to the other.
Aang crosses the piers effortlessly till he gets to the
last one. The Fire Nation guards try to follow him out,
but retreat back to the safety of the courtyard.

           V69F   V69G

Aang yells to the soldiers with anger.

                         AANG
                      (yelling)
            This is to teach us about air currents
            and how to balance using them. We learn
            to do this when we are eight.

V69E

The wind whips Aang's clothes, but he seems perfectly at
balance on the top of the posts. Aang holds out his
staff. The wings on the staff open up like they're in
slow motion. Aang turns and is about to leap off into the
darkness of the canyon. He glances back over his shoulder
and looks to the courtyard.

Fig. 6.6 Lined script page using Peter Skarratt (from Lori Grabowski).

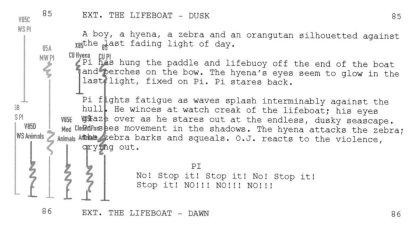

85   EXT. THE LIFEBOAT - DUSK   85

      A boy, a hyena, a zebra and an orangutan silhouetted against
      the last fading light of day.   *

      Pi has hung the paddle and lifebuoy off the end of the boat
      and perches on the bow. The hyena's eyes seem to glow in the
      last light, fixed on Pi. Pi stares back.

      Pi fights fatigue as waves splash interminably against the
      hull. He winces at watch creak of the lifeboat; his eyes
      glaze over as he stares out at the endless, dusky seascape.
      He sees movement in the shadows. The hyena attacks the zebra;
      the zebra barks and squeals. O.J. reacts to the violence,
      crying out.

                              PI
                   No! Stop it! Stop it! No! Stop it!
                   Stop it! NO!!! NO!!! NO!!!

86   EXT. THE LIFEBOAT - DAWN   86

      Silence. Morning. Hazy. Pi slumps over the oar, eyes half
      open, glazed. He has stayed up a second night for fear of
      being attacked, and now he slowly nods sideways, giving in to
      exhaustion despite himself, and tumbles into the water.

      Pi gasps in shock as the water slaps him into full
      consciousness. He climbs back onto the life ring - coughing,
      tired, wet, sad and fearful.

      The lifeboat rolls and growls beneath Pi's feet as he stares -
      and then he notices O.J. The poor orang is sitting on a side
      bench half-hidden by the tarp, and horribly seasick. Her
      tongue lolls out of her mouth and she's visibly panting.

                              PI
                   I'm sorry, O.J.; I don't have any
                   seasickness medicine for you -

      And then it strikes him.

                              PI   (CONT'D)
                   Supplies! Ah, supplies!

      Pi pulls up the edge of the tarp nearest the bow. A row of
      benches with hinged lids curve around the bow. Pi opens the
      rearmost bench and finds a "LIFEBOAT MANUAL AND NAVIGATIONAL
      GUIDE" in a plastic bag along with a pencil lying on top of
      bags of supplies. He pulls out the manual and flips through
      it - an illustration shows that the boat is lined with
      compartments. He opens the next bench - it's stuffed with
      life jackets.

Fig. 6.7 Lined script page using MovieSlate 8 (from Sean Pollock).

LINING MULTI-CAMERA SHOOTS

Multi-camera live/live-to-tape projects, such as sitcoms, interviews, and
game and talk shows, are lined differently. For these, all cameras roll

together and each line indicates when the cameras are rolling. There are no squiggles indicating off-camera content. Often there are no slates, and several passes on each take. There is less need for matching notes.

For scripted projects, name the passes with the take and pass number separated with a "/," for example: "take 1/1," "take 1/2," "take 1/3," etc. For unscripted projects, use timecode to mark each pass.

Fig. 6.8 is an example of using timecode to identify each pass in a live/ live-to-tape wild track recording. The same method is used for picture.

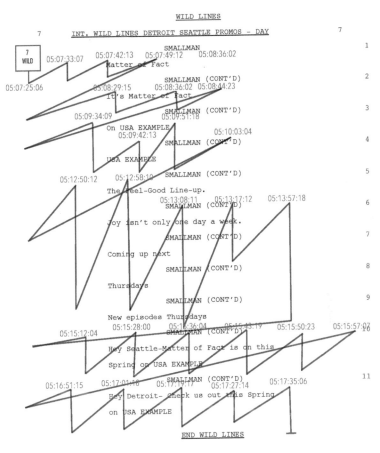

Fig. 6.8 Lined script page using MovieSlate 8, wild track lines (from Sean Pollock).

Facing Pages

Facing pages, sometimes called "opposite pages," are just that. In a paper workflow, they have holes punched on the right side of the page and sit in your notebook facing, or opposite, the lined script pages.

Facing pages are where we keep all the details of each set-up and take. In the American system, each set-up's information is entered on the page facing where that set-up begins in the lined script.[5] This convention makes it possible to see, and work into, both forms at the same time. This is especially useful when you need to keep your eye on set. Breaking your gaze to bring up a page or file, even for a second, may cause you to miss an important bit of action.

> The **facing pages** are where we keep all the details of each set-up and take.

Some script supervisors working in paper print the facing page form on the back of the preceding script page. I find this method to be too inflexible for most projects. The system falls apart when the page before is rewritten or an additional scene is added.

SETTING UP THE FACING PAGE

Here are the standard columns of the facing page:

- "Set-up number" (or "Slate")—identifies each set-up.
- "Action"—describes each set-up.
- "Lens"—logs the technical details about how the camera was set: focal length, aperture, distance from lens to subject, height from lens to floor, filters (if any), and film stock (if various stocks are used). When shooting a digital file, you may note color temperature or ASA. If there is something unusual about the shutter or film speed, this will be noted here as well.
- "CR"—names the camera roll, card, or drive that was used.
- "SR"—names the sound roll, card, or drive that was used.
- "Time"—tells how long each take ran, from action to cut.
- "Take"—numbers each take.
- "Comments"—describes each take.

These pages are a wealth of information. The picture editor scans the action column to see the nature of the coverage. They look at the comments column to see which takes are preferred, incomplete, or distinctive in any other way. The assistant editors look at the CR and SR columns to know where to

Lone Star FACING PAGES Mary Cybulski							Facing page: Dates: Scenes:
Setup	Action	Lens	CR	SR	Time	Take	Comments

Fig. 6.9 A blank facing page. From *Lone Star*.

find original media. The camera department looks at the information in the lens column when they shoot additional coverage for the scene.

Look over the examples given in Figs 6.10 and 6.11. The best notes are short, clear, and informative. The most important information is a quick guide to the media, and anything you learned on set that the editor would not know from looking at the media—which takes the director likes best and why, anything surprising about the coverage plan or actual coverage, something that went wrong and the plan to make it okay.

A facing page for a technically more complicated shoot is shown in Fig. 6.11.

"Michael Clayton"
FACING PAGES

Opp page: 63B

Dates: 4-5-06
Scenes: 4-5-06
105

Setup	Action	Lens	CR	SR	Time	Take	Comments
105	MCU 2 SHOT GABE + MICHAEL IN COFFEE SHOP	50m T3.5 6'2" 43" 18	A 396	112	1:08	1	GABE HAS JACKET ON.
					1:04	(2)	GABE IN HIS SHIRT
					1:21	(3)	START AGAIN 2x NOISEY BG.
			A 397		1:03	(4)	ADD NEW LINE "YOU BETTER GO... "
					2:09	(5)	START OVER ✪
105 A	TIGHT CU MICHAEL	135m T3.5 10' 45" 18	A 348	112	1:09	1	
					1:09	(2)	
					:59	(3)	GOOD
					1:01	(4)	✪ HEAD +TAIL STKS
					1:15	(5)	✪ "A WEEK + A HALF AGO "
105 B	TIGHT CU GABE	135m T3.5 10' 45" 18	A 399	112	1:06	(1)	
					1:08	(2)	✪
					:28	3	INCOMP SIREN SND
					1:20	(4)	

Fig. 6.10 Facing page for the simple scene (Fig. 6.1) from *Michael Clayton*.

"MICHAEL CLAYTON"
Facing Pages

Opp page: 100

Scenes: 159
Dates: 3-2-06, 2-9-06

Slate	Action	Lens	CR	SR	Time	Take	Comments
159 B	2 CAMERAS LOW ECU MICHAEL AS HE READS NEAR LAMP + FINDS RECEIPT FROM LIGHT GOING ON TO RUNNING AROUND A· LOOKING LEFT B· LOOKING RIGHT	A 180 T2.8 5'9" – 40h 18	A 187 B 102	49	:49 :49 :54 :54	① ① ② ②	WATCH OUT FOR SOFT SPOTS ON A-CAM. B- MISSLATED AS CR # B101
159 D	INSERT BOOK + RECEIPT FROM LIGHT GOING ON UNTIL "FREEZE"	75m T4.2 3'4" – 79"h 18	A 188	50	:48 :53 :09 :54	① ② 3 ④	FS + FULL TAKE HIDE NOTE INSIDE BOOK MORE. FINDING IT DOESNT LOOK RIGHT HIDE NOTE AGAIN. ADD "FREEZE" MOMENT
159 E	TIGHTER INSERT ON RECEIPT.	75m T4.2 3' 76"h	A 188	50	1:43	①	2x ACTION 2ND PASS BEST 3-2-06
WT 1005	WILD TRACK FOR Sc 159	–	–	20	3:00	1	OFF-CAMERA COP DIALOG SPOKEN BY VERNE, THEN IKER 2-9-06

Fig. 6.11 Facing page for the more complicated scene (Fig. 6.2) from *Michael Clayton*.

DESCRIBING CAMERA MOVES

Here are some standard descriptions of camera movement that you need to know:

- "Pan"—the camera stays in one place and pivots horizontally.
- "Dolly" or "track"—the camera moves horizontally.
- "Tilt"—The camera stays in one place and pivots vertically.
- "Boom"—The camera moves vertically.
- "Zoom"—The camera stays in one place; the frame size is changed by adjusting the focal length of the lens.
- "Push in" (or "Push out")—The camera moves forward (or back); the frame size is changed by adjusting the camera position.

Editors do not need a description of every step of a camera move; they have the footage. Write only enough so that the editors can tell one take from another. Too much information clogs the page and the editor's brain.

TIMECODE

When shooting to a digital file, a note for timecode should be added. Some people add a column on the far left. I prefer to write timecode in the "Comments" column (see Fig. 6.12). This gives me plenty of room to note not only the timecode at the start of a take, but also at any other point. This is helpful when you want to pinpoint a moment in a long take. Set-up 85C has just one long take, lasting almost 15 minutes. The running timecode in the "Comments" column helps locate the good parts within this long take. Many digital applications can enter timecode into your notes with a tap of your stylus. A great advantage.

3-D

Shooting in 3-D requires some additional notes. I like to write these vertically in a narrow column, as most of this information usually stays the same throughout the entire take (see Fig. 6.12).

The two notations that are written vertically here are standard: "I/O" is the interocular, the distance between the lenses of the two cameras.

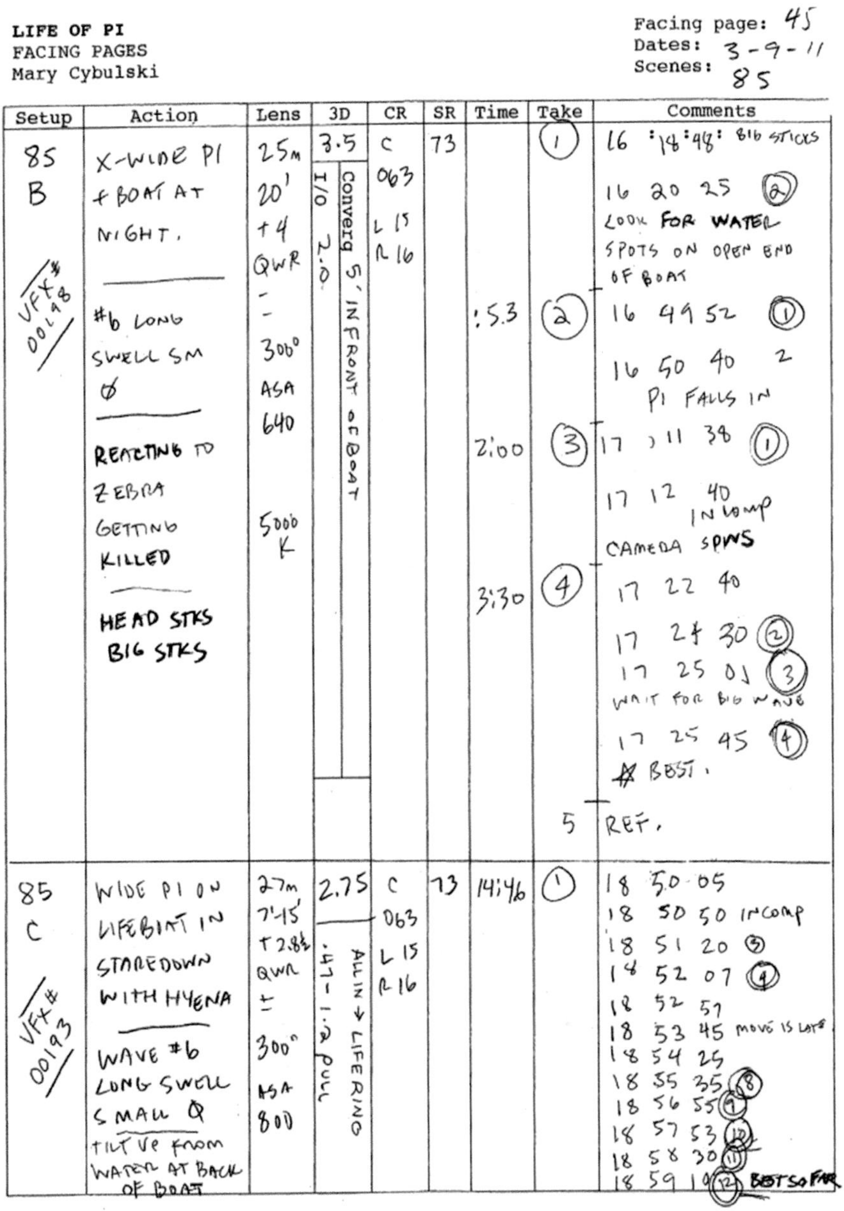

LIFE OF PI
FACING PAGES
Mary Cybulski

Facing page: 45
Dates: 3-9-11
Scenes: 85

Setup	Action	Lens	3D	CR	SR	Time	Take	Comments
85 B /VFX# 0048/	X-WIDE PI + BOAT AT NIGHT. ———— #6 LONG SWELL SM ∅ ———— REACTING TO ZEBRA GETTING KILLED ———— HEAD STKS BIG STKS	25m 20' +4 QWR - 300° ASA 640 5000 K	3.5 I/O 2.0 Converg 5' IN FRONT OF BOAT	C 063 L 15 R 16	73	:53.3 2:00 3:30	① ② ③ ④ 5	16 :18:48: BIG STICKS 16 20 25 ② LOOK FOR WATER SPOTS ON OPEN END OF BOAT 16 49 52 ① 16 50 40 2 PI FALLS IN 17)11 38 ① 17 12 40 IN LOMP CAMERA SPINS 17 22 40 17 24 30 ② 17 25 0) ③ WAIT FOR BIG WAVE 17 25 45 ④ ✗ BEST. REF.
85 C /VFX# 0093/	WIDE PI ON LIFEBOAT IN STAREDOWN WITH HYENA WAVE #6 LONG SWELL SMALL ∅ TILT UP FROM WATER AT BACK OF BOAT	27m 7'15' T 28½ QWR ± 300° ASA 800	2.75 :47-1:2 pull ALL IN ↓ LIFE RING	C 063 L 15 R 16	73	14:46	①	18 50-05 18 50 50 INCOMP 18 51 20 ③ 14 52 07 ④ 18 52 51 18 53 45 MOVE IS LATE 18 54 25 18 55 35 ⑧ 18 56 55 ⑨ 18 57 53 ⑫ 18 58 30 ⑪ 18 59 10 ⑫ BEST SO FAR

Fig. 6.12 A facing page with timecode, 3-D, and other unusual notes from *Life of Pi*.

"Converg" is short for convergence. This note records the distance between the camera and the convergence plane, where objects seen by the two cameras line up. When projected, this plane will seem to be parallel with the movie screen, neither in front of, nor behind, the screen.

On this project, *Life of Pi*, we added an additional notation to help us track the feel of the 3-D experience. This is the number at the top of the 3-D column, noted here as *3.5* in the first set-up and *2.75* in the second. This was a judgment call by the 3-D designer to help us design and understand the arcs of 3-D intensity, *1* being a shallow 3-D and *5* being a very deep 3-D.

Because we were shooting in 3-D, using two cameras for every single set-up, the notes in the camera roll column name the combined camera roll, numbered "C063," as well as two drives, one for each camera. Drive "15" is for the left eye and drive "16" is for the right eye.

This was a complicated shoot. You will find a few other unusual notes here:

- A VFX reference number in the set-up column ("VFX# 00198")
- A notation about the size and shape of the waves we made in the water tank, "#6, long swell, small, 0"
- A 300-degree shutter
- ASA ratings of 640 and 800 (unusual for this project)
- 5000K light color temperature
- "QWR" is a filter

SPECIAL ELEMENTS

An additional column may be added to track an important and unusual element. A feature film I talked about in Chapter 4 called *Thousand Pieces of Gold* was shot in the mountains of Montana. The weather changes constantly there. I made a column in my facing pages for the weather that was very useful. Once, we had rain, sun, and snow, all in the same set-up. That column made it easy to see when there was an issue with the weather.

DIGITAL FACING PAGES

After you have established a working rhythm on set and have a good feel for what is important to note on your facing pages, you may want to use a data-based digital application for this form. In some data-based applications, the facing page functions as an input receptacle, holding data for each scene (See Fig. 6.13 and Fig. 6.14). The information you input on this page can be exported as various reports, such as a Facing Page Report

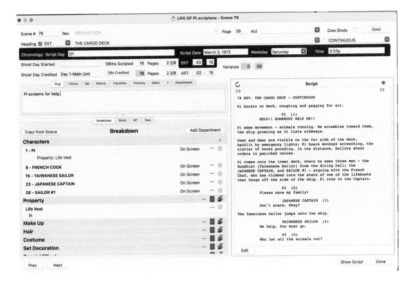

Fig. 6.13 Scene mode input page using ScriptE (from Tony Pettine).

Fig. 6.14 Input facing page using Peter Skarratt (from Lori Grabowski).

(see Figs 6.15 through 6.17), as well as the Editor's Daily Log (see Fig. 6.21 and Fig. 6.22), and the Script Supervisor's Daily Production Report (see Fig. 6.25 and Fig. 6.26). This really saves time, especially at the end of the day.

SCRIPT FACING PAGE
LIFE OF PI

Scene: 85

Slate Take	Description	CR	SR	Time	Comments
85 1ᶜ	Scene(s): 85	A11	13	0:08	FAV-"NO" (good one)
	Shot on Day: Day 1				(3D) 2, D67, L15, R16
	Crane - cu PI stares at HYENA and				
	watches it attack ZEBRA - waves shot				
	on gimbal to replicate #1 roller				
	Clip #: 17, L: 50, Fltr: 0, T: 2.8&1/3, LH: 22", CD: 22', ISO: ei800, FrR: 24 fps, Temp: 5000K, Shtr: 320°				
	Inter: .27 (conver. - Behind PI's head 5'3")				
2ᶜ				0:20	NG-"STOP IT!" (incomplete)
					(3D) 2, D67, L15, R16
	Clip #: 18, L: 50, Fltr: 0, T: 2.8&1/3, LH: 22", CD: 22', ISO: ei800, FrR: 24 fps, Temp: 5000K, Shtr: 320°				
3ᶜ				1:38	FAV-makes a better place off camera for PI to sit,
					,02:38:11:05 2nd x - good, ,02:38:32:07 3x good,
					,02:38:45:09 4x good, ,02:39:00:13 5x good
					(3D) 2, D67, L15, R16
	Clip #: 19, L: 50, Fltr: 0, T: 2.8&1/3, LH: 22", CD: 22', ISO: ei800, FrR: 24 fps, Temp: 5000K, Shtr: 320°				
4ᶜ				0:09	OK-reference silver balls
					(3D) 2, D67, L15, R16
	Clip #: 20, L: 50, Fltr: 0, T: 2.8&1/3, LH: 22", CD: 22', ISO: ei800, FrR: 24 fps, Temp: 5000K, Shtr: 320°				
85A 1ᶜ	Scene(s): 85	A11	13	0:32	Bungy cam not good
	Shot on Day: Day 1				(3D) 2.5,(D61, L17, R18)
	Bungy Cam - M/W - PI stares at				
	HYENA, watches it eat ZEBRA (gimbal				
	port beam - small 2, 85A tk 3)				
	Clip #: 21, L: 32, LH: 44" var, CD: 10', FrR: 24 fps, Shtr: 270°				
	Inter: .47 (conv. - 8'6 to 1'8" near foot)				
2ᶜ				0:17	(3D) 2.5,(D61, L17, R18)
	Clip #: 22, L: 32, LH: 44" var, CD: 10', FrR: 24 fps, Shtr: 270°				
3ᶜ				0:38	FAV-02:57:20:17 1x good, ,02:57:28:15 2x good
					(3D) 2.5,(D61, L17, R18)
	Clip #: 23, L: 32, LH: 44" var, CD: 10', FrR: 24 fps, Shtr: 270°				
4ᶜ				0:37	reference silver balls
					(m/slated as 85B #1)
					(3D) 2.5,(D61, L17, R18)
	Clip #: 24, L: 32, LH: 44" var, CD: 10', FrR: 24 fps, Shtr: 270°				

c - Take Complete

Fig. 6.15 Facing page report using ScriptE (from Tony Pettine).

The Last Airbender   Nickelodeon/Blinding Edge/Kennedy/Marshall   Page 64

Director: M. Night Shyamalan   D.P.: Andrew Lesnie

Script Supervisor: Mary Cybulski Cell: 555–555–5555   E–mail: mcyxx@xx.xxx

Take	P	Tm	Comment	CAM	LENS	SND	FPS

V69D   A CAMERA

(AANG JUMPS OUT ON PIERS, TURNS BACK)

X WIDE ---> MCU AANG

Day: 78 6/12/2009 Page: 64 Setup: 1							
Board #: FNF-070 Dist.: 15-40 T-Stop: 2.8 Height: 20'-4'3" Notes: TAIL STIX							
1		:16		A334	A23	60A	23.98
2		:15					
3		:14					
4	X	:14	Add wind.	A335			
5	X	:17	Lots of wind. Lots.				
6		:19					
7		:18					
8		:06	Inc. - Stumble				
9	X	:16		A336			
10 PU		:07					

V69D   B CAMERA

(AANG JUMPS OUT ON PIERS, TURNS BACK)

MED AANG ----> MED FIRE SOLDIERS

Day: 78 6/12/2009 Page: 64 Setup: 2							
Board #: FNF-071 Dist.: 24-290 T-Stop: 2.8 Height: 97"							
1		:16		B203	B200	60A	23.98
2		:15					
3		:14					
4	X	:14	Add wind.				
5	X	:17	Lots of wind. Lots. Shake in camera				
6		:19	So much wind his shirt blew up. // Bump on crane.				
7		:18					
8		:06	Inc. - Stumble				
9	X	:16	Same bump	B204			
10 PU		:07					

V69E   A CAMERA

(AANG OPENS THE WINGS ON HIS STAFF & TURNS BACK)

LOW M/W at PIER ---> CRANE UP --> WIDE AANG FLYING OVER SOLDIERS

Day: 78 6/12/2009 Page: 64 Setup: 3							
Board #: FNF-100 & FNF-130 Dist.: 15 - 40 T-Stop: 2.8 Height: 7 1/2' - 5'5"							
1		:17	Adjust the way Aang holds his staff.	A336	A21	60A	23.98
2		:17					
3		:20					
4	X	:15					
5		:16		A337			

Fig. 6.16 Facing page report using Peter Skarratt (from Lori Grabowski).

The Last Airbender   Nickelodeon/Blinding Edge/Kennedy/Marshall   Page 64
Director: M. Night Shyamalan   D.P.: Andrew Lesnie
Script Supervisor: Mary Cybulski   Cell: 555-555-5555   E-mail: mcyxx@xx.xxx

Take	P	Tm	Comment	CAM	LENS	SND	FPS

V69E   B CAMERA

(AANG OPENS THE WINGS ON HIS STAFF & TURNS BACK)

WIDE SOLDIERS, AANG FLYING

Day: 78   6/12/2009   Page: 64   Setup: 4
Board #: FNF-101   Dist.: 15 - 40   T-Stop: 2.8   Height: Varied

Take	P	Tm	Comment	CAM	LENS	SND	FPS
1		:17		B204	B35	60A	23.98
2		:17					
3		:20					
4	X	:15					
5		:16					

V69E   E CAMERA

(AANG OPENS THE WINGS ON HIS STAFF & TURNS BACK)

LOW SOLDIERS, AANG FLYING

Day: 78   6/12/2009   Page: 64   Setup: 5
Board #: FNF-102

Take	P	Tm	Comment	CAM	LENS	SND	FPS
1		:17	Bump, otherwise good.	E46	N/A	60A	23.98
2		:17					
3		:20					
4	X	:15	Nice jump. E cam didn't roll on Take 5.				

Fig. 6.16 *continued.*

You can ease into a digital system by writing your original notes on paper and entering the data into your digital facing pages between set-ups. Your paper notes are hard copy backups in case you have trouble with your software or there is some technical tool you don't understand at the moment. You never, ever want to be unavailable to the director, producer, actors, or crew members because you are working out a glitch in your system.

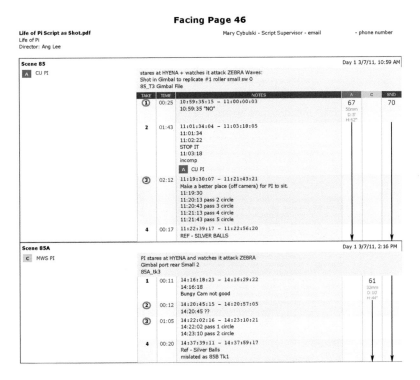

Fig. 6.17 Facing page report "facing page" report for life of pi

NOTES FOR UNSCRIPTED PRODUCTIONS

Unscripted productions have a different workflow and demands. Script supervisors are usually in a control booth or at a distance from set. They must be able to record what is happening in real time, with enough detail to find the major beats of the action and dialog. There is a lot of typing. Long takes make pinning timecode to action very important.

Working on a laptop is ideal for these shoots. Lack of portability is not a problem, and the laptop's more powerful applications and ease of typing really pay off.

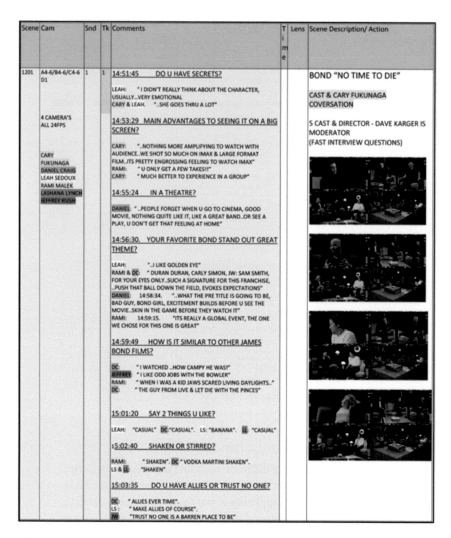

Fig. 6.18 A page of notes for an unscripted production using MovieSlate 8. From a promotional interview for *No Time to Die* (from Sean Pollock).

CHOOSING A SYSTEM

When you shop for a digital system, look for applications that fit the projects you do and the way you think. If you have established a methodology on set, you should be able to name which digital tools are important to you. Most programs have choices about sorting, adding, and arranging columns, changing colors, font types, etc.

Editors' Daily Log

The editors' daily log is a list of all the media we capture each day, in shooting order. The assistant editors depend on this log to know what they should be getting from the lab or transfer house. Other script notes (the lined script and facing pages) are dispersed throughout the script in story order and are not as useful in this regard.

> The **editors' daily log** is a list of all the media we capture each day, in shooting order.

The editors' log also goes to the film lab and/or the digital transfer house, where the technicians use it to prepare dailies.

Here are the standard columns on the editors' daily log:

- *Cam. Roll*—names the camera roll, card, or drive that was used.
- *Snd. Roll*—names the sound roll, card, or drive that was used.
- *Set-Up* (or *Slate*)—identifies the set-up number.
- *Takes*—shows the takes that were recorded.
- *Prints* (or *Select Takes*)—these are the good takes. Traditionally, this column showed which takes were printed on film from the original camera negative. Now, even productions that are shot on film usually transfer all takes to digital files. In this case, the *Print* column is renamed *Select Takes* and indicates which takes the director prefers.
- *Notes*—this is the place to put any technical notes that are helpful to the lab or assistant editor in syncing or logging the dailies.
- *Description*—this is a brief description of each set-up, so the lab and assistant editor can be certain that they are looking at the right material.

Some people have a column on their log that is a running tally of set-ups. This makes filing the total set-ups in the script supervisor's daily report fast and easy at the end of the day. I keep a running tally, casually, in the right-hand margin. That way, I get my tally and it doesn't take any page width. If you are working in a data-based digital system, the set-ups will be tallied automatically.

If you handwrite shot descriptions in the editors' log, keep them very short. They are used to identify each set-up, not name everything that happened in the shot.

In a paper workflow, blank editors' logs are made of open-ended columns. Use a ruler to draw a line across the columns whenever it helps to separate and define information: between set-ups or camera rolls, etc.

GENERATING EDITORS' DAILY LOGS FROM DIGITAL FACING PAGES

If your application uses the facing page input as a data bank, you can export that data as an Editors' Daily Log. The descriptions and comments are usually way more detailed than they need to be. Some programs let you select a lead line in your facing page description that becomes a shorter notation in the editors' daily log.

Script Supervisor's Daily Report

Script supervisors use the daily report[6] to keep notes for the production department (assistant directors, unit production manager, producers, studio executives, etc.). It contains information about the shooting crew's working hours, what material was recorded, what scenes were completed, and which camera and sound rolls were filled. It also tracks the company's day-to-day progress: what is owed, added, or deleted.

The second AD (sometimes the paperwork PA or DGA trainee) will combine information on this form with information from other departments to make the Daily Production Report, which is the definitive record of everything that happened on this production day. Here is the information you will need to complete a Script Supervisor's Daily Report:

THE CORRECT TIME

The script supervisor is the official timekeeper on set. Make sure you have a dependable watch in sync with the local standard time. Before

| "TAKING WOODSTOCK" EDITORS' DAILY LOG
Transfer All. Circled Director's Selects. | | | | | | Date:
Shoot Day:
Page   of |
Cam. Roll	Snd. Roll	Set-up	Takes	Select Takes	Notes	Description

Fig. 6.19 A blank editors' daily log. From *Taking Woodstock*.

LONE STAR   EDITOR'S DAILY LOG

DATE 5-9-95   SHOOT DAY 12

CR/SR	SET-UP	TAKES	PRINTS	NOTES	DESCRIPTION
57/37	89D	1-5	3+5		MED OTIS BEHIND BAR, GETS MONEY → CU MONEY ON BAR → CU OTIS → MED OTIS GETS MONEY DOWN.
57/37	89E	1-3	2+3		OS WADE TO MED OTIS GETS BOX DOWN. MCU WADE AS HE WINKS AT HOLLIS.
57/37	89F	1	1		MED WADE GETS SHOT, LOW ANGLE, OTIS BEHIND
57/—	89G	1	1	MOS	CU BLOODY MONEY
57/37	89H	1-5 5	2+3+4 5	HEAD OF SHOT WRONG SIDE OF LINE. NOT TO BE USED TKS 3-5 PH.	CU GUN IN BOX, TILT UP TO CU OTIS, WADE BEHIND. OTIS TURNS TO BUDDY AT DOOR
57/37	89J	1-4	3+4		MCU OTIS REACHES FOR BOX. SHOT THROUGH BOTTLES.
57/37	89K	1-2	2		MED OTIS PULLS HIMSELF UP AT BAR. WADE WALKS IN BEHIND
57/37 58/37	89L	1-2 3	2 3		MCU WADE AT BAR FROM OTIS GETS UP TO BUDDY COMES IN.
58/37	89M	1-3	1+2+3		MCU WADE WATCHES OTIS GO TO GET MONEY
58/37	89N	1-4	1+2+3+4		CU WADE AIMS, WINKS + AIMS. RACK FOCUS TO GUN.
58/38	89P	1-2	1+2		CU WADE'S GUN
58/—	89Q	1-2	1+2	MOS	MED HOLLIS. HE CROSSES BEHIND WADE. ZOOM IN TO CU
58/—	89R	1	1	MOS	MCU HOLLIS FOR REACTION TO WINK.
58/38	89S	1-2	1+2	TAIL SLATE	CU HOLLIS' GUN POINTS C.R.
58/38	89T	1-2	1+2	TAIL SLATE	CU HOLLIS' GUN POINTS C.L.
58/38	41	1-6	2+6	②	MCU SAM → WIDE WADE → MED BUDDY
59/38	41A	1	1	①	WIDE BUDDY IN YARD
59/38	41B	1-2	1+2	③	MCU SAM FOR DIALOG WITH ZACK
59/38	41C	1-5	5	④	OS SAM TO MED ZACK. PATROL MAN BEHIND
59/39		6-7	7		

END

Fig. 6.20 Two editors' daily logs, filled in. You can see the organization is a bit different, but the type of information is the same. From *Lone Star* and *Syriana*.

"SYRIANA"
EDITORS' DAILY LOG

Date: 6-14-05
Shoot Day: 5
Page 2 of 2

Cam. Roll	Snd. Roll	Slate	Takes	Prints	Notes	Description
B 1010	94	A 150 C	1	—		MED BENNETT SR. BENNETT STEPS INTO FG-.
B 1011			2-3	③		
B 1012			4	④		
B 1013			5	⑤		
B 1014			6-7	⑦		
A 1065	94	A 150 D	1	①		M CU BENNETT SR. 2 SHOT WHEN STANDING
B 1015	94	A 150 D	1	①		CU BENNETT SR. SITTING AT TABLE
A 1265	94	A 150 E	1-2	②		CU BENNETT YELLING OUT WINDOW + MCU LOOKING AT KUDO
A 1266			3-5	③④⑤		
A 1266	94	A 150 F	1-2	①②		OVER BENNETT'S RT TO INSERT HAMMER OPENING BOX.
A 1266	94	A 150 G	1	①		CLOSER - OVER BENNETT'S RT TO INSERT HAMMER OPENING BOX
A 1267	MOS	17E	1-2	①②		INSERT OF BENNETTS FANCY WATCH. FROM BOTH SIDES.
HDA2	94	C10	1	①	VIDEO ONLY	MCU MOM
HDA2	94	C10 A	1	①		CU MOM
HDA2	MOS	C10 B	1	①		GAS PUMP B-ROLL
HDA2	MOS	C10 C	1-2	①②		WIDE GAS STATION

END

Fig. 6.20 *continued*.

5/24/22

DAILY EDITOR'S LOG
LIFE OF PI

Day: Day 1 - Main Unit

Date: 5/23/22

Slate Take #	Description	CR	SR	Time	Lens	Comments	SU
78 1*	Scene(s): 78 Crane - wide shot - PI runs to side of lower deck - WIDE PI runs from stern to rail. Camera swings over railing and ocean. *** VFX #00082 ***	A11	13	0:06	25	boat rocking needs adjustment * (3D) 2&3/4, D14, L13, R14	1
	CLOSER -- med/wide into mcu PI - (runs for takes 1-2, 6&7)	C11		0:06	150	boat rocking needs adjustment	2
2*		A11		0:07	25	OK-PI falls needs bigger wave * (3D) 2&3/4, D14, L13, R14	1
		C11		0:07	150	OK-PI falls needs bigger wave	2
3*		A11		0:21	25	OK-A CAM ONLY - blocking and timing makes rocking less strong * (3D) 2&3/4, D14, L13, R14	1
		C11		0:00	150	NG-NO ROLL	2
4*		A11		0:06	25	OK-A CAM ONLY - water good, rocking not so good (take #2 still the best) * (3D) 2&3/4, D14, L13, R14	1
		C11		0:00	150	NG-NO ROLL	2
5*		A11		0:05	25	NG-A CAM ONLY - NO GOOD * (3D) 2&3/4, D14, L13, R14	1
		C11		0:00	150	NG-NO ROLL	2
6*		A11		0:28	25	FAV-PI changes his walk to straighter to camera then sharper turn to rail * (3D) 2&3/4, D14, L13, R14	1
		C11		0:28	150	FAV-PI changes his walk to straighter to camera then sharper turn to rail	2
7*		A11		0:45	25	FAV-best water — not so much wobble * (3D) 2&3/4, D14, L13, R14	1
		C11		0:45	150	FAV-best water — not so much wobble	2
8*		A11		0:25	25	FAV-A CAM ONLY — reference silver balls * (3D) 2&3/4, D14, L13, R14	1
		C11		0:25	150	NG-NO ROLL	2
78A 1	Scene(s): 78 Crane M/W to cu - PI steps out on lower deck *vfx remove wire for door closing (focus best starting at take #6)	A11	13	0:04	40	NG-focus buzzz (3D) 2, (D15, L11, R12)	3
2				0:05	40	NG-see crew (3D) 2, (D15, L11, R12)	3
3				0:14	40	OK-PI stands straighter at the end (3D) 2, (D15, L11, R12)	3

* - VFX shot

Fig. 6.21 Editor's Daily Log report using ScriptE. This report is generated from Fig. 6.13, Scene mode input page using ScriptE (from Tony Pettine).

SYRIANA   Participant / Section Eight   Edit Log

Director: Stephen Gaghan   D.P.: Robert Elswit

Script Supervisor: Mary Cybulski   Cell: 555-555-5555   E-mail: mcyxx@xx.xxx

Take	P	Tm	Comment	CAM	CAM	SND
			Day: 5 (AP) 6/14/2005			

A150C
MED BENNETT SR. ---> BENNETT STEPS INTO FG

Day: 5 (AP)		6/14/2005	Page: 79 Setup: 1			
1					B1010	94
2					B1011	
3	X					
4	X				B1012	
5	X				B1013	
6					B1014	
7	X					

A150D
A - MCU BENNETT SR --> 2/SH WHEN STANDING

B - C/U BENNETT ST SITTING AT TABLE

Day: 5 (AP)		6/14/2005	Page: 79 Setup: 3			
1	X			A1265	B1015	94

A150E
C/U BENNETT YELLING OUT WINDOW + MCU LOOKING AT KUDO

Day: 5 (AP)		6/14/2005	Page: 79 Setup: 4			
1				A1265		94
2	X					
3	X			A1266		
4	X					
5	X					

A150F
OVER BENNETT'S RT, TD INSERT HAMMER OPENING BOX.

Day: 5 (AP)		6/14/2005	Page: 79 Setup: 5			
1	X			A1266		94
2	X					

A150G
CLOSER --- OVER BENNETT'S RT, TD INSERT HAMMER OPENING BOX.

Day: 5 (AP)		6/14/2005	Page: 79 Setup: 6			
1	X			A1266		94

17E
INSERT OF BENNETT'S FANCY WATCH FROM BOTH SIDES

Day: 5 (AP)		6/14/2005	Page: 11 Setup: 7			
1	X			A1267		MOS
2	X					

C10
MCU MOM

Day: 5 (AP) 6/14/2005 Page: 7 Setup: 8						
Notes: VIDEO ONLY						
1	X			HDA2		94

Fig. 6.22 Editor's Daily Log report using Peter Skarratt (from Lori Grabowski).

smartphones, I used to make a phone call to "the correct time" (this was really a thing) at the start of each week and adjust my watch if needed. Once we had smartphones, I could just check in with the first AD at the start of a job to make sure we were in perfect sync. This becomes important when the AD calls grace and needs to know exactly when we go into penalty.[7]

My one experience of smartphone time not working happened in Morocco, deep in the Sahara desert. We were scheduled to get up and leave the hotel before dawn. During the night, the US adjusted the clocks for daylight savings time. Some of our phones automatically made that adjustment and some did not.[8]

THE CREW'S WORK DAY

- "Shooting day"—places this day in the production schedule. The first day of a 70-day shoot is "Day 1 of 70." Count only the working days, not the days off.
- "Date"—the date of this shooting day.
- "Set call" (or "Report")—the shooting crew's start time, on set.
- "Leave"—if some crew members are working out of town and getting paid for their local travel time, you may want this additional field. It records the time of day when the majority of the out-of-town crew will start their working day, usually when they are picked up from the hotel. Ask whoever is keeping the production report if they would like leave time included in your report.
- "1st AM Shot"—the time of day when the cameras first roll. This may be in the morning, afternoon, or night.
- "1st Meal" (or "Lunch")—the time of day that the crew breaks and returns for their first meal. This can be calculated and reported in various ways, which will be covered in Chapter 9, "A Day on Set."
- "1st PM Shot"—the time of day when the cameras first roll after the first meal break. This may be in the morning, afternoon, or night.
- "2nd Meal"—the time of day that the crew breaks and returns for their second meal. Most often, there is no 2nd meal, but make a field for it, so you have it if you need it.
- "2nd PM Shot"—the time of day when the cameras first roll after a second meal break. Most often, there is no 2nd PM shot.

- "Cam. Wrap"—the time of day that the first AD calls "That's a wrap!" on set. Most of the crew will have work to do after camera wrap is called. If there is more than one shooting unit working, there may be different camera wrap times for each unit.[9] You are not responsible for recording individual crew members' wrap times, except your own.

> The **script supervisor's daily report** contains information for the production department about the shooting crew's working day.

THE WORK THAT IS PLANNED FOR THAT DAY

- "Scheduled for Today"—all the scenes that are officially planned, listed by scene number, with details of page count and location. Find this information on the call sheet. Under "Time," I write my preproduction timing.

THE PROGRESS MADE THAT DAY

- "Total in Script"—lists the totals from your preproduction breakdowns: the number of scenes, minutes of screen time, and number of pages, adjusted for any script changes that have happened during production, prior to this day.
- "Added/Omitted"—show adjustments here for any script changes that happen today, which affect the script totals.
- "Revised Total in Script"—the new script totals after the day's changes are figured in. These are the numbers you will use for the next day's "Total in Script."
- "Taken Previously"—take this number from your last report. The first shooting day's "Taken Previously" totals are 0.
- "Taken Today"—today's completed work. For "Time" (or "Minutes"), I use my on-set master time for each scene (the way I think it will play when run in its entirety), not my preproduction timing.
- "Total Taken to Date"—add these last two together. These will be the numbers you will use in the next day's "Taken Previously."
- "Remaining to Take"—subtract "Total Taken to Date" from "Revised Total in Script."
- "Scheduled for Today"—to get these numbers, total the amounts listed in "Scheduled for Today," seen here at the top of the form.

"TAKING WOODSTOCK"
SCRIPT SUPERVISOR'S DAILY REPORT

Shooting Day:	Scheduled for Today			
Date:	Scene#	Pages	Time	Location
Leave:				
Report:				
1st AM Shot:				
1st Meal:				
1st PM Shot:				
2nd Meal:				
1st Shot				
A Cam. Wrap:				

	Scenes	Pages	Minutes	Set-ups
Total in Script				
Added/Omitted				
Revised Total in Script				
Taken Previously				
Taken Today				
Total Taken to Date				
Remaining to Take				
Scheduled for Today				

Camera Rolls:	Scenes completed today:
Sound Rolls:	Partially completed scenes:
Wildtrack:	Scenes scheduled & not shot:
Remarks:	Additional set-ups for credited scenes:

Fig. 6.23 A blank script supervisor's daily report. From *Taking Woodstock*.

THE DETAILS OF THE DAY'S WORK

- "Camera Rolls"—lists the camera rolls, cards, or drives that were used today, by roll number (not number of rolls).
- "Sound Rolls"—lists the sound rolls, cards, or drives that were used today, by roll number.
- "Wild Track"—lists the wild track that was recorded today, by wild track number.
- "Scenes Completed Today"—lists the scenes that were completed today, by scene number.
- "Partially Completed Scenes"—lists the scenes that were partially completed today, by scene number.
- "Scenes Scheduled but Not Shot"—listed by scene number.
- "Additional Set-Ups Shot for Completed Scenes"—these are scenes that have been previously counted as complete which now have additional material, shot today. List each scene, by scene number.

DIGITAL DAILY PRODUCTION REPORTS

This report is closely linked to your Scene/Page/Time breakdown. It requires very little understanding of your project's story, so it is a good place to try out using digital applications. Data-based script supervising systems like ScriptE, Peter Skarratt, and MovieSlate 8 can generate a daily report automatically from the project's facing pages.

If you want to ease into a digital format, you can build this form as a spreadsheet with embedded formulas that will do the calculations after you input the numbers for each day.

PRODUCTION REPORTS FOR COMMERCIALS, PROMOTIONS, AND OTHER AD AGENCY PROJECTS

Production reports for commercials are presented to the agency and client. Most commercial production companies like the daily reports to be graphically appealing and easy to read, often with pictures. An application with robust graphic functions makes this easy and fun. (See Fig. 6.18, a page of notes for an unscripted production using MovieSlate 8 from a promotional interview for *No Time to Die*.)

LONE STAR
SCRIPT SUPERVISOR'S DAILY REPORT

DATE: 5-9-95			
SHOOTING DAY: 12			
LEAVE: 7:30PM			
SET CALL: 7:40PM			
1st SHOT: 8:35 PM			
1st MEAL: 1:25 Am			
1st SHOT: 4:00 Am			
2nd MEAL:			
1st SHOT:			
CAMERA WRAP: 5:52 AM			

SCHEDULED FOR TODAY:

SCENE	PAGE	TIME	LOCATION
89	1 3/8	50/1:00	INT. BIG OS .1957
41	1 7/8	138/2:00	EXT. SAM'S BACKYARD

	SCENES	PAGES	TIME	SET-UPS
SCHEDULED TODAY	2	3 2/8	2:28	
TAKEN TODAY	2	3 2/8	3:00	19
PREVIOUSLY TAKEN	30	28 1/8	33:16	130
TOTAL TAKEN	32	31 3/8	36:16	149
TOTAL REMAINING	62	85 5/8	79:33	
TOTAL IN SCRIPT	94	117	115:49	
Added Today	—o—	—o—	—o—	
Deleted Today	—o—	—o—	—o—	
TOTAL SCENES: ADDED: —o— DROPPED: —o— RETAKEN: —o—				

CAMERA ROLLS # 57-59   SCENES COMPLETED TODAY # 41-89

SOUND ROLLS # 37-39

WILDTRACK # —o—   PARTIALLY COMPLETED SCENE# —o—

RESHOOT SET-UPS FOR SCENE # —o—

ADDITIONAL SET-UPS FOR SCENE# —o—

REMARKS:

Fig. 6.24 Two script supervisor's daily reports. From *Lone Star* and *Syriana*. These are paired with the editors' daily log examples (Fig. 6.20).

"SYRIANA"
SCRIPT SUPERVISOR'S DAILY REPORT

Date: 6-14-05	Scheduled for Today			
Shooting Day: 5	Scene#	Pages	Time	Location
JUNE ADDITIONAL	A150	1 1/8	2:00/2:00	INT BENNETT APT
Set Call: 7A	R17pt	— o —	— o —	INT PLANE
1st AM Shot: 10:10 AM	C10	5/8	:12/:12	EXT. GAS STATION
1st Meal: 1:30-2 PM				
1st PM Shot: 3:26 PM				
2nd Meal:				
1st Shot				
Cam. Wrap: 3:55 PM				

	Pages	Scenes	Minutes	Set-ups
Total in Script	148 3/8	244	200:12	
Added/Omitted	+1 1/8	+1	2:00	
Revised Total in Script	149 4/8	245	202:12	
Taken Previously	147 6/8	243	201:23	2027
Taken Today	1 6/8	2	2:12	16
Total Taken to Date	149 4/8	245	203:35	2043
To Be Taken	— o —	— o —		
Scheduled for Today	1 6/8	2	2:12	

Camera Rolls: A1255-A1267 + B1006-1015	Scenes completed today: A150 + C10
Sound Rolls: 94	Partially completed scenes: —
Wildtrack:	Scenes scheduled & not shot: —
Remarks: (T) ADD Sc A150	Additional set-ups shot for scenes: 17

Fig. 6.24 *continued.*

5/24/22	DAILY PROGRESS REPORT											Day 1 - Main Unit		
	LIFE OF PI											Date: 5/23/22		

Time			Pages	Scenes	Setups	ERT	ART	+/-	Wilds	(+)Scenes:	(+)Pgs:	(-)Scenes:	(-)Pgs:
Call:	7:00 AM	Today	2 5/8	2	5	2:38	2:38	0:00	0	0	0/8	0	0/8
Call 2:													
1st Shot:	11:43 PM	Previous	0/8	0	0	0:00	0:00	0:00	0	0	0/8	0	0/8
Lunch		To Date	2 5/8	2	5	2:38	2:38	0:00	0	0	0/8	0	0/8
Out:	1:00 PM												
In:	1:30 AM	Scripted	76 0/8	114	Added Today:								
1st Shot:		(+) 1/8ths	0/8	0	Cut Today:								
Dinner		(-) 1/8ths	0/8	0	Cam Rolls: A11 C11								
Out:													
In:		Current	76 0/8	114	Sound: 13								
1st Shot:		Remaining	73 3/8	112	Retakes:								
Wrap													

Camera:	1:19 AM	PROJECTED RUNNING TIME					ALT PROJECTED RUNNING TIME			
Sound:		Min:	2:38	Pages:	2 5/8					
Script:	2:19 AM	Ratio:	1.003175	X	72 3/8	=	72:36	Credited: 2:38	+ Remaining: 70:06 = 72:44	

SCENES FULLY CREDITED					PARTIALS	SETUPS	WILD TRACKS
#	Pages	ERT	ART	+/-	1 78	4 85	
78	2 2/8	2:15	2:15	0:00	2 78	5 85A	
85	3/8	0:23	0:23	0:00	3 78A		

Weather:	Sound stage - stormy weather high seas

NOTES:

Test shoot day for Mary's book - logged and lined only 1st 2 setups of scene 78 and 85

Fig. 6.25 Script Supervisor's Daily Production Report using ScriptE (from Tony Pettine). This report is generated from Fig. 6.13.

NOTES USED ON SOME DAYS OR SOME MOVIES

Wild Track Tally

A wild track is a piece of sound that has no picture associated with it. We use it for things like voice-over dialog, room tone, sound effects, and atmospheric sound.[10] We note wild track on the lined script, the facing pages, the editors' daily log, and the script supervisor's daily production report. We also list it in a separate tally (see Fig. 6.27).

> A **wild track tally** is a list of recorded sound that has no picture associated with it.

On the East Coast of the United States, each wild track has its own number, beginning with 1001, then 1002, etc. We start with 1001 so that the number looks different from every other number in the edit room, making it instantly identifiable as wild track.

On the West Coast, wild track is usually identified only by its scene number, as in "wild track for scene 36." The West Coast system avoids the task of keeping track of which wild track number is next. It is also easier for the

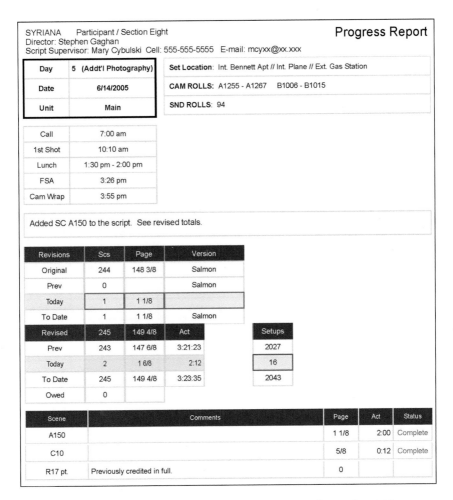

Fig. 6.26 Script Supervisor's Daily Production Report using Peter Skarratt (from Lori Grabowski).

sound mixer to program into a digital recorder. I find this system problematic when a single wild track might be used for more than one scene, or a scene has more than one wild track. I prefer the East Coast method. Ask your editors which method they like.

Do not confuse wild track with "sound run wild." The latter is sound that has corresponding picture which is not in sync. An example of this is when a camera is run off-speed (faster or slower than usual) and sound is recorded at the usual speed.

"SUNSHINE STATE"
Wild Track Log   PAGE 1 OF 3

Wt #	Scene	Description	Notes	SR#	Date
1001	2	RAW TONE	MED RAIN	1	4-25-01
1002	2	MURRAY'S 1ST LINE	PLAYS OVER Sc 1	6	4-26-01
1003	5	ROOM TONE	RECORDED WITH Sc 5CTK1	7	4-26-01
1004	64	WILD TRACK - TRAFFIC	RUN WITH 64C	9	4-28-01
1005	11	TOURIST- OFF CAMERA LINE		11	4-30-01
VIDEO INTERVIEW	91	TKS 1-4: PART 3 OF PLAYBACK	WE ALSO HAVE DAT	14	5-1-01
1006	11	NORTHRUP DIALOG BEFORE WE SEE HIM		14	5-1-01
VIDEO INTERVIEW	91	TKS 5-8: PART 1 OF PLAYBACK	WE ALSO HAVE DAT	14	5-1-01
VIDEO INTERVIEW	91	TKS 9-10: PART 2 OF PLAY BACK	WE ALSO HAVE DAT	14	5-1-01
1007	16	WALLA		16	5-2-01
1008	16	CHAIRWOMAN'S LAST DIALOG	FOR OVERLAP	16	5-2-01
1009	55	ROOM TONE		21	5-3-01
1010	53	ALL DIALOG FOR Sc 53		21	5-3-01
1011	40	ROOM TONE		22	5-4-01
1012	68	ROOM TONE - RIVER	RUN @ 68T	29	5-8-01
1013	46	AMBIANCE. PA IS DISTANT		29	5-9-01
1014	46	ANNOUNCEMENTS AT DOG TRACK		30	5-9-01
1015	46	WT OF DOG RACE		31	5-9-01
1016	15	ROOM TONE		33	5-10-01
1017	6	ROOM TONE - SHORE TONE		34	5-11-01
1018	79	WILD DIALOG "IDIOT"		35	5-11-01
1019	42	TONE - WITH LEAF BLOWER	FOR 42A TK2	36	5-12-01
1020	37	BG DIALOG FOR BUSINESSMEN		40	5-14-01
1021	37	ROOM TONE - FISH TANK		40	5-14-01
1022	33+70	WALLA FOR PIRATE SHIP		44	5-16-01

Fig. 6.27 The wild track log from *Sunshine State*.

In analog days, editors needed a minute or two of room tone to even out
transitions between different pieces of dialog and unify the sound of the
scene. After shooting each scene, the cast and crew would freeze everyone

"SUNSHINE STATE"
Wild Track Log   PAGE 2 OF 3

Wt #	Scene	Description	Notes	SR#	Date
1023	36	DUB + SHIFLETT EXTENTION		47	5-17-01
1024	36	GENERATOR TONE		47	5-17-01
1025	36	STREET WALLA		47	5-17-01
1026	37+91	BAR WALLA	MAYBE TOO ANIMATED	47	5-17-01
1027	8	TONE WITH TRUCKS + BIRDS	ROLL AT END OF 8 TK6	48	5-18-01
1028	60	STEEL DRUM		48	5-18-01
1029	60	NAIL GUN		48	5-18-01
1030	49	SOLDIERS DRILL		53	5-21-01
1031	2-19 20-21	SOUND TRUCK LOUD SPEAKER	MM NEED RE-RECORDING	61	5.24.01
1032	32	KIDS LEAVE THEATER	AIR CONDITION ON 1ST V2	69	5-29-01
1033	31	RT- LOUD MILL - RECORDED AT END OF 31 TK4		71	5-29-01
1034	21	DESIREE'S LINE "YOU HOLE"	SERIES	72	5-30-01
1035	20+21	CAR ENGINE TONE		72	5-30-01
1036	24.24A 24B	FACTORY TONE		74	5-30-01
1037	9	TONE - FOR SET UPS AT MRS. P'S HOUSE		76	5-31-01
1038	34	ALL DIALOG	SERIES	78	5-31-01
1039	47	TONE - WITH WEIRD TONE		79	6-1-01
1040	71	BOYS PLAY FOOTBALL	GOES WITH SET-UP 71D	84	6-5-01
1041	71	BOYS PLAY FOOTBALL - "KILL THE MAN"	GOES WITH SET-UP 71	84	6-5-01
1042	74	WAVE TONE ON RADIO MIKES		87	6-6-01
1043	74	WAVE TONE POINTED TOWARD OCEAN	FOR GENERAL USE	87	6-6-01
1044	74	WAVE TONE PARALLEL TO SHORELINE	FOR GENERAL USE	87	6-6-01
1045	GENERAL USE	WIND + SURF - MED PERSPECTIVE	NOT TRANSFERRED	88	6-6-01
1046	GENERAL USE	WIND + SURF - DISTANT PERSPECTIVE	NOT TRANSFERRED	88	6-6-01
1047	GENERAL USE	WIND + SURF - CLOSER PERSPECTIVE	NOT TRANSFERRED	88	6-6-01

Fig. 6.27 *continued.*

and everything as it was, so the sound of the room would be the same as it was during the recording of the scene.[11] Recording room tone is less common now, as sound editors can usually take a teeny moment of tone found

"SUNSHINE STATE"
Wild Track Log   page 3 of 3

Wt #	Scene	Description	Notes	SR#	Date
1048	GEN CRU USE	WAVES - VERY NEAR	NOT TRANSFERED	88	6-7-01
1049	65	CHURCH-GOERS LEAVE CHURCH		89	6-7-01
1050	58/59	BOTH VERSES OF SONG		89	6-7-01
1051	58/59	2ND VERSE + CHORUS OF SONG		90	6-7-01
1052	63	"GOOD MORNING" FROM CONGREGATION		90	6-7-01
1053	58/59	SHARON SINGS SOLO		91	6-7-01
1054	69	RAIN TONE FOR 69TK6		91	6-7-01
1055	48	ALL OF UNDERHILL'S DIALOG	1 1/2x	99	6-12-01
1056	48	ALL OF SMOOT'S DIALOG	2x ACTION	99	6-12-01
1057	48	KIDDIE TRAIN RIDE		99	6-12-01
1058	FOR JOHN	SND TRUCK AUDITION	NO PRINTS	100	6-12-01
1059	57	ROOM TONE - THUNDER + RAIN		106	6-13-01
1060	3-19-20 21-44	SOUND TRUCK ANNOUNCEMENT	PART 1	107	6-14-01
1061	3-19-20 21-44	SOUND TRUCK ANNOUNCEMENT	PART 2	107	6-14-01
1062	39	ROOM TONE - OCEAN + CRICKETS		107	6-14-01
1063	76	ROOM TONE		108	6-14-01
		END OF PRODUCTION WILD TRACK.			

Fig. 6.27 *continued.*

within the recorded takes and expand it digitally to build enough track to do the job. Check with the edit room and sound mixer to understand what will be needed on your project.

There are times when the tone of a location has a lot of character, like the chatter in a restaurant,[12] or the machines in a factory, and the mixer will want to get that room tone wild as an atmospheric element.

Wild Picture Tally

Sometimes we grab a shot not knowing where it will go in the script. This sort of set-up is called "wild picture," because it has no scene or scene number associated with it. The shot could be something like a sunset that is too pretty to pass up or general atmosphere that could play in several places.

> A **wild picture tally** is a list of set-ups that are not associated with any particular scene.

Often we give a grabbed shot like this a tail ID that is a literal description of the shot, something like "Sunset."[13] If I think there will be more than a few wild picture grabs on my film, I like to get more organized and give them "W" numbers. The first grabbed wild picture is "W1," then "W2," etc. This organization pays off if by the end of production you have several different sunsets in your media.

I invented this system on a film we shot in Montana, *Thousand Pieces of Gold*. We had a DP, Bobby Bukowski, who loved the mountains and would pop off a shot of any beautiful thing he saw. We slated them with W numbers; birds, the moon, snow falling, hundreds of images. They all went onto the wild picture log. They were easy to tag on set, easy to find in the edit room, and were really useful for the film. I have used this system ever since.

Even if you only have a few bits of wild picture and don't give them W numbers, list them in a tally so they don't get lost.

Wild picture may or may not have sound.

Owed List

Sometimes we officially finish shooting a scene, giving it full credit in the daily report, and then decide to add a set-up or a bit of soundtrack. It is the script supervisor's job, along with the first AD, to keep a running list of the owed bits so they are not forgotten.

If we do not shoot a scheduled scene, I will include that scene on my owed list, until it is incorporated in a new shooting schedule or it is completed.

Around the middle of the production, I start distributing the updated owed list to the director, ADs, and producers (on Fridays if I can, so they can

"THE TEMPEST"   **WILD PICTURE LOG**   Page:
                                                    M. Cybulski

W#	CR#	Description	Notes	Date
1	B4	SUNSET	SERIES	11-17-08
2	B 29	SUNSET	2 FPS	11-21-08
3	B30	WAVES		11-22-08
4	B35	WAVES, TIDAL POOLS. SERIES	48 FPS 6 FPS 45° ✗	11-24-08
5	B38	CLOUDS TK1 3FPS, TK2 2FPS		11-23-08
6	B38	CLOUDS 2FPS	MISSLATED w3A	11-25-08
7	B40	HILLSIDE GARDEN OF THE GODS	EARLY LIGHT	11-26-08
8	B41	CLOUDS - WINDY - GARDEN OF THE GODS	WINDY	11-26-08
9	B48	CLOUDS, BLUE SKY + GRAY		12-1-08
10	A142	VARIOUS FOREST CUT AWAYS	FOR ARIEL	12-9-08
11	B60	SHOTS OF SEA	2ND UNIT	12-11-08
12	A292	ARIEL FLIES	NG. INCOMPLET NOTHING USEFUL	1-27-09

Fig. 6.28 A wild picture log filled out mid-production. From *The Tempest*.

look at it over the weekend). If it is a long list or if it is toward the end of the shoot, I also give it to the department heads. That way they won't wrap any item we need for the shoot. Check with the producers and director before you hand an owed list to anyone. They may not want this information to be public.

> An **owed list** keeps track of incomplete scenes and set-ups that are not on the AD's shooting schedule.

POSSIBLE OWED SHOTS & TRACK   9/9/04

To: Steve, Georgia, Jen, Michael, Dan, Simon, Alison, Robert, Louise, John, Richard, Marina, Tim, Waldo, Kay, Todd, Chrissie, Barry, Phil, Fran, Petur
From: Mary Cybulski

Please let me know if anything else should be on this list.
Thanks
Mary

SCENE   OWED   (WT is WILD TRACK only)

17   Bennett's POV out plane window
26   WT: Overlapping dialog clean
62   WT: TV cover for Stan in parking lot
65   Beater boys loading carcass into truck
                   CGI Animal falling and dying
                   WT: Danny Dalton new dialog?
93   Insert Blackberry 'Sunshine' on display
110   Insert Lilly school document
                        Lilly school
                        Translation on post it
                        Money Wire
132/133   CLI sign
195   Oilman of the year sign
A194   WT: Reza sighing in appreciation
                        Small giggle from Mary Alice?

MAYBE:
66   Hand on bloody plant
141   Reshoot with Chris???

Fig. 6.29 An owed shot list. From *Syriana*.

Lined Storyboards

A script is made of words. While this is great for most scenes, words are often not the best way to describe choreographed action like a fight, stunt, or visual effect. If your film has a lot of this sort of thing, you may be given storyboards to help explain what is going on. In this case, I like to line

> **Line a storyboard** when it describes a sequence better than the written script.

the storyboards in a system that I borrowed from working on TV commercials. I do this in addition to the usual lined script, not as a replacement.

Figs 6.30 and 6.31 are examples of lined storyboards from *The Happening* and *The Last Airbender*. The set-ups are lined and named with the set-up number, matching the lined script. Note that unlike the lined script, these lines mark only the frames that illustrate that particular set-up. They don't start with the first action on that set-up or end with the last action on that set-up.

LINING ACTION BEAT BY BEAT

When I have a sequence with complicated and consistent action but no storyboard, I might write out a description of the action, one line of description for each beat, and then draw set-up lines over that description as if it were dialog with straight or wavy marks. This is especially useful when there is a lot of coverage that shows specific moments in close-up. See Fig. 7.1c on page 223 for an example of this.

Visual Effects

A VFX sequence can be part of a scene or it can include several scenes. Each visual effects shot has its own name. These names (the VFX numbers) are generated by the VFX department and are not related to the slates from set. VFX shots can be completely computer generated, a composite of various live action elements, or a combination. Every live action element in a composite shot keeps the set-up number it was given when captured, so that it can be traced back to its beginning. Usually there will be a sequence of letters that will identify the VFX sequence, then a number that will identify the composite shot in that sequence.

Here are notes from two VFX-heavy movies: Fig. 6.32, a facing page and lined script from *The Last Airbender* and Figs 6.33 and 6.34, a lined VFX breakdown, facing page and lined script from *Life of Pi*. The two systems of

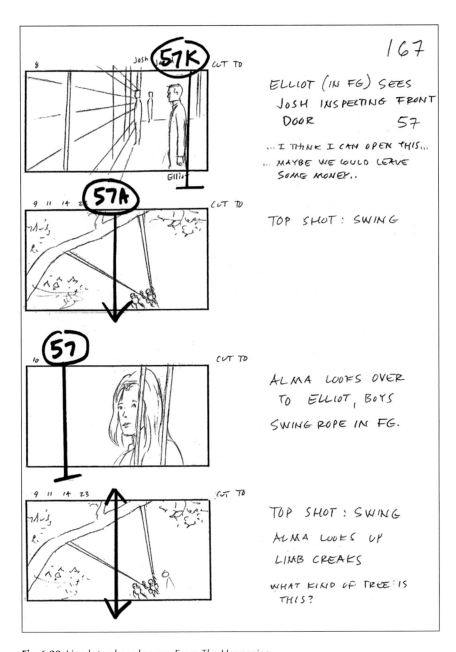

Fig. 6.30 Lined storyboard pages. From *The Happening*.

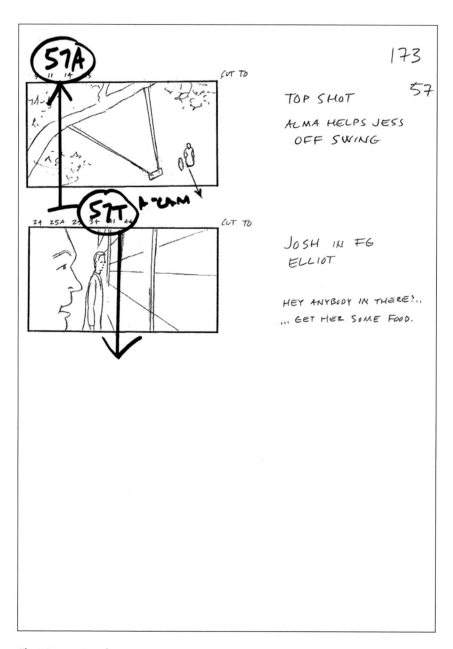

173

57

TOP SHOT

ALMA HELPS JESS
  OFF SWING

JOSH IN FG
ELLIOT

HEY ANYBODY IN THERE?...
... GET HER SOME FOOD.

Fig. 6.30 *continued.*

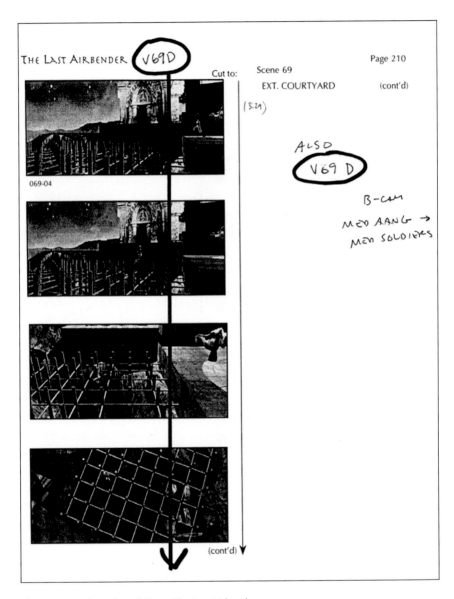

Fig. 6.31 Lined storyboard. From *The Last Airbender*.

notes are a bit different, but they contain the same essential information. Talk to the VFX and editing departments in preproduction to work out a system that gives everyone notes that they will like to work with. Whatever

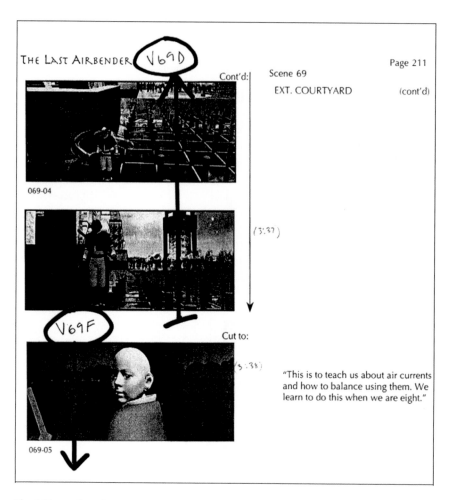

THE LAST AIRBENDER   V69D   Page 211

Cont'd: Scene 69

EXT. COURTYARD   (cont'd)

069-04

(3:37)

V69F

Cut to:

(3:38)

"This is to teach us about air currents
and how to balance using them. We
learn to do this when we are eight."

069-05

Fig. 6.31 *continued.*

your system is, it should identify each composite shot and make clear what
live action set-ups are to be used in that composite.

The three-letter, three-digit numbers in the set-up column of Fig. 6.33
are VFX numbers. These are multiple camera set-ups. The letter above
each VFX number links it to a specific camera angle. The VFX numbers
are also noted as part of the labels at the top of the set-up lines in the
lined script.

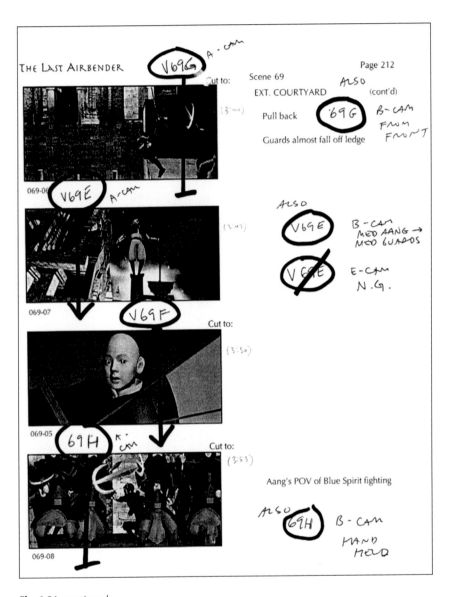

Fig. 6.31 *continued.*

Set-up V69E has no prints on the E camera, as seen on the facing page. I noted that set-up on the lined script, but crossed it out. This reminds the editors that the set-up exists but that Night didn't like it.

"THE LAST AIRBENDER"
FACING PAGES

Facing page: 64
Dates: 6-12-09
Scenes: 69

Setup	Action	Lens	CR	SR	Time	Take	Comments
V69 D	2 CAMERAS AANG JUMPS OUT ON PIERS + TURNS BACK	A 23 15-40 T2.8 20'-43 CRANE	A 334 B 203	60 A	:16 :16 :15 :15	1 1 2 2	
A FNF-070	FIRE STKS A - X-WIDE →	—			:14 :14	3 3	
	MCU AANG	B	A 335		:14	④	ADD WWD.
B FNF-071	B - MED AANG → MED FIRE SOLDIERS.	200 24-290 T2.8			:14 :17 :17	4 ⑤ 5	LOTS OF WWD. LOTS. SHAKE IN CAMERA
		97"4 —			:14 :19	6 6	SO MUCH WIND HIS SHIRT FLIES UP BUMP ON CRANE
					:18 :18	7 7	
			A 336 B 204		:06 :06 :16 :16	8 8 ⑨ 9 /0SPH	INCOMP SCRMBLE. SAME BUMP
V69E A FNF-100 B FNF-101 E FNF-102	3 CAMERAS AANG OPENS THE WINGS ON HIS STAFF + TURNS BACK A - LOW M/W AT PIER. CRANE UP → WIDE AANG FLYING OVER SOLDIERS	A21 15-40 T2.8 24-55 -20' 53i T24-290 T2.8 VAR. E 46	A 336 B 204 E 46 B —	60 A	:17 :17 :17 :17 :17 :17 :20 :20 :20 :15 :15 :15	1 1 1 2 2 2 3 3 3 ④ 4 4	BUMP. OTHERWISE GOOD ADJUST THE WAY AANG HOLDS HIS STAFF - PRE JUMP
A-CAM ALSO COVERS PNF-130	B WIDE SOLDIERS + AANG FLYING B. LOW SOLDIERS + AANG FLYING		A 337		:16 :16	5 5	NO MORE E-CAM

Fig. 6.32 The facing page and lined script for this action from *The Last Airbender*.

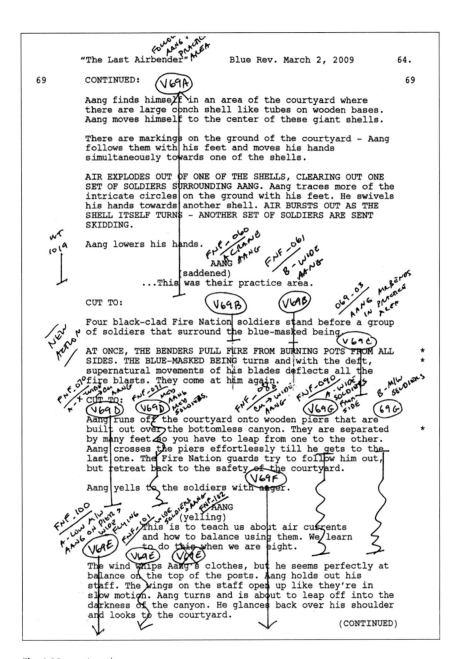

"The Last Airbender"   Blue Rev. March 2, 2009   64.

69   CONTINUED: V69A   69

Aang finds himself in an area of the courtyard where
there are large conch shell like tubes on wooden bases.
Aang moves himself to the center of these giant shells.

There are markings on the ground of the courtyard - Aang
follows them with his feet and moves his hands
simultaneously towards one of the shells.

AIR EXPLODES OUT OF ONE OF THE SHELLS, CLEARING OUT ONE
SET OF SOLDIERS SURROUNDING AANG. Aang traces more of the
intricate circles on the ground with his feet. He swivels
his hands towards another shell. AIR BURSTS OUT AS THE
SHELL ITSELF TURNS - ANOTHER SET OF SOLDIERS ARE SENT
SKIDDING.

Aang lowers his hands.

                    (saddened)
          ...This was their practice area.

          CUT TO: V69B   V69B

Four black-clad Fire Nation soldiers stand before a group
of soldiers that surround the blue-masked being.

AT ONCE, THE BENDERS PULL FIRE FROM BURNING POTS FROM ALL   *
SIDES. THE BLUE-MASKED BEING turns and with the deft,   *
supernatural movements of his blades deflects all the
fire blasts. They come at him again.

          CUT TO:

Aang runs off the courtyard onto wooden piers that are
built out over the bottomless canyon. They are separated
by many feet so you have to leap from one to the other.
Aang crosses the piers effortlessly till he gets to the   *
last one. The Fire Nation guards try to follow him out,
but retreat back to the safety of the courtyard.

Aang yells to the soldiers with anger.

                    (yelling)
          This is to teach us about air currents
          and how to balance using them. We learn
          to do this when we are eight.

The wind whips Aang's clothes, but he seems perfectly at
balance on the top of the posts. Aang holds out his
staff. The wings on the staff open up like they're in
slow motion. Aang turns and is about to leap off into the
darkness of the canyon. He glances back over his shoulder
and looks to the courtyard.

                                                 (CONTINUED)

Fig. 6.32 *continued.*

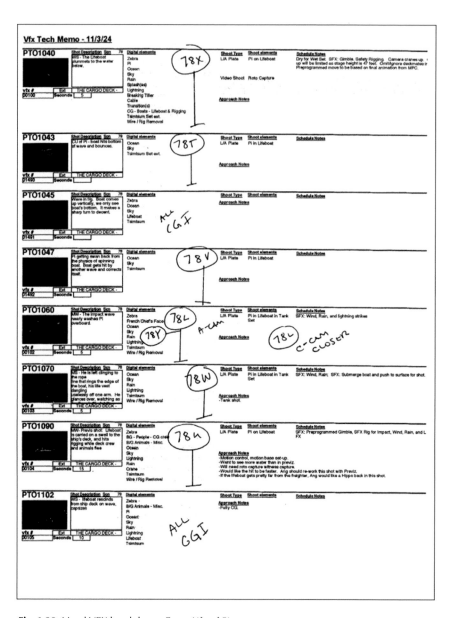

Fig. 6.33 Lined VFX breakdown. From *Life of Pi*.

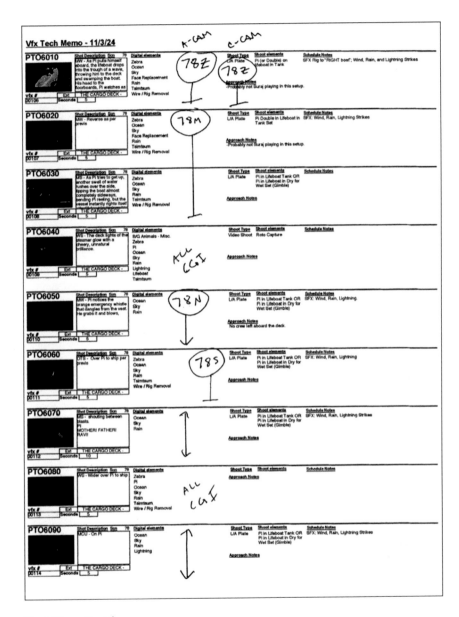

Fig. 6.33 *continued.*

LIFE OF PI
FACING PAGES
Mary Cybulski

Facing page: 39
Dates: 4-29-11
Scenes: 78

Setup	Action	Lens	3D	CR	SR	Time	Take	Comments
78 Z VFx* oo1o6	2 CAMERAS LIFEBOAT RIGHTS ITSELF A - M/W PI C - WIDE PI RATIO 1.185 VFX WILL PUT IN OARS + LIFE RING + FIX TARP TIM - WE THINK WE WANT TK1 ON C-CAM FOR THE ROLL OVER + TK3 ON A-CAM FOR PI BOUNCING AROUND ON TOP OF TARP.	A 75M 22' 35' T2½ 6'-8½ VAR 50↓ 270° 3400K ASA 800 C 32M 36' +2⅔ — 270° 3400K ASA 800	BUILT c2.25 I/O A: .33 Converg A: A↔Z C: .75 C: FRONT OF BOAT	A 115 L 17 R 18 C 106 L 15 R 16	136	;12 ;12 ;11 ;11 ;12 ;12	① ① ② ② ③ ③ 4 4	ROLL :22:46:00 ACTION 22 47 00 TAIL STKS 22 47 37 LIFEBOAT TRAVELS AWAY FROM CAMERA AFTER FLIP. ROLL 23 08 30 ACTION 23 09 45 TAIL STKS 23 10 18 2ND STK 23 10 27 ROPE STAYS ON TOO LONG, TIPPING BOAT TO CAMERA RIGHT. TAIL STKS 23 31 19 BOAT GETS HUNG UP DURING FLIP. SEE PI BEST ON A-CAM THIS TAKE REF - BALLS+STUFFY LIGHTS ARE TURNED OFF DURING TAKE, BUT ONLY IN BLUE SCREEN. TAIL STKS 23 43 41

Fig. 6.34 The facing page and lined script for this action. From *Life of Pi*.

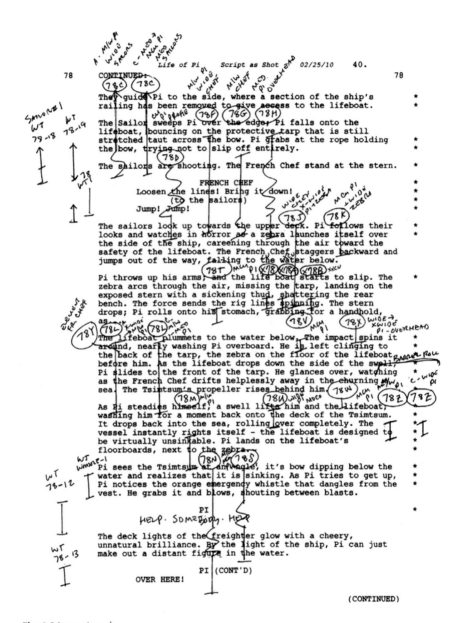

Life of Pi   Script as Shot 02/25/10   40.

78 CONTINUED: 78

They guide Pi to the side, where a section of the ship's
railing has been removed to give access to the lifeboat.   *
                                                             *

The Sailor sweeps Pi over the edge; Pi falls onto the
lifeboat, bouncing on the protective tarp that is still
stretched taut across the bow. Pi grabs at the rope holding *
the bow, trying not to slip off entirely.   *

The sailors are shooting. The French Chef stand at the stern. *

                    FRENCH CHEF   *
        Loosen the lines! Bring it down!   *
            (to the sailors)   *
        Jump! Jump!   *

The sailors look up towards the upper deck. Pi follows their *
looks and watches in horror as a zebra launches itself over *
the side of the ship, careening through the air toward the
safety of the lifeboat. The French Chef staggers backward and
jumps out of the way, falling to the water below.

Pi throws up his arms, and the life boat starts to slip. The *
zebra arcs through the air, missing the tarp, landing on the
exposed stern with a sickening thud, shattering the rear
bench. The force sends the rig lines spinning. The stern
drops; Pi rolls onto his stomach, grabbing for a handhold,
as

The lifeboat plummets to the water below. The impact spins it
around, nearly washing Pi overboard. He is left clinging to *
the back of the tarp, the zebra on the floor of the lifeboat
before him. As the lifeboat drops down the side of the swell
Pi slides to the front of the tarp. He glances over, watching *
as the French Chef drifts helplessly away in the churning
sea. The Tsimtsum's propeller rises behind him.

As Pi steadies himself, a swell lifts him and the lifeboat,
washing him for a moment back onto the deck of the Tsimtsum.
It drops back into the sea, rolling over completely. The   *
vessel instantly rights itself - the lifeboat is designed to
be virtually unsinkable. Pi lands on the lifeboat's   *
floorboards, next to the zebra.   *

Pi sees the Tsimtsum at an angle, it's bow dipping below the *
water and realizes that it is sinking. As Pi tries to get up, *
Pi notices the orange emergency whistle that dangles from the *
vest. He grabs it and blows, shouting between blasts.

                    PI
        HELP. SOMEBODY. HELP   *

The deck lights of the freighter glow with a cheery,
unnatural brilliance. By the light of the ship, Pi can just
make out a distant figure in the water.

                 PI (CONT'D)
        OVER HERE!

                                            (CONTINUED)

Fig. 6.34 *continued.*

In Figs 6.33 and 6.34 you can see that live action set-up 78Z is a two-camera set-up, offering two different frame sizes for composite VFX# 00106.

Composite VFX# 00102 (frame PTO1060), requires two live action elements, 78L and 78Y. Look at Fig. 6.33 and Fig. 6.34 to see how I noted that.

Keep in mind that some VFX elements, or even entire final shots, may be computer generated, and therefore have no set-up numbers from set. I make a note of these as well, so it is clear that nothing is missing from production.

> Whatever system you design to track **VFX composite shots**, it should identify each composite shot and make clear what live action set-ups are to be used in that composite.

You may notice that the facing page in Fig. 6.34 is not set up in the standard American system. Our editor for this project, Tim Squyres, prefers his notes in a slightly British way, with the facing pages in a separate binder and all the set-ups for each scene grouped together at the start of that scene. I am happy to do this. I made a facing page format that has room on each side of the notes for punched holes. That way I can use a right-sided hole punch in my set book and he can have a left sided hole punch for his edit room folder.

There is another unusual thing in this facing page. Ang Lee had two levels of selects: takes he liked and takes he really liked. To keep track of this, I made up a new system of circled takes and double circled takes. When working with Tony Gilroy, we had a similar system of circled and starred takes.

ON-SET MATCHING NOTES

We script supervisors have developed our own personal methods for keeping track of the many things we need to match on set. There is no standard.

Here are the notations that I use most often. They are noted on the set-up lines of the lined script at the exact moment of dialog or action that they refer to. I pencil them in during rehearsals, as the timing usually shifts a bit when the actors feel their way through a scene.

- Two slashes, //, when a character stops.
- A circle-shaped arrow when a character turns, showing a clockwise or counter-clockwise turn.

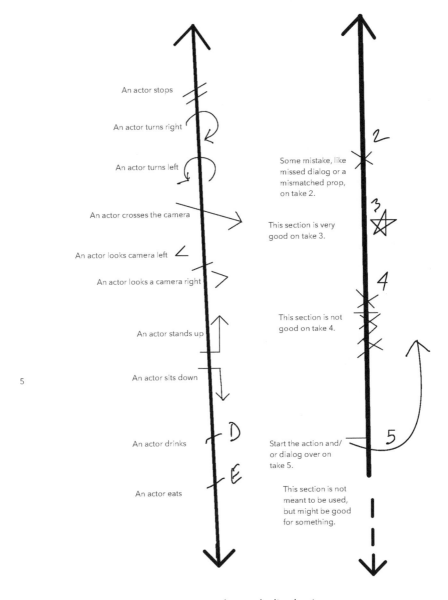

An actor stops

An actor turns right

An actor turns left

Some mistake, like missed dialog or a mismatched prop, on take 2.

An actor crosses the camera

This section is very good on take 3.

An actor looks camera left

An actor looks a camera right

An actor stands up

This section is not good on take 4.

An actor sits down

5

An actor drinks

Start the action and/ or dialog over on take 5.

An actor eats

This section is not meant to be used, but might be good for something.

Fig. 6.35 The matching notations I use most often on the lined script.

- An arrow across the line when a character crosses camera.
- Side arrows, > and <, showing which way a character is looking (this is better noted on frame drawings, if you use them. More about this at the end of this chapter).
- An arrow up or down when a character stands or sits.
- A circled "D" when a character takes a drink.
- A circled "E" when an eating character takes a bite.

Matching notes become really useful when we resume work after there has been a break, such as after turning around or coming back from lunch. When the furniture and light have shifted and different dramatic moments are featured, things can feel unfamiliar. The muscle memory that actors depend on can be thrown off. Having the specifics written down will save you and them.

> When the furniture and light have shifted and different dramatic moments are featured, **things can feel unfamiliar**.

Points of Action

Along with matching notes, I mark the lined script along the relevant set-up line when something significant happens at a specific point in the action. These comments are also noted on the facing pages. Feel free to invent any notations that you find personally helpful. Here are the ones I use the most:

- "X" for mistake, with take number noted.
- Star for a favorite, with take number noted.
- Cross-outs, *XXXX*, along the set-up line where a set-up is no-good.
- "Repeat arrow," with take number, noted at the point an actor stops and goes back to repeat some dialog or action.
- A broken set-up line, instead of a solid line, when a section of the set-up is not meant to be used; maybe the eyeline is wrong for a moment or the character is talking off-camera before they enter the frame. It is worth making a note here in case there is a bit of sound or an isolated close-up that could help the editor get out of a jam.

Examples of Matching Notes

See Fig. 6.3 (near the beginning of this chapter) for these matching notes:

In two takes, 53 take 6 and 53C take 2, the actors backtracked in the dialog, repeating a line or two. This is indicated by the curved arrows, labeled with take number and drawn near the dialog where the backtrack occurred.

Set-up 53A take 4 starts late (this is called a "pick-up") just after dialog line 25. Take 3 ends early, after dialog 52.

We see that set-ups 53D (at the end) and 53E (at the beginning) have short sections where the camera is rolling but the coverage is not useful in the usual way. This is indicated by a broken set-up line.

The actor playing Wesley was not consistent with his action. There are some notes on the right-hand side about when he has his glasses on and off.

Working Script Page vs. Final Script Page

I keep a lot of matching notes in my working script: things like action or dialog that changes before settling into a constant, drawings of clothing or makeup details, and matching back notes that I want to make sure I won't forget. This makes a very crowded page, good for me but too cluttered for the editor.

In order to have my cake and eat it too, I make a new cleaned up version of my lined script for the editors. That way I can make all the notations I want without driving the editors crazy. I think the benefit of having many matching notes is worth the extra work. It is the only form I clean up before handing in.

If you are lining a script using certain digital applications, you can set up your workflow to accommodate both private and public notes on the same document. At this writing, MovieSlate 8 has a function that will display and publish two ways, with and without private notes. If you are using Scription, you can keep your private notes on a dedicated layer. By the time you read this, there should be more choices available.

> I can make **all the notations I want** without driving the editors crazy.

Figs 6.36 through 6.40 are a handful of the pages from my set book on David Mamet's *Heist* and the corresponding pages from my final (clean) script that I turned in to the editors.

Set-Up Frames

I make a notation that is not standard in our craft but is extremely useful. I draw every set-up. These are very rough and sparse drawings that include whatever information I think is important and is better described in pictures than in words (see Figs 6.41 through 6.44).

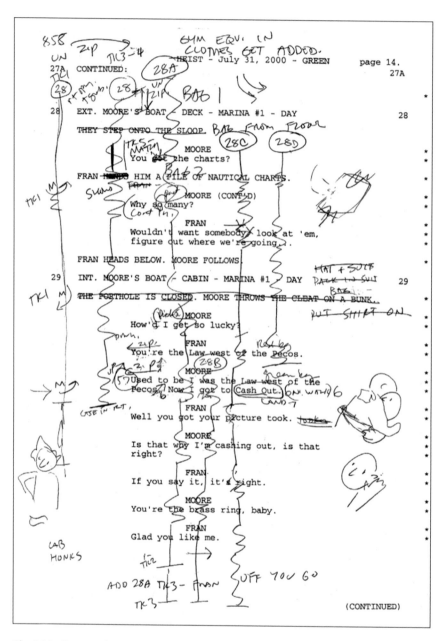

Fig. 6.36a Page 14, from my set book of *Heist*.

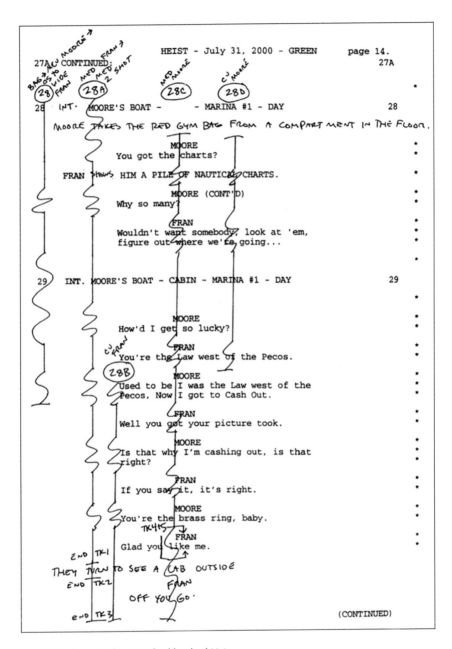

Fig. 6.36b Page 14, from my final book of *Heist*.

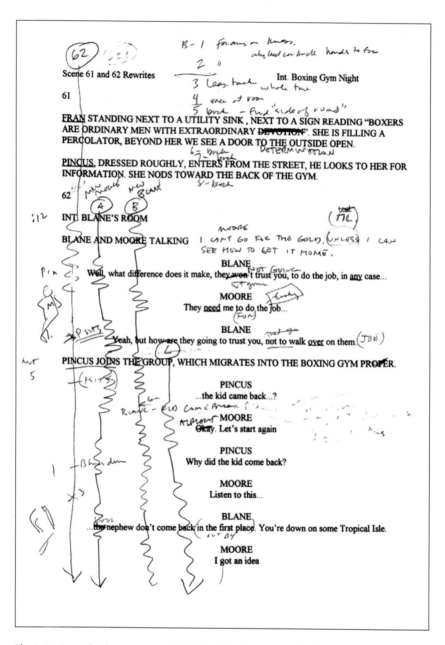

Fig. 6.37 Pages that became pages 54B, 55 and 56 from my set book of *Heist*. These are pages that were written on set, unformatted. They were later incorporated into the official draft.

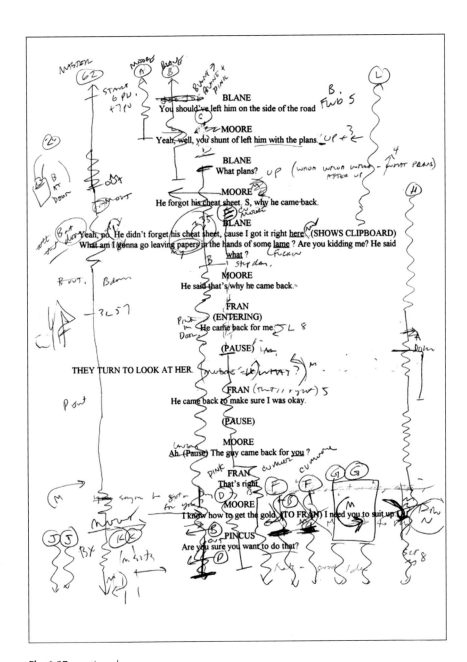

Fig. 6.37 *continued.*

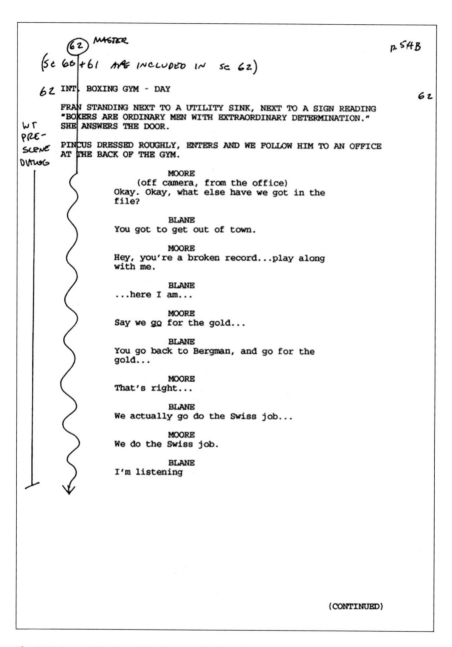

Fig. 6.38 Pages 54B, 55 and 56, from my final book of *Heist*.

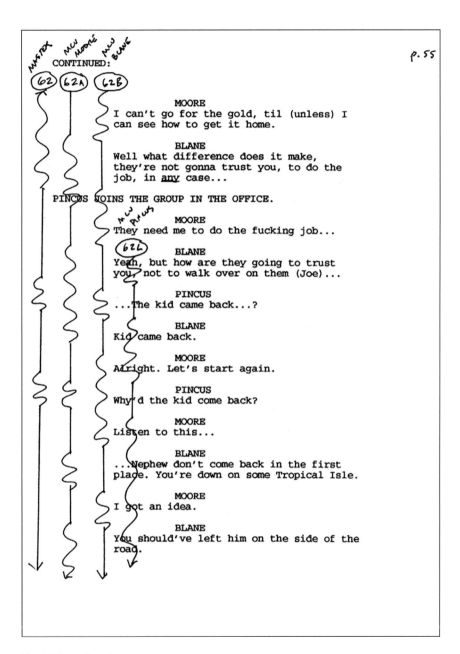

CONTINUED: p. 55

MASTER   MCU MOORE   MCU BLANE

62   62A   62B

                    MOORE
            I can't go for the gold, til (unless) I
            can see how to get it home.

                    BLANE
            Well what difference does it make,
            they're not gonna trust you, to do the
            job, in any case...

PINCUS JOINS THE GROUP IN THE OFFICE.

            MCU PINCUS
                    MOORE
            They need me to do the fucking job...

            62C   BLANE
            Yeah, but how are they going to trust
            you, not to walk over on them (Joe)...

                    PINCUS
            ...The kid came back...?

                    BLANE
            Kid came back.

                    MOORE
            Alright. Let's start again.

                    PINCUS
            Why'd the kid come back?

                    MOORE
            Listen to this...

                    BLANE
            ...Nephew don't come back in the first
            place. You're down on some Tropical Isle.

                    MOORE
            I got an idea.

                    BLANE
            You should've left him on the side of the
            road.

Fig. 6.38 *continued.*

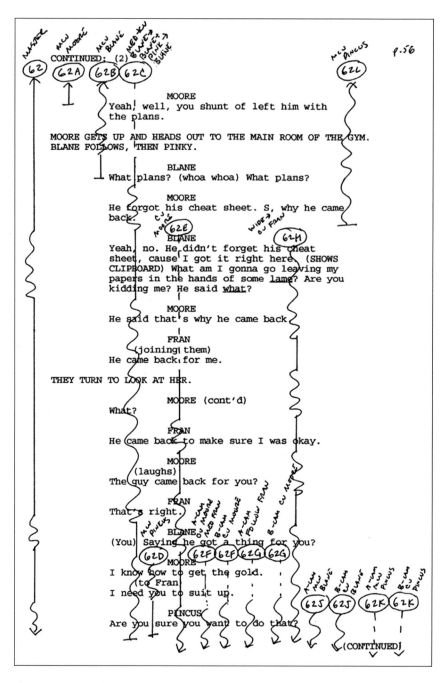

Fig. 6.38 *continued.*

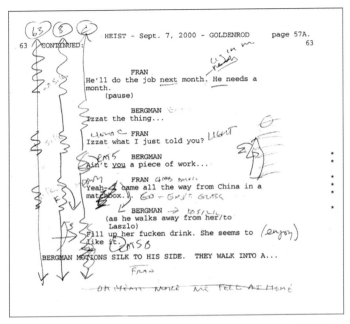

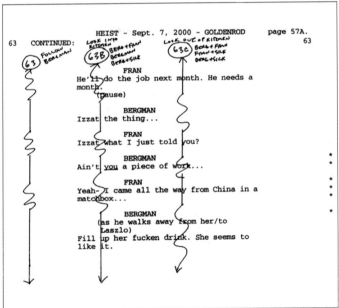

Fig. 6.39 Page 57A from my set book and final book for *Heist*.

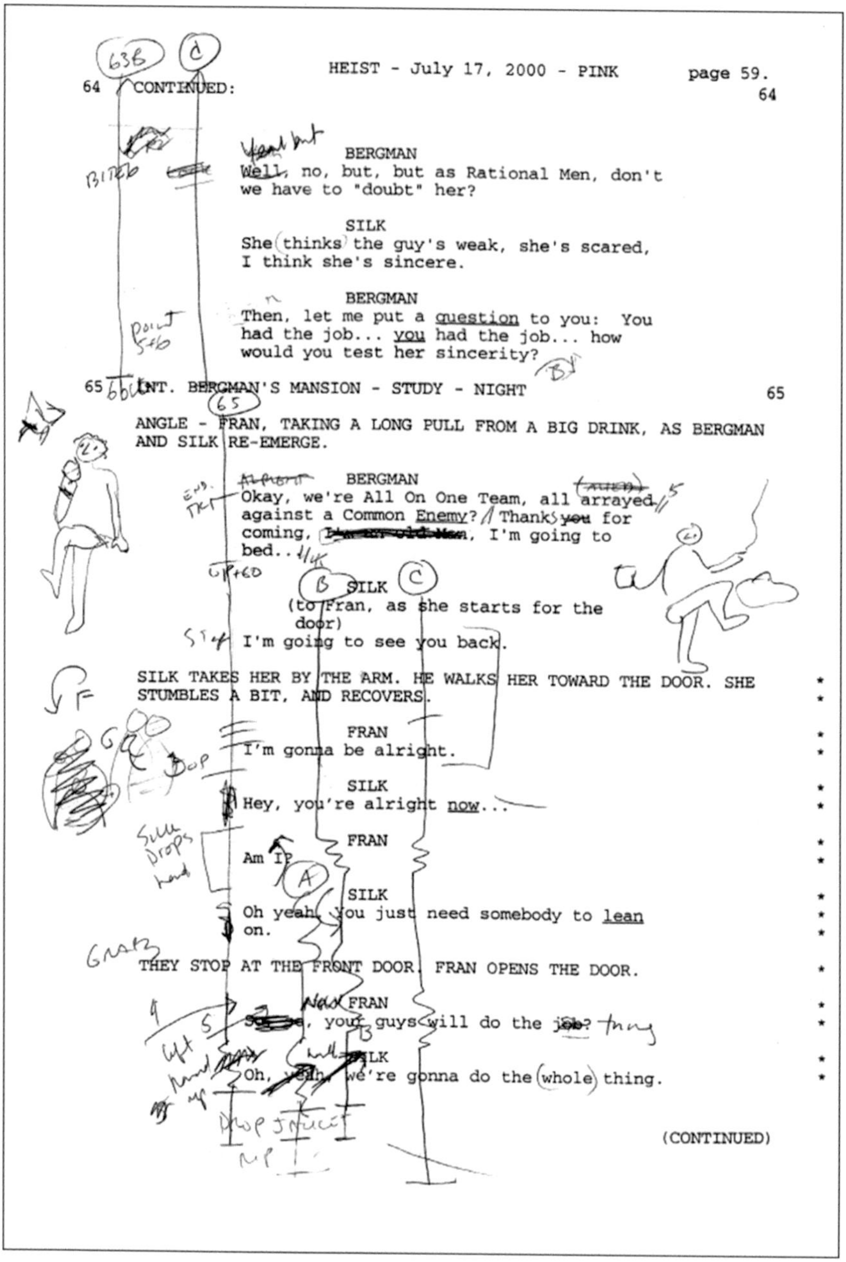

HEIST - July 17, 2000 - PINK   page 59.

64   CONTINUED: 64

          BERGMAN
Well, no, but, but as Rational Men, don't
we have to "doubt" her?

          SILK
She thinks the guy's weak, she's scared,
I think she's sincere.

          BERGMAN
Then, let me put a question to you: You
had the job... you had the job... how
would you test her sincerity?

65   INT. BERGMAN'S MANSION - STUDY - NIGHT   65

ANGLE - FRAN, TAKING A LONG PULL FROM A BIG DRINK, AS BERGMAN
AND SILK RE-EMERGE.

          BERGMAN
Okay, we're All On One Team, all arrayed
against a Common Enemy? Thanks you for
coming, I'm going to
bed..

          SILK
(to Fran, as she starts for the
door)
I'm going to see you back.

SILK TAKES HER BY THE ARM. HE WALKS HER TOWARD THE DOOR. SHE
STUMBLES A BIT, AND RECOVERS.

          FRAN
I'm gonna be alright.

          SILK
Hey, you're alright now...

          FRAN
Am I?

          SILK
Oh yeah, you just need somebody to lean
on.

THEY STOP AT THE FRONT DOOR. FRAN OPENS THE DOOR.

          FRAN
So, your guys will do the job?

          SILK
Oh, yeah, we're gonna do the whole thing.

                              (CONTINUED)

Fig. 6.40 Page 59 from my set book and final book for *Heist*.

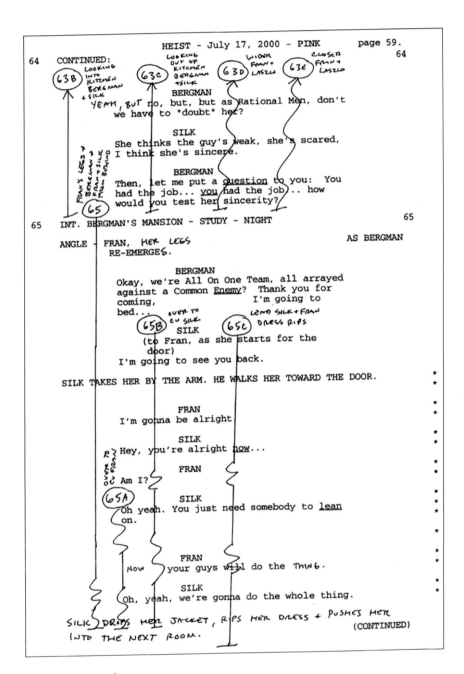

HEIST - July 17, 2000 - PINK   page 59.

64 CONTINUED: 64

63B (LOOKING INTO KITCHEN BERGMAN + SILK)
63C (LOOKING OUT OF KITCHEN BERGMAN + SILK)
63D (WIDOW FRAN + LASZLO)
63E (CLOSER FRAN + LASZLO)

BERGMAN
YEAH, BUT no, but, but as Rational Men, don't
we have to "doubt" her?

SILK
She thinks the guy's weak, she's scared,
I think she's sincere.

(FRAN'S LEGS → BERGMAN → FRAN + SILK FRAN BEHIND)

BERGMAN
Then, let me put a question to you: You
had the job... you had the job... how
would you test her sincerity?

65

65 INT. BERGMAN'S MANSION - STUDY - NIGHT   65

ANGLE - FRAN, HER LEGS   AS BERGMAN
        RE-EMERGES.

BERGMAN
Okay, we're All On One Team, all arrayed
against a Common Enemy? Thank you for
coming,   I'm going to
bed...

65B (OVER TO CU SILK)
65C (LEAD SILK + FRAN DRESS RIPS)

SILK
(to Fran, as she starts for the
door)
I'm going to see you back.

SILK TAKES HER BY THE ARM. HE WALKS HER TOWARD THE DOOR.   *
                                                            *

FRAN   *
I'm gonna be alright.   *

SILK   *
Hey, you're alright now...   *

(OVER TO OC FRAN)
FRAN   *
Am I?   *

65A
SILK   *
Oh yeah. You just need somebody to lean
on.   *

FRAN   *
NOW your guys will do the THING.   *

SILK   *
Oh, yeah, we're gonna do the whole thing.   *

SILK DROPS HER JACKET, RIPS HER DRESS + PUSHES HER   *
INTO THE NEXT ROOM.   (CONTINUED)

Fig. 6.40 *continued.*

Fig. 6.41a A page of set-up frames from my *The Ice Storm* set book. The circular arrows in the second row show the direction a character is turning.

Fig. 6.41b Another page of set-up frames from my *The Ice Storm* set book, a dinner table scene. The letters on the sides of the frames note which characters are on the left and right side off-camera.

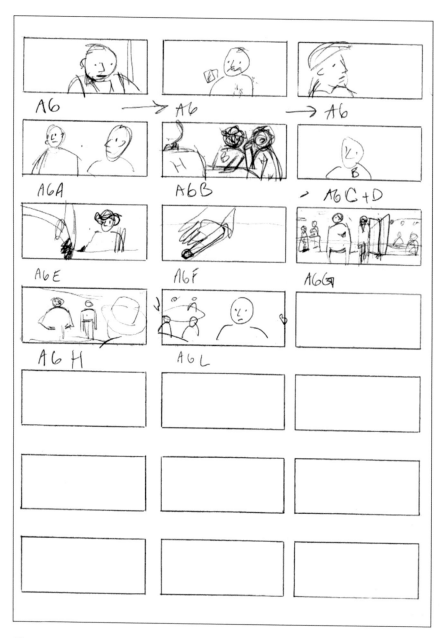

Fig. 6.42 Two pages of set-up frames from my *Lone Star* set book. The second page includes a lighting diagram. This was the only note like this I took on the project. Usually an electrician keeps the record of the lighting, but if a DP asks me to write anything down, I am happy to do it.

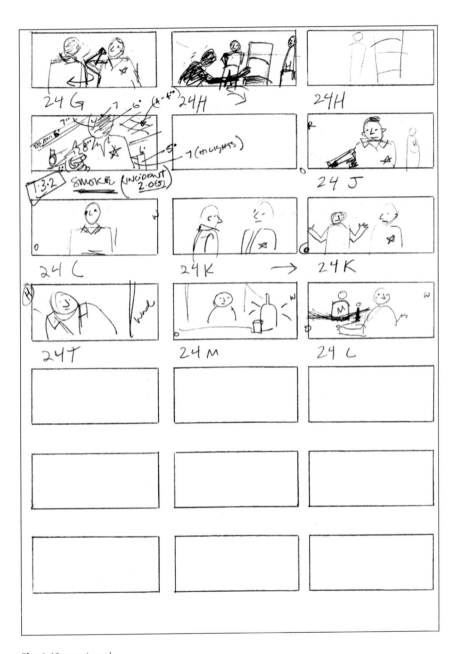

Fig. 6.42 *continued.*

Fig. 6.43 Two pages of set-up frames from my *In the Cut* set book.

Fig. 6.43 *continued.*

Fig. 6.44 Two pages of set-up frames from my *The Spanish Prisoner* set book. Notice the drawings for set-ups 62 and 62B have several drawings, showing the major compositions of long, changing set-ups. The small numbers next to the set-up numbers indicate the lines of dialog that correspond to each composition. Again, the letters on the edge of the frame show me where the off-camera characters are for each moment.

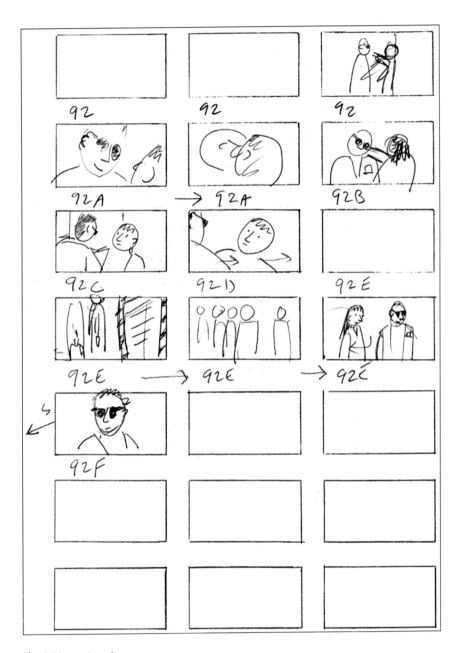

Fig. 6.44 *continued*.

This information may include how the main characters are positioned in the frame, which way they are looking (indicated by the direction their triangle nose is pointed), what is included in the background, which hand a prop is in, body position—especially elbows, knees, and hair. If our camera moves a lot,

> **Set-up frames** are most useful for information that is better described in pictures than in words.

I try to draw a frame at each of the major camera positions or at the camera positions that I think are most likely to be cut points.

If we are shooting in an unrehearsed documentary style, drawing frames is not usually possible; there are just too many other things to do. In cases like this, I will draw one or two very important moments, or a moment that I know I will have to match, after a take is complete.

I print storyboard boxes on the back of my working script for this purpose. If you are working in a digital PDF format, it is easy to make the same digital forms and slip them into your book wherever they are useful. Ask your first assistant camera person or the DP what aspect ratio they will be using, so that the height and width of the frame boxes will be correct.

SLATING

An essential part of organizing and cataloging the bits of media is naming each piece. It is the script supervisor's job to do this.

The American System

The most common system for naming set-ups is the American system, which is based on scene number. In this system, the name of the first set-up of each scene will be that scene number. Additional set-ups for that scene will start with that scene number followed by a letter (or two). The first set-up for scene *16*, for

> The **most common system** for naming set-ups is the American system.

instance, will be called set-up *16*. The second set-up for that scene will be called *16A*, the third *16B*, etc.

This system has the advantage of instant identification with the scene in which it belongs. It has the disadvantage of someone (the script supervisor) having to name the set-up in the heat of production and getting that information to other members of the crew. In particular, the second assistant cameraperson (2nd AC) and the sound mixer must have a correct set-up number for every take before we start shooting it.

Naming the take is straightforward for scenes that are shot at one time, in their entirety. The naming becomes more complicated when scenes are shot over many days, with action that is continued into other scenes, and for set-ups with cross-cutting or ad-libbed action that may be used in more than one scene. In these cases, the basic rule is to name the set-up for the scene in which that set-up begins. A variation of this rule is when cross-cutting.

SLATING FOR CROSS-CUTTING MULTIPLE SCENES

Sometimes a sequence of two (or more) scenes that cut back and forth, such as a telephone conversation, will come to you with a new scene number every time the script shows a cut between the characters. This looks fine on the page but when you get to set, chances are you will capture each side of the conversation as a continuous action. If you do, those progressing scene numbers (based on the writer's guess of a final cut) will be messy and meaningless.

Other times, a cross-cutting sequence will be written with one scene number for the first bit of dialog, lasting maybe 1/8 of a page, and a second scene number for the other side, lasting maybe three pages. This is not ideal either, as it misrepresents production time and progress.

In both cases, I give the sequence a scene number for each side of the conversation or action. All the set-ups on the first side of a phone call have one scene number (and the usual progression of set-up numbers for further coverage). All the set-ups on the other side have a second scene number. I will split the page and time count between them, in the ratio that I think best represents production time and progress. I note all this in the facing pages and daily report. Something like: "Slates for sc. 56 also cover sc. 58 and 60." And "Slates for sc. 57 also cover sc. 59 and 61." Of course, the lined script will show this as well.

An exception to this exception is cross-cutting a chase sequence where each cut back and forth is a new location or contains a specific stunt, VFX, or other element that should be recognized and tracked. In this case, each cut will be captured separately. You can name each bit as it is written.

We give each set-up one (and only one) scene's name, even when the set-up covers action that is carried into a following scene. You don't want a slate with a run-on of scene numbers. Call it by the first scene that it covers. Note the details of this on the facing page, lined script, and daily report.

> We give each set-up only **one scene's name.**

SKIPPED LETTERS

The American system does not use the letters I and O as they may easily be mistaken for the numbers *1* and *0* when written by hand or on a fuzzy copy. Set-up 16H is followed by 16J, and 16N is followed by 16P. Some script supervisors also skip the letters Q and S, because they may look like *0* and *5*. I do this if the slates are handwritten and the slating AC has sloppy handwriting.

> The American system does not use **the letters *I* and *O*.**

SLATING ADDED SCENES

As I said in Chapter 5, new scenes that are added to a locked script probably have numbers followed by one or two letters, such as "7A" or "7AA." This labeling works very well for preproduction and shooting scripts. Numbers followed by letters sort well on most data bank systems and are helpful for making breakdowns and schedules. This configuration will not work for slating on set. If we leave these scene numbers as they are, the first set-up of scene 7A will have the same name as the second set-up of scene 7 (as in: 7, 7A, 7B, etc.).

> It is important that each piece of media has a **distinct name.** Added scene 4A becomes scene A4 when it is shot.

Because it is important that each piece of media has a distinct name, when we slate added scenes, we move the added letter(s) to the front, before the number. The scene 7A in the script becomes "A7" on the slate. Scene 7AA in the script becomes scene "AA7" on the slate. This new scene number is now the scene's official name. It will be known as such from here on; on the slate, the "script as shot," the facing pages, the editors' daily log, the files in the edit room, everywhere.

When we shoot more than one set-up for these scenes, the convention is the same as it is for the plain numbered scenes. The sequences look like this: A7, A7A, A7B, A7C, etc. and AA7, AA7A, AA7B, AA7C, etc.

Naming Set-Ups for Added Scenes:	
Before shooting:	During and after shooting:
7A	A7, A7A, A7B, A7C
7AA	AA7, AA7A, AA7B, AA7C

SLATING TWO-CAMERA SET-UPS

When two cameras roll together and shoot the same action, they share the same set-up number, with an added distinction indicating which camera is shooting which angle. The slating for a two-camera set-up looks like this: "16E, A-Cam" and "16E, B-Cam." Labeling them together like this tells us that the

> When **two cameras roll together** and shoot the same action, they share the same set-up number.

two cameras have perfectly matched action and dialog, as they were shot at the same time.

See Fig. 6.2, a lined script, and Fig. 6.11, its opposite page, for *Michael Clayton* to see how a two-camera set-up is notated on these forms. A two-camera set-up is counted as two set-ups on the Daily Production Report.

Sometimes we shoot a two-camera set-up, get in a few takes, and then change only one of the camera positions. Is this a new set-up or not? The A-camera is dominant. If the A-camera changes, it is a new set-up and both cameras will be given a new set-up number. Note that the B-camera did not change. If the B-camera changes, keep the set-up number as it is for both cameras and note that the B-camera has changed its shot.

We use this awkward system because it is very helpful to identify two-camera set-ups. A pair of matching set-ups, with exactly the same action and dialog, is a beautiful thing.

SLATING SCENES WITH MANY SET-UPS

When we have a scene with so many set-ups that we work through the alphabet (all the way to 16Z) and still need more set-up names, we go to double letters starting with 16AA, next 16AB, 16AC, etc. to 16AZ. When we need more set-ups than that, we go through the alphabet again starting with B, as in 16BA, 16BB, 16BC, etc.

> After we work to the **end of the alphabet**, we use double letters.

SPECIAL SET-UP DISTINCTIONS

The American system has a few other conventions that will tell you something about the set-up at a glance. Here are the most important ones:

Reshoots

When we reshoot a set-up, we use the original slate number, for instance "16E," and put the letter R in front of the number. The slate "R16E" tells everyone instantly that there is another set-up exactly like this one, that this is the second try and is assumed to be the preferred version.

If we were to reshoot it again, at a different time, exactly the same (but better), we use "RR16E."

When the entire scene is rewritten or when a major element of the scene, such as the coverage or performance, has changed so much that the original footage cannot be used with the new, we treat the new material as if it were a new scene and give it a new scene number. If the original scene is 16, the new scene is "A16." We do this even if the scene is listed on the call sheet as "R16." This is, of course, assuming there is no previous scene with the name of "A16." If there is, we call the new scene "B16."

> When we **reshoot**, we put an R in front of the set-up number, as long as the new media will work with the other existing media.

There are times when a scene is completed but, for any number of reasons, a set-up is added at a later date. If a new set-up is designed to cut into the original material, it takes the next letter in the scene's coverage, no matter when it is shot. If the last slate for scene 16 was "16E," the next slate up is "16F," not "R16E." This is true even if the new set-up is shot months later, is called "R16" on the call sheet, and is designed to fix a problem.

Slating for Second Unit

When a set-up is shot without the director present, it is officially a second unit shot. We signify this by putting the letter X before the set-up number, as in "X16."

With an X before the scene number, the second unit starts from the beginning of the alphabet, "X16," "X16A," "X16B," etc., no matter what letter the main unit is on for that scene.

> When we shoot **without the director**, we put an X in front of the set-up number.

This system has a big advantage for second unit crews shooting at a distance from the main unit. The X makes all of their set-up numbers distinct from the main unit, ensuring that there are no repeated slate numbers due to miscommunication between the units. For instance, both units may use the letter E while shooting scene 16 because the main unit set-up will be called "16E" and the second unit set-up will be called "X16E."

Slating for Visual Effects

The visual effects team will want you to tag the set-ups from production that will be reworked in post-production. In this case I put a V at the front of the set-up number. This makes it easy for the lab or transfer house to pull the correct takes and keep them together. It also makes it easier for the visual effects producer to keep an up-to-date cost analysis. I do this even when the camera team has a "VFX" label on the slate. The slate is not always seen in post-production, but the set-up number is.

> **VFX shots** have a V in front of the set-up number.

To slate for visual effects, keep your set-up numbers progressing as they would for any other scene, and simply add a V to the shots that will be reworked. For instance, in a scene with six set-ups, when two of them are visual effects shots, the slates might look like this: 16, 16A, V16B, 16C, V16D, 16E.

The British System

Another common slating system is the British system. In this system the set-ups are numbered consecutively in shooting order. The first set-up of the production is called 1, no matter what scene it belongs to. The second set-up is 2, the third 3, etc. If the first day of production ends on set-up 25, the second day will start with set-up 26.

This system has the advantage of requiring less work on set. It is so simple that it is almost impossible to make a slating mistake.[14] It is, however, more cumbersome in the edit room, as the editors need to look at the notes to know what scene each set-up belongs to, if it is a reshoot, etc.

> In the British system, the set-ups are **numbered consecutively** in shooting order.

What we call the facing pages in the American system are called "script notes" or "continuity sheets" in the British system. They don't face their corresponding scene and set-up in the lined script. Instead, they are collected in a separate notebook, in shooting (not cutting) order.

I have never worked with an American post-production team that had a general preference for the British system of slating, though some British editors like the American approach. When you work with a mixed US/British post-production team, ask them which system they would like you to use. The editors have to work with the material for many months. It is only fair to give them notes they are comfortable with.

European Slates

In most of continental Europe, the set-up numbers are constructed from scene numbers, as they are in the American system, but instead of adding letters, they add a number. For example, what would be 22, 22A, 22B in the US system would be 22-1, 22-2, 22-3 in the European system.

An American/British Hybrid

I used a hybrid American/British system once on an American film. It was for Michel Gondry's feature film *Be Kind Rewind*, which was shot in a very unusual way.

Be Kind Rewind is a story about a group of friends who make movies using an old VHS video camera. The actors shot video on prop cameras during the filming of scripted scenes. That footage had no predetermined place in the story. It could have been used as a set-up in the original scene, as playback in another scene, or as part of a finished home movie in a stand-alone scene. Some set-ups were shot with 35mm film cameras only, some with just the VHS cameras, and some with both.

Even more confusing in the "how to organize the media" puzzle, we had storyboards for home movies that were not part of the script at all. Michel didn't know yet where they would play. They had no script pages, let alone scene numbers.

I thought that trying to impose scene numbers on a shoot like this would lead to all kinds of confusion, mistakes, and maybe misplaced media, so I recommended using consecutive set-up numbers like in the British system.

It worked really well. We needed a constant somewhere in the system. We didn't have continuity in scene numbers or camera rolls, but with consecutive set-up numbers we had a spine to hang the media on, a thread that started at 1, moved forward, and included all the media, however it was recorded or meant to be used. This was super helpful as we jumped between formats, hopped around the script, and especially when we shot outside the script. We did everything else using the American, East Coast system: facing pages, wild track numbers, etc.

> Our systems usually work well in their standard form but if you have a **special case** you can adapt them to solve your problem.

Limitations on Making Set-Up Names

You may be limited in what you are able to name your set-ups by the formatting demands of the software which the camera, editors, and sound mixer are using. Talk to the departments in preproduction to see what their restrictions are as far as how many digits can be used and if there are any restrictions in the use of numbers or letters.

Some script supervising platforms have a function that can send your notes to the edit room in a report that their particular software can read. This will cut down the assistant editor's work inputting your data into their system. If you are experienced and comfortable with using your digital system and want to offer this to your editors, talk to them in prep and set up a smooth workflow for this.

CAMERA AND SOUND ROLL NUMBERS

Multiple Cameras

When a production uses more than one camera, each camera will have a name. The principle camera will be the "A-Camera," the second will be the "B-Camera," etc. The A-Camera first assistant will name the camera bodies. The A-Camera

> The names of the **camera bodies** will come from the camera department.

second assistant will label them. The camera roll numbers will correspond to the name of each body. The A-Camera rolls will be A1, A2, A3, etc. The B-Camera rolls will be B1, B2, B3, etc.[15]

Second Unit

Camera rolls (cards and drives) shot in second unit are named with an "X" in front of their letter. This is true even when the second unit takes a camera body from the first unit. An "A" camera roll from the second unit will look like XA1, XA2, XA3, etc. Camera rolls shot in the second unit, using the C camera from the main unit, will be called XC1, XC2, XC3, etc. Check with the second AC to find out how they have named the second unit camera bodies. The second unit camera assistants will find out from you what roll they should be on.

Test Rolls

We often shoot test footage in preproduction. These tests may be for hair, makeup, wardrobe, set dressing, visual technique, sync, or lenses. Whatever the tests are for, the camera and sound rolls (cards or drives) are usually marked with a T: TA1, TA2, TA3, etc. We start with camera roll A1 the first time we shoot footage that is to be used in the film. This may be on Day 1 of the production schedule or in preproduction.

SETTING UP YOUR BOOK

Each script supervisor sets up their book to their own liking. Whatever form you prefer, it is a good idea to keep a backup file of current and past projects. This might be photocopies, a file on a home desktop, an external hard drive, or any other dependable backup system you like to use.

A Paper-Based Notebook

Some script supervisors, myself included, like to carry an entire working script with them all the time. I put the forms and breakdowns that I use most often in front of my script. These include the day's call sheet, the day's script supervisor's production report, the editors' daily log, the master breakdown, and whatever time breakdown is most important to this particular production. If I am working with storyboards, I will put the day's boards there too. Behind my script, I put my page/time/scene tally, a one liner, a crew list, blank forms, and any reference material (photographs, lined and facing pages from previous shoot days, etc.) that I may need for that day. I use page dividers between sections and tag the day's work with big paper clips so I never have to riffle through the script looking for one of the day's scenes.

Other script supervisors like to keep a lighter book. They pull just the script pages and references that they think they will need for the day's work. Some like a three-ring binder because it is easy to add, subtract, and move pages around the book. Others like a spring-back binder as it is less likely to tear the holes in the page. Everyone working on paper has a ruler on a string, so it doesn't get lost.

Any book that you are comfortable with is fine. The idea is to keep the most current information very handy and have the background reference close. I almost never put my script down. I take it with me when I get coffee and walk to the bathroom. I keep a catalog case at the foot of my chair that holds my final script, secondary reference material, and backup office supplies.

> Keep the most current information **handy** and the background reference **close**.

A Digital Notebook

A digital notebook is a bit more complicated to set up but once it is done, you will have everything you need at the ready in a lightweight, compact, and portable package.

The organization of your digital notebook will vary depending on your devices and applications, as well as the overall design of your workflow. When using a laptop, you can organize folders by whatever criteria you choose: project, shooting day, or scene. All of your applications will be able to draw from the primary folders. Tablets organize their files by application. To work on a script in Scriptation, MovieSlate 8, ScriptE, etc., you must download that script from an email directly into the specific application.

Some people like to work with all their notes in one platform. A unified system streamlines the coordination of the notes. Others like to spread the data and functions across a few different applications and tailor a system more exactly to the ways they like to work. Whatever workflow you design for yourself, make sure it is technically dependable, that you can access and work on your notes quickly, and that the notes can be backed up regularly.

NOTES

1 More about this in Chapter 9, "A Day on Set."

2 A set-up is all the media that is recorded of the same action, shot from the same camera position and lens size. Don't confuse this with a take, which refers to each time you roll on that set-up.

3 Different types of projects have different ways to ID a set-up. There are a few different slating systems, as well. See pages 194–201 in this chapter.

4 Thank you to the veteran script supervisor, Mary Kelly, for her historic knowledge and confirmation of my own shadowy memory.

5 Facing pages are standard for the American system of keeping notes. The British system is a little different and is described later in this chapter (see pp. 199)

6 This report is also known as the Progress Report, or Daily Progress Report.

7 More about calling grace in Chapter 9, "A Day on Set."

8 The second AD called us when we were still asleep saying that the call time had changed and we needed to get up now. He was startled and sleepy and got the math wrong. The call time was fine, his phone was wrong. After some mass confusion, we had a long breakfast at the hotel—on the clock.

9 If the additional unit is sizable, they will have their own script supervisor and a separate Script Supervisor's Daily Report. If the additional unit is a small breakaway crew grabbing a shot or two, the crew usually returns to finish the day with the main unit, and their work can be folded into the main report. If the additional crew's work is minimal but they camera wrap early, you can just add a note to the report saying that.

10 "Room tone" is the background sound of a room or exterior environment. More on this in Chapter 9, "A Day on Set."

11 The recording of room tone is always a weird moment on set, both frustrating and reflective as the company that had just been racing hard against the clock is forced to stop, standing hard against its own momentum. My favorite representation of this is in the wonderful movie *Living in Oblivion*.

12 Background chatter is called "walla."

13 A "tail ID" is an identifying slate that is recorded at the end of the shot, instead of at the beginning of the shot, as is usual. The slate is held upside down to make it clear to the editors that the slate is referring to the media that comes before, not after.

14 The British system can be a good choice for loosely scripted, run-and-gun documentary style productions.

15 On multi-camera sitcoms and live/live-to-tape shoots, the three cameras will be numbered by their position on the floor. They are named left to right: A, B, and C. If there is a fourth camera, it is often called "X," as it is an extra camera for inserts and special angles.

Chapter 7
Production Overview
Maintaining Continuity

WHY WE NEED CONTINUITY

A movie builds a world and invites us in. The more convincing that world is, the easier it is to engage. Good continuity supports the illusion of natural action unfolding as we watch the story. Bad continuity reminds us that what we are watching is constructed, not real. It takes us out of the story and destroys the easy flow of our pretend world. Good continuity is not perfect continuity. It is good enough to keep us believing and engaged in the story.

> Good continuity is **not perfect continuity**.

True Love, the first movie I worked as a script supervisor, taught me a lot about continuity. The most important lesson I learned was to be careful that continuity does not get in the way of performance (and whatever else will make the movie worth watching). *True Love*'s continuity is all over the place, and mostly, it is fine.

But sometimes it is not fine at all.

For instance, we had a two-person scene, a father and daughter sitting across a table in an intense and aggressive conversation. We shot it as two over-the-shoulder medium close-ups. The man playing the father was, in real life, a teacher of the woman playing his daughter. This brought a powerful, natural, and appropriate dynamic to the scene. When we shot the dad's coverage, he physically leaned in and let his daughter have it. She reacted naturally to the force of his performance and leaned back, away from him. Next, we turned around to shoot coverage on the daughter. After a break for lighting, the actors came back and played the scene again. We were all glad to see that when it counted, in the daughter's coverage, she stood up to him and let *him* have it. She physically leaned in and met the force of his on-camera performance with a mighty force of her own. Her dad reacted naturally to the new reality and dialed back his aggression.

While we were shooting, everything felt good and right on the mark. After the two set-ups were cut together, it became obvious that the scene was unusable. It was a long scene with lots of emotional volleys, calling for

DOI: 10.4324/9780367823665-7

many cuts. At every cut the actors ping-ponged back and forth, leaning in and leaning out, depending on the coverage.

True Love was the first feature film for everyone on set that day. I couldn't cut a scene in my head yet—and didn't even know that I should. If we had been more skillful, we would have recognized the problem, made an adjustment in the moment, and all would have been fine. As it was, there wasn't the budget for a reshoot and the scene is not in the movie.

You can see how something that feels good on set can be a big problem in the edit room, often when it is too late to fix. A skillful script supervisor will save time and money by understanding when continuity matters and how to adjust the action in order to protect the scene. This is another example of why our most important work is as filmmakers, not secretaries.

Another lesson I learned on that shoot was to use the superpower of matching back. We added a scene mid-production, and because I didn't look at my master breakdown and match back, we shot a minor character in two places at the same (story) time. Another scene that was not usable!

TWO KINDS OF CONTINUITY

There are two kinds of continuity: matched action and progressive continuity.

Matched Action

We match action within a scene.[1] A finished scene in a narrative movie is usually cut together from a number of different set-ups. We shoot some action, stop, move the camera, adjust the light, and shoot the same action again from a new angle. We sometimes shoot dozens of set-ups for a single scene.

This repeated action has to match from take to take and set-up to set-up. Of course every take will be a little different, but they need to match closely enough that, when the set-ups are cut together, all the action looks like the same moment seen from different angles.

Progressive Continuity

A narrative story also needs continuity between scenes. This sort of continuity is usually more concerned with maintaining a narrative flow than matching action.

Take, as an example, a sequence that includes a fistfight. As we plan the action that comes after the fight, we need to think about the following sorts of things: how long will the characters be out of breath? When will they change out of their ripped clothes? How will their injuries change over time? This is progressive continuity. It is a combination of matching and logic.[2]

Your preproduction work, breaking down the script to find production elements and forming a timeline, is essential for finding the logic of this flow. Logical thinking is especially important when scenes are shot out of story order.

WHAT TO MATCH

Checklists for Matching

When we talk about matching action, we are really talking about matching many details within that action. Here is a list that may help you remember what to look for. The list is long and intimidating. Take a deep breath before reading it and meet me on the other side for some ideas of how to deal with it all.

DIALOG

Matched Action	Progressive Continuity
• Match the right words, in the right order. • Match the right sequence in exchanges between characters. • Captured dialog may or may not deviate from the script. • The director will decide how much the dialog will be allowed to change. • The script supervisor will track it.	• Are there any inconsistencies in the logic within the dialog from scene to scene? • Are there any inconsistencies between dialog and the action from scene to scene? • If an actor is using a non-native dialect or accent, make a plan to develop and maintain the dialect. • If you are working with a dialect coach, make a plan for incorporating their notes with yours.

MOTION

Editors like to cut on motion because it makes the edit less noticeable. To find likely cut points, imagine the finished scene playing. When you feel that a change between camera angles may be useful, look for a bit of motion in the frame. If a character stands up, sits down, stops, starts, turns, or makes a grand gesture, that moment is a likely cut point. The matching should be solid at that point.

MOTION AND DIALOG

Matched Action	Progressive Continuity
• Match the characters' dialog to the same place in their movement and body position.	• If dialog continues from one scene into the next, match the point of transition between scenes to the exact words in the dialog.

MOTION AND BLOCKING

Matched Action	Progressive Continuity
• Match the characters' movements to the **same physical place**: where do they stop, turn around, break into a run? • **If on a staircase**, note the step. If on a long walk and talk, note the closest background elements, a door, gate, or fence. • **Match the major traits** of the characters' movements: clockwise or counter-clockwise turn? A step taken with the right or left foot? What is the speed and attitude of a character walking or running? • **Sitting down and getting up**: on what word? Leaning forward or straight torso? Hands on arm of chair?	• Remember the pace and attitude of a character's movement if that movement will be continued from scene to scene. For instance, in a chase scene, a traveling montage, or a character moving through a doorway or gate: which foot leads through the doorway? Which hand on gate? • If a group is traveling: what is their order and spacing? Do they change positions in regard to one another or walk locked together?

BODY POSITION

Pay attention to and match the characters' posture, especially in over-the-shoulder and group shots. Many actors change their energy levels when it is time for their close-up, which may affect their physicality.

Matched Action	Progressive Continuity
• **General posture**: very erect? Slouched? To what side and how much?	• Note everything in the matched action column for direct cuts, such as walking from room to room.
• Loose limbs or uptight? Aggressive or reticent?	• Which foot forward going through the door? Pace and body lean? Which hand on the doorknob?
• Anything peculiar? Tight shoulders? A limp? Lots of hand gestures?	• Is there any emotional influence that will affect the character's body language? Happiness or sadness?
• Hands on hips? Weight on one foot? Which one, when shifted?	• Any recent physical exertion that will affect body language?
• Arms crossed: right over left? Hands holding elbows or tucked in?	
• Hand in which pocket and when? Does this affect the drape of the wardrobe?	
• **Hugging and holding**: arms on shoulder or waist? Hands clasped? Whose arms are over and under? Heads cross on right or left? When does it start and stop?	
• **Holding babies and kids**: which hip or shoulder? How are the grown-up's arms and hands? How are the kid's posture and limbs? The kid's clothes or blanket?	
• **Fights**: most fight sequences will be choreographed, which makes things easier. If not, match as in any other sequence. There may be wild variations. Think about where the cut points will be and concentrate on matching those points.	
• Photograph how the bodies fall in every take. Detail any surprises or variations.	

TONE AND PACE

Matched Action	Progressive Continuity
• A set-up that takes a character from sleepy to agitated has to start out sleepy on each take.	• Does the tone and pace of this scene fit in with what has been going on with the character physically and emotionally in related scenes?

EMOTIONAL PERFORMANCE

Track the arc of a character's performance.

Matched Action	Progressive Continuity
• If a character breaks into sobs at the end of one take and at the beginning of the next, it will be difficult to intercut those takes.	• Think about how much time has elapsed after an emotional scene. If a character has had a strong emotion recently, it may be correct to have a trace of the feeling in the current performance, especially at the beginning of the scene.

MAKEUP AND HAIR

Matched Action	Progressive Continuity
• What is the **overall impression**? Fresh or worn? Ruddy? Crisp or soft? • **Any particularities**? Smeared lipstick? A cowlick in the hair? • **Injuries**? Where (right or left!) and in what stage of healing? • How long is **the hair**? • On what side is the hair parted? • Does it fall in front of or behind the shoulders? • In front of or behind the ears? • If this changes in the scene, when?	• Depending on how much time has elapsed, some or all of the inter-scene matching will apply. • Know when each character **changes the look** of their makeup and hair. • If the character has injuries, **track the healing** progress against your timeline. Work with the makeup department to design a plan. • Has the character been in any **situation that would alter** the makeup and hair: rain, dust, wind, hot weather, a fight?

Matched Action	Progressive Continuity
• How short is the beard? • How thick are the braids? • If there is a **headband or scarf**, how high on the forehead does it sit? • Any barrettes or ribbons? Where?	• If the character's look is going to be hard to maintain without interfering with performance or production schedule, **talk first** to the on-set person from that department and then mention it to the director and/or showrunner, so everyone knows what they are getting into.

COSTUME

Matched Action	Progressive Continuity
• What part of the **shirttail** is out? • Which **buttons** are buttoned? • How are the **sleeves** rolled up? • How is a **scarf** or tie tied? • Any **jewelry**? • Any **purse or bag**? • On which shoulder? • Buckle forward or back? • Flap in or away from body? • **Hats**: how high or low on brow? Tilted or straight? To which side? • Is there **anything unusual**? A belt loop missed? A hem showing? • Any **stains, wrinkles or rips**?	• Know when each character changes their wardrobe. • Has the character been in any **situation that would alter** the wardrobe: rain, dust, wind, hot weather, a fight? • Has there been enough time between scenes that placement of **wardrobe might normally change**? If so, this will buy you some freedom from matching.

PROPS

Matched Action	Progressive Continuity
• Any **jewelry**? Earrings? Pins? Tie tacks? Where and how are they presented? • **Necklaces**: clasps back or showing? • **Watches**: Which wrist? Face in or out? • **What time is it** in the scene? • Check that hand props are placed in the scene so **they can be available** to the characters when needed. • How will the props function in the scene? **Set them up** to be able to do what they must.	• Do the props **age, get soiled, bent, or broken** over time? • When a prop is mentioned in one scene, **match back** to see what other scenes should include it.

HANDLING PROPS

Matched Action	Progressive Continuity
• **Which hand**? • What is the position of the prop in that hand? • What is the position of the prop when it is picked up, put down, or handed to another character? • When handed off, which hand to which hand? • If a prop is **handed from on-camera to off-camera**, does it leave via camera right or left, top or bottom of the frame? • For a **book or magazine**, note the open page and how the fingers rest on which edges.	• For **matched cuts**, as in walking from one room to the next: be as exact as matching within a scene. • When and **how did we last see this prop?** • What has happened to the prop during the preceding scenes? Between scenes? • What does the prop have to do in future scenes? Where and how does it need to be, at the end of this scene, to **set it up correctly**?

Matched Action	Progressive Continuity
• Holding **folders and envelopes**: address up or down? Open edge towards or away from body? • **At table**: how is the plate placed? When and what is eaten? Right or left handed? • **On the telephone**: which hand? Which ear? How is the hand on the phone?	

SET DRESSING

Matched Action	Progressive Continuity
• Times on **clocks**? • Dates on **calendars or documents**? • **Doors** open? Which way? In or out? Hinges on left or right? How far open and when? • What do we see on the other side? • Is an **address or apartment number** visible? Is it correct? • **Windows** open? How much and when? • **Window dressing**: shades up, down, partway? Curtain position. • Is anything **around the window** affected by wind or other weather? • **Light fixtures**: Lit? Position of shades and cords.	• What action happened in this scene or **previous scenes** that changed the set dressing? Evidence of a fight? A meal? • Does the character have an **emotional arc** that will affect their surroundings? • What are the character's **habits**? Do they always lock the door? Leave projects half done? • What **scenes in the future** require specific set dressing? • When will that dressing be set?

TIMES OF DAY AND DATE

Matched Action	Progressive Continuity
• Are there indications in the dialog or action of the script that indicate time of day or date? • Are there props or set dressing (clocks, calendars, letters, or newspapers) that need to have a time of day or date on them?	• Is there any **logical reason** in your preproduction breakdowns that places a scene in a particular time of day or date? • Is that flexible?

CARS AND OTHER VEHICLES

Matched Action	Progressive Continuity
• **Windows**: up or down? How much and when were they adjusted? • **Mirrors**: angle and tilt? What do you see reflected in them? • **Lights**: on or off? High or low beam? Any broken? • **Decorations** and **trash**: what's on the dashboard? Hanging from the mirror? Visible on the seats? • **Windshield**: any decals? Smears? Cracks? Do dusty and clean glass define the wiper area?	• How dirty or clean: think about **where the vehicle has been**. • Is there **any reason** for the windows and lights to be set in a particular way? If so, anticipate and set them the same for the scenes in continuity. • Is there dialog that will be covered from the car interior? Is it better for **sound** to have the windows up? Check with the director before the windows are established. • Is there coverage that will see a bad **reflection** in a window? For instance, a close drive-by that will see the camera and crew reflected as the car passes the camera position. Check with the DP or camera operator before the window position is established. Rolling the window down may solve that problem.

SCREEN DIRECTION

Matched Action	Progressive Continuity
• Note which direction (camera left to right, or camera right to left) a character is **looking** toward other characters or objects in the scene. • In which direction do the characters **exit and enter** a shot, reach, or throw? • Screen direction is important for matching between set-ups and is discussed in detail in Chapter 8.	• Note which direction (camera left to right, or camera right to left) a character **enters and exits** a room. • Which direction is a character **traveling**? • Screen direction is important for matching between scenes and is discussed in detail in Chapter 8.

BACKGROUND ACTORS

Officially, the ADs are responsible for matching background actors. We can help them by noticing any individuals that stand out, where they are, and when they move.

We can photograph crowd scenes from an angle that shows the position of key background players. These pictures will help the ADs reconstruct the crowd if necessary. Photos of a crowd are really useful in classroom and theater audience situations, where there will be lots of intercutting and people are expected to stay in the same place.

Matched Action	Progressive Continuity
• What is the general **feel** of the crowd? • Thick or sparse? • **Moving** fast or slowly? • Animated or subdued?	• Does the **general character** of the crowd fit the flow of the story? • The **time of day**? • The **character of the place**?

Nobody Is Perfect

This list can make you crazy. How can you see all that, let alone help actors match everything they do? You can't. It is physically impossible to have absolute continuity.

Actors are not robots or puppets, and we don't want them to be. Actors need to match well enough for the media to cut together and maintain the illusion of the story. We script supervisors try to help them do that without getting in the way of their performance. That means knowing when the action should match, giving matching notes when it counts, and leaving everyone alone when it doesn't.

> **The most important skill for matching** is knowing what matters and what doesn't matter.

"Continuity Is for Sissies"

I hate when people say that.

I used to hear that phrase on set. People who said it were usually inexperienced and not able to cut in their head. They didn't know when continuity mattered and so, afraid to talk about it, they aggressively batted away the whole concept.[3] As I worked with more skillful filmmakers, I heard it less and less, and finally, not at all.

As you start out, you will probably come in contact with some of these frightened cowboys. Usually they have more authority than you have. What can you do? If you really know that a mismatch will be a problem in post, try to walk your fellow filmmakers through the problem in a way that will help them visualize it. If you are not sure that it will matter, don't pretend you are. Once your credibility is shot, it is hard to get it back.

If you have made a good case, and the director doesn't want to listen, make a note in the facing pages, x-out the affected sections of the set-up lines on the lined script, and let it go. It is their movie. They get to do what they want. Months later, in the edit room, they will be in a jam and read the note. Be nice about it. You will make mistakes too.

THINKING LIKE AN EDITOR

Pay Attention to the Cut Points

The first concept to understand about when to match is that continuity only matters at a cut point. If there is no cut, there is no need to match. The action is continuous by definition. How can you tell where the cut points will be? Sometimes it is clear. Sometimes it isn't.

Thinking like an editor will help you identify likely cut points. Here is an introduction to get you started. You will get better at recognizing cut points with experience.

> **Continuity only matters at a cut point.**

Different Styles of Coverage

MASTER AND COVERAGE

The classic American way to cover a scene in a dramatic narrative story is to shoot a master shot and coverage.[4]

A master shot is a set-up that includes all or most of the action of the scene. It is usually pretty wide and serves as an overview of the scene, letting the audience see the physical dynamics of the situation including location, blocking of characters, atmosphere, and geographic context. Coverage in this case is the group of other set-ups that present the details of the scene's action. These may be medium or close-up shots of characters, point of view shots, insert shots, etc. Traditionally, we shoot these shots one after another, with one camera, re-staging the action for each set-up. This style of shooting can be done with more than one camera. The more cameras in a set-up, the more difficult it is to design lighting and sound recording that is specifically tailored to each angle.

The "master and coverage style" is very demanding for matching, as there are many possible cut points throughout the action. The most apparent action should match at all likely cut points.

MASTER TO MASTER

Another way to cover a scene is "master to master." This is more common in European and American independent movies. In this technique, one set-up follows the action until it is no longer useful. Then, another set-up is made to take the action forward. There is a bit of overlap in the action between these set-ups to allow for a range of cutting points between shots. The action must match at these overlapped cutting points.

In this style of coverage, it is not necessary to match every little action *between* overlapped sections. As long as each take starts and ends the same (these are the cut points) the actors can be relatively free in their matching for the rest of the take. This freedom makes master to master a useful strategy for working with non-professional or less technically experienced actors.

MASTER ONLY

There will be a few scenes in almost every movie that are covered entirely by one shot. These master-only scenes have no additional coverage. One set-up covers all the action in that scene.

In master-only scenes, it is not necessary to match the action within the scene. If a director and actor want to change dialog, action, emotional performance, etc., from take to take, it is not a continuity problem.

Each take must start and end in a way that will maintain continuity with the scenes before and after. But within the scene, master only coverage gives you a lot of freedom to experiment.

MULTI-CAMERA AND LIVE/LIVE-TO-TAPE

In a multi-camera, live/live-to-tape shoot, three cameras run at the same time. Matching is less critical, as there are always three angles of the same exact action. The action often stops, backs up, and starts again without cutting the cameras. These new starts are a sort of cut point. Action should match here if you want to cut the new start into the established media.

Multi-camera, live/live-to-tape coverage is possible by using a more generalized lighting plan and placing all the cameras on one side of the action. These conventions make it possible to run all those cameras together and gives the live/live-to-tape shoot the classic look of a sitcom or talk show.

MATCHED ACTION BETWEEN SCENES

When one scene cuts to another with little or no time between, the action must match.[5] A character that goes into a doorway must come out the other side with the same part in their hair, their bag on the same shoulder, walking at the same pace and posture, with the same hand on the doorknob. This can be tricky when one side of the door is in a studio in New York City and the other is on location in Rome.

How to Find the Cut Points

Most movies use a combination of all these coverage styles. Let's look at a scene that uses a combination of coverage styles and identify some probable cut points.

Here's a scene with four set-ups:

1. Exterior. Introduction. Crane into a window showing two people in a kitchen, cooking, talking, and moving around the room. This shot holds for the first two lines of dialog.
2. Interior. A medium two-shot of the same two people cooking. This action lasts for the first page of dialog. Then the characters sit at a table and continue talking for another page.
3. Interior. Medium close-up, first person at table.
4. Interior. Medium close-up, second person at table.

When we think about the possible ways these shots can be cut together, we can discover some important things about when we have to match carefully and when we don't. For instance:

5. The actors need to pay very close attention to their matching during the first two lines of dialog. There must be a cut point here, going from the exterior two-shot to the interior two-shot. Because both actors are seen on both sides of the cut, they both have to have good continuity for the cut to work.
6. We have almost a page of dialog where the two actors move around the kitchen cooking and talking in a master-only segment within the scene. This is a great opportunity not to match. Don't bug the actors about saying a line at the exact same position or picking up a certain prop on the exact same line. They should follow the basic moves as established, handling the props so they end up in the same place when the master-only part of the scene is over and there is, again, a cut point. They also should sit at the table on the same line of dialog in the two-shot and at least one close-up. The physical act of sitting will change the dynamic between the characters, which will often be reflected in a change of camera angle and therefore a cut.
7. The actors will have to maintain decent continuity while they are sitting. This section is shot as master and coverage: a two-shot and two singles. The action in the close-ups should match the two-shot pretty well, especially at any point when the drama gets more intense. These rises in drama are good points to cut from the two-shot to a single or from one single to the other.
8. If the singles at the table are over-the-shoulder shots, the off-camera character must match in posture and any action that can be seen from over their shoulder. If the singles are clean, this is not so critical.

In a scene with more complicated coverage, there will be more possible cut points, and thus more points within the scene where maintaining continuity is important.

If there is a moment within a set-up that is out of continuity, the shot may still be useful. If the set-up's action goes back into continuity before the next cut point, there is no problem. I will say it again because it is so important: continuity only matters at the cut point.

> **Continuity only matters at the cut point.**

Easy and Difficult Matches

WHAT MAKES A DIFFICULT MATCH?

The more shared action on both sides of the cut, the more details have to match, and the more fussy the match will be.

For instance, when a wide four-shot cuts to a medium four-shot of the same action, all four actors need to match. When that wide four-shot cuts to a close single of one character in the same action, only that one character has to match. Think about what you see on both sides of a cut. That is what has to match to make the cut work. A cut that works is a cut that maintains the illusion that this is the same action seen from different angles.

PROTECTING A DIFFICULT MATCH: EXAMPLE 1

This understanding becomes very useful when a movie's shooting style is scrappy, like a documentary, or a comedy that is full of ad-libs. Shooting some set-ups with isolated action can get the editor out of a jam and allow a more free style of shooting on set. A clean single of the lead or secondary character is often ideal. Sometimes, even just a reaction shot can save the day. To be useful, the shot must be something that the director wants to actually have in their movie.

We did this a lot when shooting Michel Gondry's *Be Kind Rewind*, a movie about a frenetic group of friends. We shot it in a madcap style: two cameras that could look anywhere at any time, mostly wide, group shots, with wild ad-libs. When I felt we were shooting ourselves into an uncuttable situation, I recommended that we grab some isolated action so the editor had someplace to go without shared action on both sides of the cut.

PROTECTING A DIFFICULT MATCH: EXAMPLE 2

We had a similar tricky matching situation in the robbery scene of David Mamet's *Heist*. This long scene also had frenetic action, captured mostly in

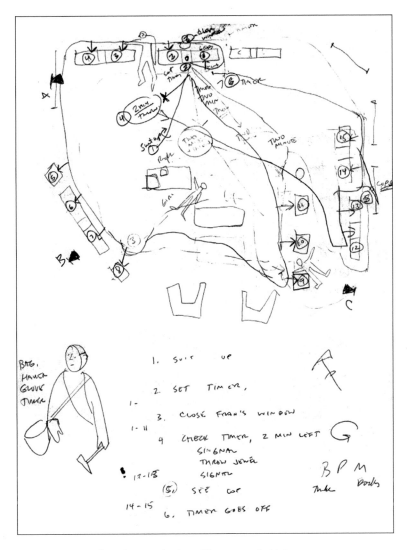

Fig. 7.1a A rough floor diagram for the robbery scene in *Heist*.

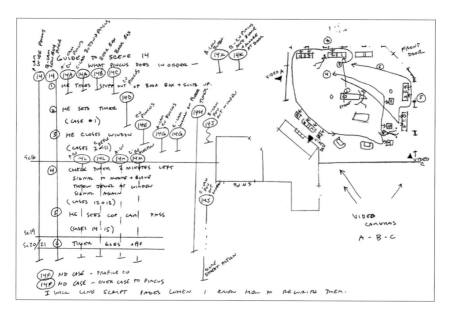

Fig. 7.1b A polished floor diagram for the robbery scene in Heist.

wide, group shots. The difference here was that this scene was built from very specific actions captured from specific angles. In addition to the core scene coverage, we had three surveillance cameras that saw pretty much the whole room all the time. Any time these cameras were used, there was matched action on both sides of the cut.

To make sure the room stayed in continuity, we made a floor plan. We mapped out the choreographed action of the most active character. This was Pincus, played by Ricky Jay. Once Ricky's action was settled, we could hang the action of the other characters from that spine.

Here is my rough map of Ricky's action, which I made as we were working it out (Fig. 7.1a), and the cleaned-up version I distributed to the cast and crew and included in my final lined script (Fig. 7.1b).

When I have action that is this complicated and this specific, I usually rework the script to describe the character's physical action step by step. This helps me on set to match the coverage and then helps the editors find the pieces.

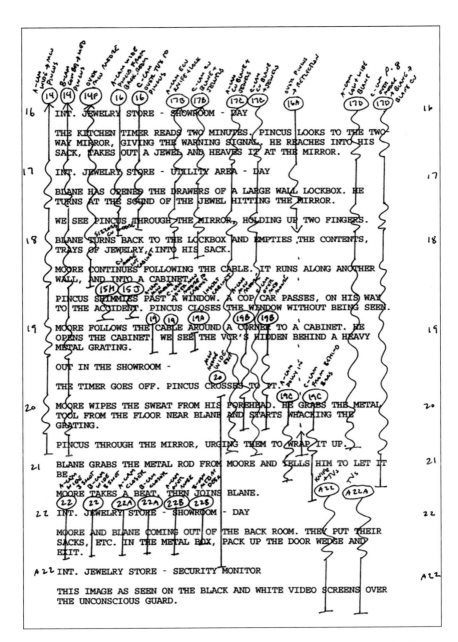

16 INT. JEWELRY STORE - SHOWROOM - DAY

THE KITCHEN TIMER READS TWO MINUTES. PINCUS LOOKS TO THE TWO-WAY MIRROR, GIVING THE WARNING SIGNAL. HE REACHES INTO HIS SACK, TAKES OUT A JEWEL AND HEAVES IT AT THE MIRROR.

17 INT. JEWELRY STORE - UTILITY AREA - DAY

BLANE HAS OPENED THE DRAWERS OF A LARGE WALL LOCKBOX. HE TURNS AT THE SOUND OF THE JEWEL HITTING THE MIRROR.

WE SEE PINCUS THROUGH THE MIRROR, HOLDING UP TWO FINGERS.

18 BLANE TURNS BACK TO THE LOCKBOX AND EMPTIES THE CONTENTS, TRAYS OF JEWELRY, INTO HIS SACK.

MOORE CONTINUES FOLLOWING THE CABLE. IT RUNS ALONG ANOTHER WALL, AND INTO A CABINET.

PINCUS SHIMMIES PAST A WINDOW. A COP CAR PASSES, ON HIS WAY TO THE ACCIDENT. PINCUS CLOSES THE WINDOW WITHOUT BEING SEEN.

19 MOORE FOLLOWS THE CABLE AROUND A CORNER TO A CABINET. HE OPENS THE CABINET. WE SEE THE VCR'S HIDDEN BEHIND A HEAVY METAL GRATING.

OUT IN THE SHOWROOM -

THE TIMER GOES OFF. PINCUS CROSSES TO PT.

20 MOORE WIPES THE SWEAT FROM HIS FOREHEAD. HE GRABS THE METAL TOOL FROM THE FLOOR NEAR BLANE AND STARTS WHACKING THE GRATING.

PINCUS THROUGH THE MIRROR, URGING THEM TO WRAP IT UP.

21 BLANE GRABS THE METAL ROD FROM MOORE AND TELLS HIM TO LET IT BE.

MOORE TAKES A BEAT, THEN JOINS BLANE.

22 INT. JEWELRY STORE - SHOWROOM - DAY

MOORE AND BLANE COMING OUT OF THE BACK ROOM. THEY PUT THEIR SACKS, ETC. IN THE METAL BOX, PACK UP THE DOOR WEDGE AND EXIT.

A22 INT. JEWELRY STORE - SECURITY MONITOR

THIS IMAGE AS SEEN ON THE BLACK AND WHITE VIDEO SCREENS OVER THE UNCONSCIOUS GUARD.

Fig. 7.1c Lined script page for the robbery scene in *Heist*. Without this much detail in the action, the set-up lines don't have much meaning.

Understanding Dominance and Visibility

One of the difficult things about matching is judging just how noticeable a mismatch would be in the final cut. As I said, we don't want our actors to be robots, but we have to match the things that we think will be truly distracting and thereby destructive to the story.

Here are some factors that attract attention to a mismatch, making the mistake more damaging.

VISUAL

When a mismatched item is brightly colored, brightly lit, large in the frame, in the center of the frame, or moving, it will be more noticeable.

STORY

When a mismatched item is central to the story, mentioned in the dialog, or highlights a significant trait of a character, it will be more noticeable.

REPETITION OF CUT

When a mismatch between two set-ups cuts back and forth repeatedly, the mismatch will be more noticeable.

GET OUT OF JAIL

Keep in mind that the opposite is also true. If the audience's attention is focused intently on something else, even gross mismatches may go unnoticed.[6] Similarly, a mismatch that exists over a single cut is surprisingly forgiving.

VARIATIONS IN CONTINUITY STYLE

Each film has its own style of matching just as it has its own style of camera movement, color palette, and performance. A carefully constructed costume drama, or a very quiet story, will usually call for precise continuity. Balanced framing, deliberate dialog, and a general orderliness usually mean you should be strict about matching.

Scrappy, documentary-style narrative films that depend on fresh performances and lots of ad-libs might be hampered by strict continuity. Their style may be so wild and forgiving that you can get away with blatant mismatches.

Setting the style of continuity is not a decision that script supervisors make by themselves. Talk to your director about what they expect as far as matching, then do your best to deliver that.

If a loose style of continuity is chosen, make sure your director is clear what the results will be and that they are choosing to live with some mismatches. Check in with the editor, so that they know what is going on and have a chance to weigh in if they want. You don't want to get in a situation where the director says matching doesn't matter on set, then blames you in post-production for footage that will not cut together easily.

Some Actors Do Not Have a Clue about Matching

Inexperienced actors who have been trained only for stage work may not understand why they should match. They may not even know that they should. If an actor is having big trouble matching, make sure the director is aware of it, even in a master-only scene. The director may be privately thinking about adding a shot and should know that in this case, it would be a problem.

CHEATING: WHEN WHAT'S WRONG IS RIGHT

Many times the director, DP, or someone else on set will want to change an already established element. This is called a cheat, as in "Can we cheat that vase a little forward?"

We cheat things all the time. Really. Something gets cheated on almost every set-up: a candle is moved out from in front of someone's face, an actor is repositioned to take better advantage of natural light, a prop is held differently to show an important detail. All these cheats help the movie and should be welcomed.

How can we get away with making things wrong on purpose? Try this demonstration: Walk around an object that is close to you (like a chair or a tall glass on a table) and watch what happens visually to the objects behind and around it. Everything in the background slides in relative position to the close object. The same thing happens when you move closer or farther away from the object. Space between the featured object and its neighbors seems to expand and contract.

In real life this relationship changes slowly, with each step you take. In a movie, this relationship can also change on the cut, and when it does, the sliding background changes in leaps. Cutting from camera angle to camera angle, a viewer can lose track of exactly what the physical relationship is—or was.

This change of perspective on the cut is the reason we can cheat successfully. The more extreme the change of perspective, the bigger the cheat we can get away with. Our goal is to use this spatial confusion to make the movie better but not push it so far that the presented reality breaks. At that point, a good cheat becomes a continuity mistake.

Some Common Cheats

REPOSITIONING INTO OR OUT OF THE FRAME

When a hand prop sits awkwardly on the edge of frame, it is often cheated in or out. A piece of set dressing may be cheated the same way.

When a close-up feels too crowded, surrounding players and set dressing may be cheated away from the main player or out of the frame.

Removing a foreground object altogether will work if the viewer feels that the camera's perspective is from between the subject and the removed object. This can work even if it is impossible to put a camera in that physical space.

The opposite is true as well. Surrounding objects may be cheated in to make a more cluttered frame.

TO ADD DETAIL

Sometimes we add physical detail to an object, such as a document or an injury, when we shoot an insert or another very close shot. This works because when we look closer at something in real life, we naturally see more detail.

BODY POSITION

When there is a group of actors of uneven height, one may have their height adjusted in the close-up coverage to make a better composition. This can work even if a master shot has been taken that shows the real relationship between the actors' heights.

Actors are often repositioned in relationship to the set or location. The purpose could be to take advantage of a different background, for better light, to present a visual or thematic feature in that background, or to stretch an otherwise limited location.

TO LIMIT OR EXAGGERATE MOVEMENT

An actor's gestures are often cheated to be smaller in close-ups, larger in wide shots. If they were not adjusted, the gesture might overwhelm a tight frame or get lost in a wide frame.

CHEATING LOOKS

When looking in a mirror, actors should look at the camera's reflection, not their own.

When aiming a gun, actors aim at where the camera sees the target, not where the actor sees it. The actor will need guidance from the camera operator to find the right spot.

When we want an intimate look from an actor, they will often look at the side of the lens instead of the off-camera player.

Audacious Cheats

CHEATING THE BACKGROUND

Sometimes we have to reshoot a scene with background actors who are not present. Here is where the photos you took for the ADs come in handy. The ADs can use these photos to comb through a group of extras and find the closest match on hand. Sometimes matching clothing is more important than matching faces, especially if the background players are out of focus.

I was on an extremely low-budget shoot where the actors were responsible for bringing their own wardrobe. An actor came the first day with a white V-neck T-shirt, and the second day with a white crew neck T-shirt. We cut a V on the front of his crew neck shirt and got away with it. Of course this would not work on a more professional project.

David Mamet's *The Winslow Boy* has a number of courtroom scenes. The location they were using only had one wall that looked right. That one good wall was cheated to play as two. The crew shot all the coverage in one direction, with the good wall as a background, then turned the whole set around and shot the complementary coverage looking at the same wall, now playing as the opposite side of the room.

CHEATING LIGHT

Lights are moved around *a lot*. It is breathtaking how much mismatching you can get away with when cheating the lighting plan. I have been on sets where the key light has changed sides completely, and the cut still works because the balance of light and shadow, as well as the general tone, remained the same. Give your DP the authority here. It is their job to know what will play.

Will This Cheat Work?

Some cheats are seamless; no one could ever tell things were changed. Some cheats are obviously so wrong that no one would want to use them.

The cheats you will spend time thinking about are the ones that fall between these camps.

As a script supervisor, you will be one of the people on set who are asked, "Do you think this cheat works?" Here are some things to consider when you are trying to figure that out.

LOOK THROUGH THE LENS

The lens's optics will change how the subject is seen. Look through the lens, either at the camera or at a monitor with a video tap.

A NON-SPECIFIC, NON-REPEATING BACKGROUND WILL HIDE A GEOGRAPHIC CHEAT

A sky, forest, or something out of focus is more forgiving than sharp architecture or striped fabric.

THE MORE THE FRAME CHANGES, THE MORE YOU CAN GET AWAY WITH

A greater change of angle, frame size, or distance to the subject will help you.

ATTITUDE IS OFTEN MORE IMPORTANT THAN DETAILS

If an overall attitude stays the same, a small change will be less noticeable. If the shot is wide enough, a hand resting on the wrong knee is less distracting than a character that sits upright in one set-up and leans forward in the next.

DEVELOP YOUR VISUAL IMAGINATION

Finally, all you really have to go on is your visual imagination. Make the cut in your head. Imagine one set-up running and then cut to the next. Does the mismatch jump out or not? Do this even if you are not good at it. The more you practice, the better your visual imagination will get. Drawing the cut as a storyboard can help you see it. Watching each set-up carefully is essential. When you can cut in your head, you will have a superpower.

WHEN YOU DISAGREE WITH A CHEAT

Sometimes a director or DP thinks that a cheat will work but you think it has been pushed into a mismatch. Again, it is the director's movie; they get to do what they want. Make a note in the facing pages and x-out the affected sections on the set-up. Anytime there is a difference of opinion about a cheat working, it is worth talking to the editor about it. Whichever side the editor agrees with, their insight will help you sharpen your skills in judging cheats.

Sometimes a director chooses to push a cheat into a mismatch. This is different from the dismissive "continuity is for sissies" situation. Maybe a set-up was shot with a mistake that they don't want to repeat. Maybe they had a better idea after most of the scene has been shot; so much better that it outweighs having a mismatch.

See if you have the coverage to cut around it. When that is the case, note the mismatch on the facing pages and explain the work-around. X-out the no-good sections of the affected set-ups in the lined script. If you don't have coverage that can fix it, try to think of something you can do to make the mismatch less damaging—maybe a clean single that can act as a spacer between two shots that are bumping up against each other, or a small gesture that can be added near the cut that makes the logic work.

Notes for Matching

I have three ways to notate for matching, which I mentioned in Chapter 6. Here is the logic for each.

I make my blocking notes on the lined script: when actors stop, turn, cross camera, etc. This is basic information and should always be written down. These are mostly private notes. The editor only needs to see them if there is a variation in the action.[7]

I make my frame drawings.[8] Besides being a record of the most prominent visual elements, the act of drawing helps me see what is most evident. I draw what I notice. If I notice something, most likely the general audience's attention will go there, too.

I take a wide photograph of every set-up. Later, if there is a question about something I did not consider, this picture will at least show me something about it. This wide frame is different than what the camera sees, and works with the set-up frames to form a more complete set of information.

NOTES

1   Remember, a scene is all the action that takes place in a continuous time and place.

2   See Chapter 4 "Breaking Down the Script" for examples.

3   See the *True Love* stories earlier in this chapter on page 206.

4   The term "coverage" is used a couple of different ways. 1) When we talk about "covering a scene" or a "scene's coverage," we are talking about the collection of set-ups that are shot to record that action. 2) Coverage, as in "Master and Coverage," refers to all the set-ups used for that action, except the master.

5   Remember, a new scene starts whenever either time or place changes.

6   This phenomenon, "selective attention," was famously demonstrated at Harvard University in 1999. Christopher Chabris and Daniel Simons presented test subjects with a film clip of a basketball game where two teams of three players passed two balls back and forth. The test subjects were asked to count the number of times one team passed the ball. Because the test subjects were intent on counting the passes, half of them did not notice a person in a gorilla suit, who walked through the game, stopped and beat his chest, then walked out. It's pretty funny. You can see it online here, and try it on your friends: www. theinvisiblegorilla.com/gorilla_experiment.html

7   See Chapter 6, pages 172–194 for more about private notes.

8   See Chapter 6, pages 186–193.

Chapter 8

The Language and Grammar of Filmmaking

One of our jobs as script supervisors is to make sure that all the little pieces of action fit together. This includes maintaining continuity, as we discussed in the last chapter, but it also includes making sure the pieces fit the language and grammar of film.

If you are working with an inexperienced director and DP, you might be the go-to crew member for this subject. An experienced, visually inclined director will need you only as a safety net. Either way, you need to know how the language of film works; the various choices of film grammar and how each choice affects the media you are recording. Just as important, you need to understand the particular grammar of your project.

WHAT ARE THE RULES OF FILM GRAMMAR AND WHAT ARE THEY GOOD FOR?

The work of film grammar is, first, to clarify intent, so that the audience can understand the dynamics of your action, and, second, to present that action with a unique and appropriate spirit.

We have some basic principles that help the viewer understand the meaning of the media (for instance, that two characters are looking at each other, even when they are not in the same frame), but after you get past the ABCs, film grammar is more like a map than a set of instructions.

As a place to start, directors and editors generally favor unobtrusive cuts, which give you smooth transitions and a neutral flavor to the filmcraft of your story. This way the mechanics of film production stay in the background until they are needed to make a specific impression that supports the narrative.

This general truth leads some people to mistakenly think of film grammar as following the rules. As a result, some doggedly obey all the "rules"; others want to tear them down. Both ways of thinking miss the point and throw away the power of film grammar.

> The basic rules of film grammar are **designed to minimize attention** to the mechanics of film production.

DOI: 10.4324/9780367823665-8

USING FILM GRAMMAR EXPRESSIVELY

Sophisticated film grammar is a toolkit of qualifiers that sharpen the intention and tone of the media. Think of it this way: a business letter and an E. E. Cummings poem each have a grammar. They are not the same grammar, but they are not arbitrary either. Both sets of conventions, though very different, help the reader understand the content and meaning of the work.

So it is with film grammar. When used well, film grammar adds a layer of meaning to the recorded action. There are grammatical choices that add an epic feel to *There Will Be Blood* and *The Revenant*. Different choices help deliver psychological intimacy in *The Silence of the Lambs*. Still others ramp up tension in *The Shining* and *Get Out*. Every movie's grammar is a bit different, and designed for that story.

> Film grammar is a **toolkit of qualifiers** that sharpen the intention and tone of the action.

It is not the script supervisor's job to design a project's grammar, but we must understand the process well enough to recognize what the director and DP are up to. Our job is to help them make the movie they want to make.

To that end, this chapter will focus on the principles of basic neutral grammar. When your team makes an intentional departure from this basic grammar, they add some flavor to that neutral base. To do this well, they must understand film grammar and bend the rules with intent and meaning. If they are skillful, this is a lot of fun to watch. If they are not so good at this yet, it is still very interesting.

> The trick to using the rules of film grammar is to **bend the rules with intent and meaning**.

WHAT'S IN THE FILM GRAMMAR TOOLKIT?

Let's start with a foundational concept: filmmakers tell us what is important by what they choose to show on camera. *How* they present that information tells us how they feel about it.

Here are some grammar basics that filmmakers use to add clarity and tone to what the camera sees.

> 1. What is shown = **what is important**.
> 2. How it is shown = **what we are meant to feel about it**.

Camera Positions

SYMPATHETIC AND OBSERVANT CAMERA POSITIONS

When filmmakers want their viewers to psychologically identify with characters within a scene, a "sympathetic" camera angle will usually be used. In a scene with two characters using sympathetic camera angles, each character is seen from an angle near the other character. The viewers feel that they are in the conversation because they stand in the shoes of each character in turn.

If the filmmakers want to present the action without a feeling of intimacy, the camera will be set away from all the characters. We call this an "observant" camera. Both types of camera angles are common.

Fig. 8.1 A pair of sympathetic close-up singles and an observant two-shot.

If a distant camera is used in an observant camera position, the shot will feel like a surveillance camera, or as if someone is watching the action from afar.

Fig. 8.2 A surveillance angle.

The choice of sympathetic or observant angle is fundamental, and the first question to address when planning your coverage.

Wes Anderson often uses an observant camera in situations that would normally call for sympathetic angles. This choice of grammar supports the stylized, absurd, and alienated feeling he uses so well, and is a great example of breaking the rules with intent.

CAMERA HEIGHT

A low camera angle looking up at a character will tend to make that character heroic. A high angle, looking down, can belittle its subject.

An angle at an unusual height, shooting horizontally, will place the viewer in sympathy with that character, as an eye-level shot of a small child, or a sailor in a crow's nest.

Frame Size

The names we give to the basic frame sizes are shown in Fig. 8.4.

Matching Frame Sizes and Variations

The standard way to size a pair of shots is to match them, a close-up with a close-up, a wide shot with a wide shot (see Fig. 8.5). This presents a balanced, neutral flavor to the match, with an equal measure of sympathetic attention to each shot.

Fig. 8.3 A low angle looking up and a high angle looking down.

a Macro
Tiny detail fills the frame.

b Extreme Close-up (XCU)
Frame closer than full face.

c Close-up (CU)
Full head with some neck and shoulder.

d Medium Close-up (MCU)
Shows people from mid-chest up.

e Medium (Med)
Shows people from waist up.

f Med Wide (M/W)
Shows people from mid-thigh or knee up.

g Wide
People are full figure in frame.

h Long
People are smaller in frame than full figure.

i Vista (or Extra Long)
If there are people in the landscape, they are tiny.

Fig. 8.4 Names of frame sizes.

Fig. 8.5 Matched close ups, Mr. A . . . and Mr. B.

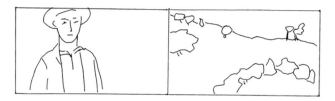

Fig. 8.6 MCU Mr. C . . . and a vista.

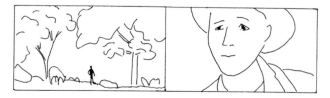

Fig. 8.7 Long shot Mr. D . . . and CU Mr. C.

Deviating from this standard introduces a new flavor to the pair. For instance, in Fig. 8.6, the viewers sympathize with Mr. C and understand that he is looking at the mountainside.

In Fig. 8.7, we feel like we are standing with Mr. C looking at Mr. D. The close-up framing gives us an opportunity to read Mr. C's expression and puts us in close sympathy with him. The feeling of "looking at each other" in this pair of angles is helped by sympathetic camera positions. Fig. 8.8 shows what happens when an observant camera position is used.

Fig. 8.8 Long shot Mr. D . . . and CU Mr. C.

We may or may not understand that the men are looking at each other. This will depend on the particulars of the action and the context of the scene and shots. If they are talking or reacting to each other, if there is a master shot that places them in the physical space, we will understand their relationship pretty quickly. In a different context, we may understand that Mr. C is looking at Mr. D, who is looking in a completely different direction, perhaps keeping his eye on his flock of sheep.

Lens Choices

Lenses are named for their focal length, which describes the distance from the middle of the lens to its focal point, in millimeters. The focal point is the place in the camera where the film or digital sensor is exposed to light coming through the lens.

The smaller the number, the wider the lens will be. You can see why that is true in the examples in Fig. 8.9.

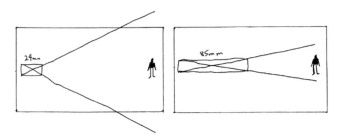

Fig. 8.9 Focal length; 24mm lens and 85mm lens.

Here are some of the most commonly used lenses and a general way to think about them in a 35mm film or full-frame digital format.

- **Fisheye**: 8mm, 10mm
- **Very wide:** 14mm, 18mm
- **Wide:** 24mm, 28mm
- **Neutral:** 35mm, 50mm, 65mm
- **Long:** 75mm, 85mm, 100mm
- **Very long:** 135mm, 200mm
- **Telephoto:** 300mm, 600mm

If your film format or sensor is smaller (like 16mm film or an APS-C digital camera), the smaller capture area will, in effect, crop the image as it hits the focal point, and change the framing of these focal lengths. How much it is cropped will depend on the size of the sensor or film.

Each of these focal lengths has characteristics that will change the look of the captured image, thereby influencing the choice of lens. The most important are depth of field, perspective, and cropping.

Depth of Field

When we focus a lens at a specific distance, there is an area in front and behind that distance that is also seen as in focus. That range of distance is called depth of field. Depth of field varies with focal length. All else being equal, the wider the lens, the deeper the depth of field will be.[1]

> All else being equal, the **wider the lens**, the **deeper the depth of field**.

A wide lens is a good choice for a group shot if the filmmakers want everyone to be clearly seen. A long lens can isolate a single figure by placing a narrow depth of field on the featured player and letting everyone else go a bit soft.

Perspective and Cropping

Perspective and cropping, used together, are very important tools in film grammar. They place us in proximity to our subject and focus our attention on that subject with a particular tone.

PERSPECTIVE

A wide lens at a close perspective will exaggerate spatial relationships. A close-up portrait taken with a wide lens will pull the nose forward, making it bigger and more present. The ears and sides of the head will recede. If

Fig. 8.10 Depth of field in a wide lens and a long lens.

exaggerated, this is the look you get through those little peepholes in apartment front doors.

A long lens at a distant perspective will flatten space. The nose and ears seem like they are on the same plane. A long lens is as glamorous as a wide lens is goofy. This is why long or longish lenses are usually used to shoot fashion photos and beautiful close-ups.

Objects close to us have a deeper spatial dynamic than objects that are farther away. You can see this for yourself by looking at something (say a chair) that is one foot away from you, then looking at something similar that is 200 feet away. Lenses see the same way. A medium close-up taken with a 28mm lens from five feet away will have more spatial depth, and so will

> Objects close to us have a **deeper spatial dynamic** than objects that are farther away.

Fig. 8.11 Extreme wide and long focal lengths.

intuitively feel closer, than a medium close-up of the same subject taken with a 100mm lens from 15 feet away.

CROPPING

A long lens will crop an image, capturing a smaller field of the subject. A wider lens will show more of the subject, as shown in Fig. 8.9. Cropping brings our attention to whatever detail is in the smaller frame without changing the spatial dynamic of the subject.

How Perspective and Cropping Are Used in Coverage

Here is an example showing how perspective and cropping can add intuitive information to the action of a scene:

Say we have a woman at a party. Her coverage, as seen from her date sitting across a small table, is a medium close-up. We use the 28mm taken from five feet away. That camera feels physically close but is not very flattering. Her coverage from a man across the room, who loves her, is also a medium close-up, but it is taken with a 100mm lens from 15 feet away. The long lens, with its cropping and perspective, help

> Two medium close-ups taken from two different distances will have **unique perspectives**.

us feel that, despite the physical distance, he is just as connected to her, that he sees (and understands) the woman just as much as her date does. As an added bonus, the longer lens makes the woman look more glamorous from her lover's point of view than from her date's. Maybe we add an extreme close-up of the woman from the lover's viewpoint, using a very long lens. If we do, we see "through his eyes" every little gesture and breath she takes. He sees her better, understands her better. This angle has both intimacy and distance, which equals longing.

Conversely, if we wanted to show the lover's alienation from the woman, we might widen the lens. A 35mm shot from 15 feet away would show her as part of the crowd. We would lose the feeling of intimate, special understanding that the close shots gave us.

Close and Wide Eyelines

When we shoot an actor looking to another actor who is off-camera, we have the option of adjusting the on-camera actor's eyeline. Adjusting this eyeline will influence the intimacy and intensity of the set-up.

The closer that eyeline is to the camera, the more sympathetic the camera will be. A wider look will give you some emotional distance.

Fig. 8.12 Close eyeline and wide eyeline.

We sometimes want a look that is so close to camera that the off-camera actor cannot physically get close enough to the lens. In this case the camera crew will put a mark just off the edge of the lens, usually a piece of bright tape, and the on-camera actor will play to the mark.

There is an emotional borderline between a look that is extremely close to the lens and a look into the lens. Once an actor's look goes into the lens, the tone of the shot becomes very strong and stylized. The association to the off-camera character is left behind, and we feel that the on-camera actor has broken the fourth wall and is speaking directly to the audience. This can be done, of course, but make sure this strong flavor is one that is useful to the story and the tone you want to express.

CAMERA MOVEMENT

How we move the camera adds feeling as well.

How the Camera Follows the Action

Say we have two seated characters, Amy and Bert. We want a single of Bert, taken from near Amy, that pans with Bert as he stands up and walks across the room. If the camera booms up, the audience psychologically stays with Bert. If the camera remains at the seated height of Amy, and tilts up, the audience psychologically stays with her.[2]

If the camera moves with Bert as he walks away from Amy, the audience stays with Bert even more, psychologically leaving Amy behind.

> Choices of camera movement can help an audience **stay with a character or leave that character behind**.

Matching Camera Movement and Speed

There are gentle and violent camera movements; moves that start gradually or abruptly, with consistent or variable speeds. The first consideration, when cutting between two moving cameras, is whether the cut is meant to be seamless or to add impact. Like almost everything else in continuity, matching the characteristics of two moving shots will give the cut a neutral feel. A mismatch will add flavor to the cut.

Say we have two dolly shots tracking with a character running down the street; one is wide and one is close-up. To set up for a seamless cut, the direction and speed of the shots should match. This will allow the viewer to track the character smoothly through the cut, providing a feeling of forward motion and velocity. As the script supervisor, you should track and note this speed.[3]

If the filmmakers want to slow down the camera's travel speed, for example to let the runner move away from the camera, in most cases the change should be done within a set-up, not on the cut. When the camera's direction or speed changes between shots, the transition will jump. This will be visually disruptive to the viewer. While this is not a good choice for most situations, it may be the perfect thing if the runner is emotionally conflicted or confused (change of direction), or if the runner at that moment steps into a newly dangerous situation (change of speed). We see cuts like this often at decisive moments in battle scenes.

If there is a possibility of a cut during a camera move, the script supervisor needs to know when the camera move starts and stops as well as its speed, acceleration, and deceleration. This should be tracked in relationship to the dialog and actors' blocking as well as against any other significant action during that time.

COMPOSITION

Match the compositional elements in paired shots for a neutral feel. Any difference will add a flavor to the coverage. Two over-the-shoulder medium close-ups will feel balanced. One over-the-shoulder medium close-up and a clean close-up will give the clean close-up more power. I find my frame drawings to be a big help in remembering the composition of each set-up.

THREE DIMENSIONS

When tracking coverage in 3-D, there are two important things to pay attention to: the inter-ocular distance and the convergence plane.

The "interocular" is the distance between the lenses of the two 3-D cameras. All else being equal, the greater the interocular distance, the deeper the 3-D space will be. If we want a neutral feel between cuts, we will balance the depth of the 3-D in pairs of shots.

The "convergence plane" is the distance in front of the camera where the images from the two cameras line up with each other. This plane will be seen by the viewer as in line with the projection screen. Everything closer than this distance will be seen as in front of the screen and closer to the viewer's personal space; everything farther away will be seen as receding behind the screen, and outside of the viewer's personal space.

A cut with a mismatched convergence plane can add power to a transition. This sort of mismatch is often used in 3-D suspense movies when cutting to a jump scare, to bring some object or character suddenly and aggressively in your face.

WORKING WITH COVERAGE

Let's exercise our film grammar in an example. Take a scene of two kids in a convenience store. One kid is shoplifting. The other watches uncomfortably. The checkout lady is looking in their direction but chatting with a friend on the telephone. There are two types of information that need to be expressed in this scene. One is factual, that is, what is happening; the other is subtext: how the film feels about what is happening.

Factual Information

Viewers need enough hard information to follow the physical action of the scene. Factual information for this scene includes:

- This scene takes place in a convenience store.
- One kid is shoplifting.
- A second kid watches her uncomfortably.
- There is a person of authority who could catch them, but is distracted.

Part of your job as a script supervisor is to check that these essential story elements are seen in the coverage. Of course this is mostly the director's job; we provide backup and support.

If there is a shot list, checking for these elements should be pretty easy. If there is a wide establishing shot or a shot panning through the store on the shot list, chances are either will include enough information to place us in a convenience store. If not, does the introduction of the shoplifting kid or the checkout lady show enough set dressing to do the job? Usually the setting is established near the beginning of the action to establish context for the drama.

If there is no shot list, you must check each story element on a shot-by-shot basis. If there is no shot wide enough to show the shoplifting kid picking up what she steals, check to make sure her physical action is clear in the coverage. Is there a shot where we can clearly see the uncomfortable kid's emotions? If not, the audience will never know she is uncomfortable, no matter how much she plays it on set.

Subtextual Information

The subtext is trickier. You must know your director's intention. There are thousands of choices, all potentially correct. If the director wants the uncomfortable kid to be the center of the scene, you will need a good amount of coverage on her. This may be one long very close shot that follows her the entire scene, or it may be a number of subjective shots, one from the stealing kid, one from the checkout lady, maybe even one from the stolen item. If the physical action is shot from the uncomfortable kid's point of view, make sure to get a close-up of the kid, or we will never know who is doing the watching.

It is not up to us to say what the coverage will be. We see what the director wants and check to make sure that the coverage will provide that particular information with that particular feeling.

You must be able to back up your director without pestering them. This is really important. No director wants to spend time on set explaining the coverage to the script supervisor. If you can follow the coverage without being disruptive, you will be a good safety net for your director and you will have a lot of fun.

THE 180° LINE

If you have spent any time on a film set, you have probably heard about the rule of the 180° line. All across the world, film sets are brought to a halt as the director, cinematographer, and script supervisor argue about the 180° line: Where is the line? Which way should the actors look to agree with the line? When did the line change?

What is this line? Why is it so important? And what makes it so elusive to even experienced filmmakers?

Why the 180° Line Is Important

The rule of the 180° line helps the audience assemble separate shots into a smooth narrative flow. Here is a simple example of how that works:

We have a two-shot of a couple talking to each other. We also have two different sets of close-up singles covering the same action. In the first pair of singles, the characters look at each other (Fig. 8.13). In the second (Fig. 8.14), they do not. The first pair of close-ups creates a better visual and narrative flow. This is because the eyelines, the direction of the looks between the characters, are maintained between all three shots.

Fig. 8.13 Two-shot and a pair of CUs looking toward each other.

Fig. 8.14 Two-shot and a pair of CUs that do not look toward each other.

A Little History of the 180° Line

Our film grammar developed directly from the tradition of watching live theater. When watching a play, each audience member has, at each moment, the choice of taking in the entire stage, following the action of a certain player, or concentrating on a player's facial expression. We do this intuitively, looking where we feel the most important bit of drama is taking place. This is what filmmakers recreate as we decide which shots we need in order to cover a scene.

Filmmakers have an advantage over theater audiences: we are able to take the best seat in the house for each story beat and put the camera there. When the dynamics of the action change, we find a new best seat for that new moment. Sometimes we come right up on stage and set the camera next to one of the players. Sometimes we fly around the stage.

But popping around from seat to seat can be disorienting. If, at each cut, the camera stays in the same general orientation to the action, we can pop around without the audience losing the dramatic tension between players. If Juliet looks to Romeo in various right-to-left directions and Romeo looks to Juliet in left-to-right looks, the tension between them holds and all the small pieces of action work together as one compound audience point of view.

The 180° rule helps us do this. It is a convention we use to keep all of our camera angles on "the audience side of the stage." This basic principle sometimes leads to the misunderstanding that there is just one line that has to be adhered to for the entire scene. In fact, we can choose a different line for every cut, if we do it right. This fluidity is what allows us to choose the perfect angle to express every dramatic moment.

How the 180° Line Works

Imagine an axis, going from one character to another. If the camera stays on one side of this line across a cut, the eyelines will agree and the viewers will retain the visual dramatic tension between these characters. Cross over the line to set a camera within the other 180° and that tension will be interrupted.

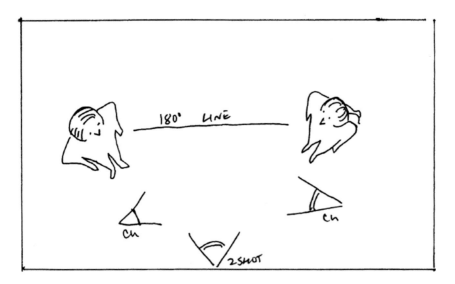

Fig. 8.15 A floor plan for shots that agree. These are the camera angles for Fig. 8.13.

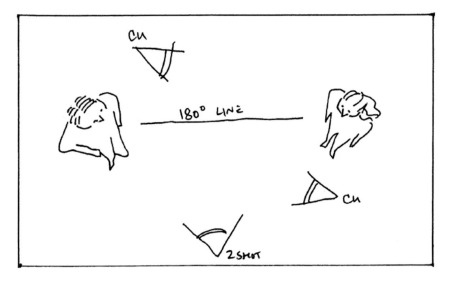

Fig. 8.16 A floor plan for shots that disagree. These are the camera angles for Fig. 8.14.

Filmmakers who are new to the concept of the 180° line sometimes have the misunderstanding that camera placement is determined by the line. This is not true. Camera placement is decided by the aesthetic and emotional impact of each angle. The 180° line is used as a check, to make sure the preferred camera angles will work together.

Camera Right and Camera Left

On a film set, when we talk about right and left, we usually mean right and left as seen from the camera. When we want to clarify this, we will say "camera right" and "camera left." On occasion, when we talk to an actor, we might say "your right" or "your left," which is the opposite of camera right and left when the actor is facing the camera.

> On a film set, when we talk about **right and left**, we usually mean right and left as seen from the camera.

Common 180° Line Coverage

Here are some examples of simple, commonly used coverage plans that use the 180° line.

THREE PEOPLE IN A LINE

When we have three people in a scene, the coverage may be one three-shot, a two-shot and a single, or three singles, depending on the emotional dynamics and blocking of the scene. If a single character is interacting with a couple, Fig. 8.17 is a good choice.

THREE-PERSON INTERROGATION

A classic set up for an interrogation (or any scene with a strong two-against-one feel) is a direct single of the interrogated and a two-shot of the

Fig. 8.17a Three people; three-shot, a two-shot, and a single.

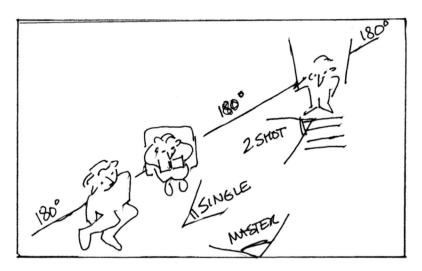

Fig. 8.17b Floor plan for Fig. 8.17a.

interrogators. The single character will split their look to the interrogators. Figs 8.18a and 8.18b show an example of this sort of coverage. This works best if there is a dominant interrogator in the two-shot. Match the looks between this dominant interrogator and the single. The looks to the second interrogator in the two-shot will not match the single, but the sympathetic connection we get from the head-on single of the interrogated character is usually more important. If both interrogators' relationships to the subject are important, you will need to add more shots.

Note that the single character is seated. This helps to show his lack of power. Don't forget to match eyelines vertically as well as horizontally.

Fig. 8.18a Interrogation coverage in two shots. The male interrogator's eyeline in the two-shot does not match the interrogated character's eyeline in the single. They both look camera right.

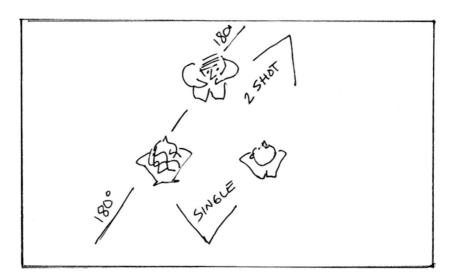

Fig. 8.18b Floor plan for Fig. 8.18a.

THREE IN A TRIANGLE OF SINGLES

You can cover a three-person scene in a triangle of singles. This is a good way to emphasize the individual nature of the characters. Place the camera for each character centered between the other two. All the eyelines will agree, but the looks will be wide.

If you add a master shot to this plan, not all the singles will agree with it. That is fine. Like all continuity, the 180° line only matters on the cut. If you know which single you want to cut with the master, check that the master and that single work together. Once you are in the singles, they will all work with each other. If you want to go back out to the master, you can do that from a matching single.

Fig. 8.19a Three angles in a triangle of singles. The letters at the sides of each drawing show the position of the off-camera characters.

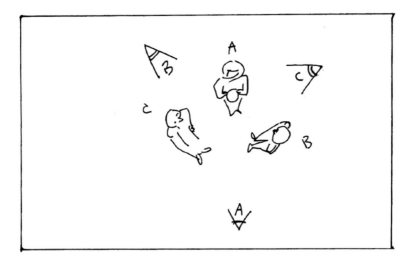

Fig. 8.19b Floor plan of 8.19a, three-person triangle in three singles.

You can adjust this coverage to be more sympathetic by moving the camera closer to an off-screen character. An angle like that, with a closer eyeline, will make a stronger emotional connection between the character near the camera and the one on camera, but will not be as versatile. You will need more set-ups to cover the same amount of story beats if you want to emphasize the emotional connection between all the characters.

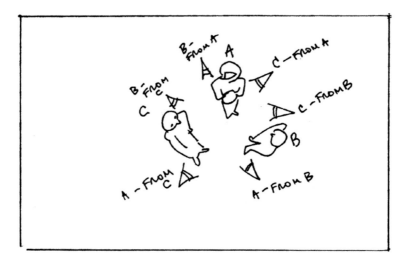

Fig. 8.20 Six singles in a three-person triangle, with closer eyelines.

Fig. 8.20 shows sympathetic coverage for all three characters, from the perspective of the other two characters. This is too much coverage for most scenes. To avoid over-covering a scene, think about which camera angles give you the story beats you really need, and shoot just those. Which of these angles are fine with wide eyelines, and which need the intimate feeling of a close eyeline? Your coverage may be a combination of wide and tight eyelines, depending on the feel you want at each moment. This is for your DP and director to decide.

To identify where the line is at the time of a cut, let the drama guide you. Who are we paying attention to right then, and who or what is that character paying attention to? Between those two points is where the 180° line is at that moment.

A GROUP IN A LINE

If you have a group of people in a line, it is easy to make all the coverage agree with the master. See Figs 8.21a and 8.21b.

Fig. 8.21a A master shot of six people. Coverage in a five-shot and a three-shot.

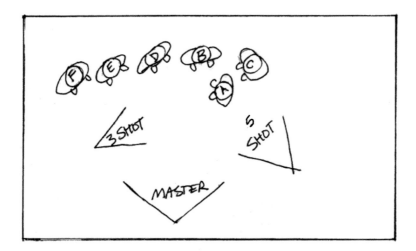

Fig. 8.21b Floor plan for Fig. 8.21a.

USING THE LINE IN A COMPLICATED SCENE

When a group is not arranged in a straight line, things get more difficult. The 180° line will change as we work our way through a complicated scene. As long as the eyelines on each side of each cut agree, the dramatic tension of the scene will hold. This takes some planning and agreement about how the scene will likely be cut.

Breaking the Scene into Beats

Start like this: Break the scene into dramatic beats. Each beat is a unique dramatic exchange that brings a new opportunity to choose the best camera angles. Who are the important players in each beat? They may include characters that do not speak and are not even mentioned in the script at that point. Set an eyeline for each beat and make sure all the camera angles needed to express that beat agree with each other. To cut between beats, you'll need a camera angle that agrees with the 180° lines for both beats.

Fig. 8.22 shows a short scene that can benefit from more complicated coverage.

```
Three characters sit around a table:
  Character A (Adam)
  Character B (Bonnie)
  Character C (Carol)

                BONNIE
        How was your day, Adam?

                ADAM
        It sucked.

Bonnie laughs and looks at Carol, who laughs as well.

                ADAM
        What's so funny?

                CAROL
        Nothing.
            (to Bonnie)
        Should we tell him?

                BONNIE
        Not yet.
```

Fig. 8.22 A short scene we will use to discuss camera placement and complicated eyelines.

Here are the beats as I would lay them out:

- **Beat 1:** Our three characters are sitting together at a table.
- **Beat 2:** Adam is in a bad mood. He snaps at Bonnie when she asks him about his day.

- **Beat 3:** Bonnie is not hurt; in fact, she seems delighted. Carol is enjoying herself as well.
- **Beat 4:** Adam wants to know what is going on. . .
- **Beat 5:** . . .but it is their secret for now.

Planning the Coverage

Fig. 8.23 shows the floor plan and possible coverage for this scene. Figs 8.24 to 8.28 show how the set-ups look on camera.

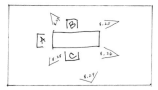

Fig. 8.23 A floor plan of three characters around a table, with the following shots noted.

Fig. 8.24 The master three-shot. **Beat 1:** Our three characters are sitting together at a table.

Fig. 8.25 Adam from Bonnie. **Beat 2:** Adam is in a bad mood. He snaps at Bonnie when she asks him about his day. "How was your day, Adam?" "It sucked." **Beat 3:** Bonnie is not hurt, in fact, she seems delighted. Carol (laughing from off camera) is enjoying herself as well.

Fig. 8.26 Single Adam from Carol. **Beat 4:** Adam wants to know what's going on. "What's so funny?"

The eyeline between Adam and Bonnie agree with the master. All eye-lines in this shot agree with 8.26.

As Adam turns from Bonnie to Carol, we have an opportunity to estab-lish a new 180° line. Changing the line can strengthen a shifting dramatic moment like what comes next. This is the set up that will make the shift work. Adam and Bonnie should be engaged with each other at the start of this shot and their eyelines must agree with previous shot. At the end of the shot, Adam and Carol are engaged and their eyelines must agree with the following shot. This establishes a new 180° line between Adam and Carol, isolating Bonnie, which we can use to pivot the coverage to the other side of Bonnie.

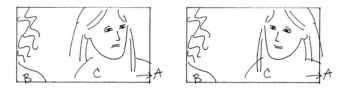

Fig. 8.27 Single Carol from Bonnie. **Beat 5:** "Nothing. . . Should we tell him?"

Cutting into this shot with a strong dramatic connection (and eyeline) between Carol and Adam will keep the audience oriented. When Carol turns to Bonnie, now on the left, we have added new visual subtext to the scene. Adam is no longer the scene's focus. He is not even in the picture. We have literally turned our back to him. We end the scene with a strong feeling of conspiracy between Bonnie and Carol.

Fig. 8.28 Single Bonnie from Carol. **Beat 5:** (continued): "Not yet." It is their secret for now.

Checking Eyelines Using the 180° Line

Follow Fig. 8.29 to check that all the planned cuts will work for eyelines.

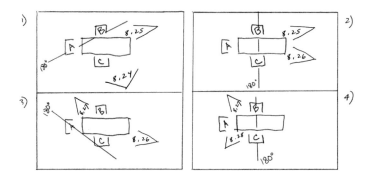

Fig. 8.29 A step-by-step cutting plan for the coverage in Figs 8.24 to 8.28, showing the 180° lines.

1. The cut between the master (8.24) and Adam as seen from Bonnie (8.25). Adam is left looking right, Bonnie is right looking left on both sides of the cut.
2. The cut between Adam as seen from Bonnie (8.25) to Adam as seen from Carol (8.26). Adam is center, Bonnie is right, Carol is left on both sides of the cut.
3. The cut between Adam as seen from Carol (8.26) to Carol as seen from Bonnie (8.27). Carol is left, Adam is right on both sides of the cut. If there is a strong connection between Carol and Adam at the cut point from 8.26 to 8.27, it won't matter that Bonnie's looks do not agree.
4. The cut between Carol as seen from Bonnie (8.27) to Bonnie as seen from Carol (8.28). Bonnie is left, Carol is right on both sides of the cut.

Hopping around the table like this can get complicated, but it lets you get your characters out of a line and into a more natural arrangement. When the shots are cut together, the audience gets a feeling of plasticity, which puts them in the middle of the action, a very different feeling than watching characters in a line, on a stage.

Big Groups

Planning your coverage beat by beat becomes more complicated and more necessary as the number of characters and dynamic tensions grow. When shooting *To Wong Foo, Thanks for Everything! Julie Newmar*, we had nine principal characters sitting at a round table in an energetic scene that went on for many pages. The way we found the coverage was to split the scene into a dozen sub-scenes, plan coverage for each of them separately, then adjust that coverage if we had to, so that each sub-scene would cut to the next. It worked out great.

If you have more than three characters forming a closed group, like around a table or camp fire, it is common to block the action so that the character most central to the action is on one side and the least important characters are opposite. A master from behind the least important characters features the central character and makes it easy to build coverage around that central spot, which is where the most powerful dynamics will be taking place.

COURTROOMS AND AUDITORIUMS

When we cover a courtroom or auditorium, the room is usually presented formally in a characteristic tableau. The coverage agrees with the master even as the coverage changes from tableau to something more intimate.

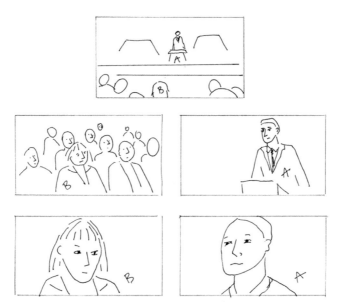

Fig. 8.30a Courtroom coverage. Row 1: Master tableau. Row 2: Coverage, with medium shots. Row 3: Coverage, with close shots.

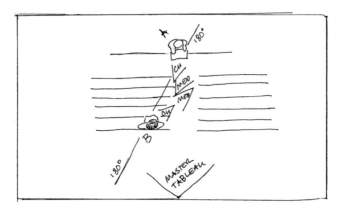

Fig. 8.30b Floor plan for Fig. 8.30a.

READING, WRITING, AND LOOKING

When a character is reading, writing, or looking at an object, dramatic tension will be maintained if the eyelines match, just as if that character was looking at another person.

Fig. 8.31a Master and coverage between a person and the object she is looking at.

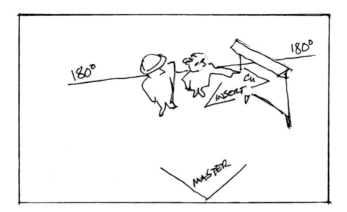

Fig. 8.31b Floor plan for Fig. 8.31a.

MAINTAINING SCREEN DIRECTION IN MOTION

In some scenes, like chases or battles, a character's motion is the most dramatic element. The momentum of that motion is more powerful when travel direction is maintained across cuts. The 180° line is useful for this too.

Fig. 8.32a A series of three shots: the character maintains a left-to-right momentum throughout.

The variations of shots in Fig. 8.32a (a close up, a medium from the back, moving through a doorway) could feel choppy and disorienting if the left-to-right momentum were not consistent.

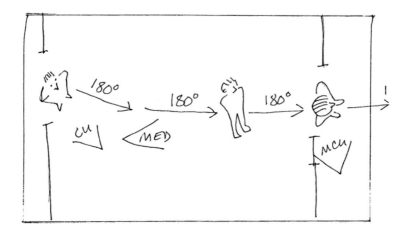

Fig. 8.32b Floor plan for Fig. 8.32a. The 180° line is used to define and maintain travel direction across cuts.

Matching Direction in a Chase

When one character is chasing another, they should both be traveling in the same direction.

Fig. 8.33a A chase. Both characters move from camera left to camera right.

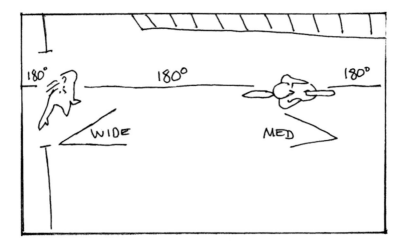

Fig. 8.33b Floor plan for Fig. 8.33a.

Moving Characters toward Each Other

If characters are walking toward each other, they should be moving in opposite directions.

Fig. 8.34a Walking toward each other. One character travels camera right, the other two, camera left.

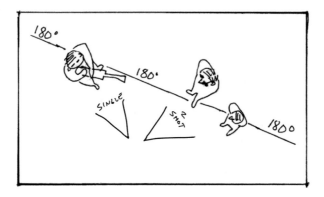

Fig. 8.34b Floor plan for Fig. 8.34a.

Traveling Objects

We maintain screen direction between cuts when something is thrown, caught, or dropped, or when a character reaches for something outside of the frame.

Fig. 8.35a Traveling object (a launched explosive) traveling camera right.

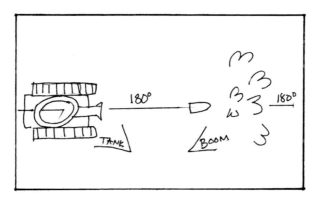

Fig. 8.35b Floor plan for Fig. 8.35a.

Changing Direction to Reduce Momentum

You might want to make a character's progression more meandering or tentative. Changing the direction of travel will do that. If the change of direction happens inside a set-up (not on the cut), the change will not be disorienting.

Fig. 8.36 Changing traveling direction within a set-up.

Fig. 8.37 Traveling right (frames A and B), neutral (frame C), then traveling left (frame D).

In frames A and B of Fig. 8.36, the character moves to the left. In frame C, he changes direction, from moving left to moving right. In frame D, he moves right.

Neutral Bumpers

Another way filmmakers change travel direction is by using a neutral shot. This could be a shot of a character coming straight toward or away from the camera. An overhead shot with a character traveling in the center of the frame will do the same thing. Once a neutral shot has been used, travel direction has been paused and the next shot can have any travel direction you like. The directional momentum will not be as strong as a constant travel direction, but that is a choice of grammar that might be just what you want.

UNUSUAL MATCHING SITUATIONS

Here are a few situations where matching screen direction is not so obvious.

Full Reverse

It is not confusing to go from exactly behind a character, or characters, to exactly in front of them. This works for a group or a single character in an environment, not for cutting between characters. It is similar to the neutral travel direction in Fig. 8.37.

Fig. 8.38 Full reverse: A wide figure from the front. CU from behind.

Hugs, Kisses, and Other Embraces

When two characters are in a tight embrace, both of their heads will go to either the right or left side of their partner. That's okay.

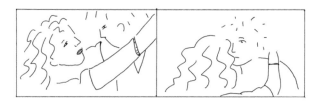

Fig. 8.39 A very close two-shot. Screen direction holds.

Fig. 8.40 Once they embrace, both faces will be on either the left or the right.

Vehicles

Scenes that take place in cars, buses, and trains have two kinds of screen direction working at the same time: 1) travel direction, and 2) eyelines between the characters in the scene. Use the dynamic that is most central to each particular story beat. This gives you a lot of options to play with.

Fig. 8.41 A vehicle, exterior and interior, a mix of eyelines in cutting order, all correct.

In frame A of Fig. 8.41, the car travels right, which agrees with frame B, a two-shot. Here the boy is on the left, mom on the right.[4] They travel right. The next two-shot, frame C, agrees with frame B, boy on the left, mom on the right. They travel left, which agrees with frame D, the last traveling shot.

Behind Camera Travel

When a character is looking at something that travels behind camera, like a parade or someone running away, the on-camera character's looks will not agree with the travel direction in the coverage of the action behind camera.

For example, in Fig. 8.42 the parade is moving left to right in the first shot. In the second shot, when the parade is behind the camera, the on-camera characters should follow the natural motion of the parade, even though their eyelines will sweep from right to left.

Fig. 8.42 A parade and the crowd watching it.

Telephone Conversations

Characters talking to each other on the telephone will have a stronger connection if they are looking in opposite screen directions. It doesn't matter that they never see each other.

Fig. 8.43 Telephone singles matching eyelines.

Screen Direction and Maps

When a character's progress is shown with a map, the direction they travel in their coverage should agree with that map.

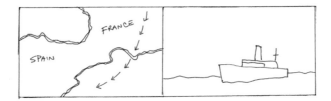

Fig. 8.44 A map and the action it illustrates, both traveling right to left.

WHEN ACTORS MOVE THE LINE

When a character's movement shifts the 180° line, the coverage should follow the shift. Note the moment exactly in relationship to the dialog and blocking, and make sure the director and DP are aware of the change.

Figs 8.45 to 8.50 illustrate this character-driven shift. Let's start with the master shot, Fig. 8.45. A woman enters a room on camera left, crosses to a chair, and sits on camera right. The man sitting at the desk remains static. His looks to her are camera left at the start and camera right after she crosses in front of him. When she exits the room, his looks to her are once again camera left.

Fig. 8.45 A master shot, as a moving character shifts the 180° line.

If there is coverage that will cut into the master, the eyelines should match the master at each probable cut point (Figs 8.46–8.50).

Fig. 8.46 Close-up coverage, when the woman is at the door, camera left.

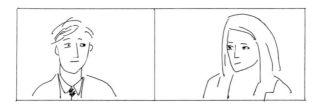

Fig. 8.47 Close-up coverage, when the woman sits in the chair, camera right.

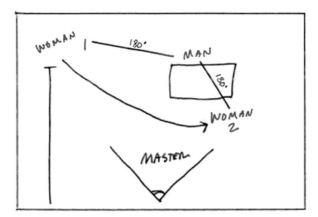

Fig. 8.48 Floor plan for Fig. 8.45, the master.

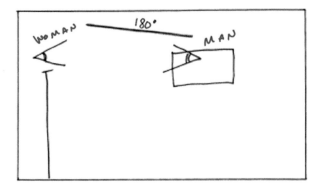

Fig. 8.49 Floor plan for Fig. 8.46, close-ups when the woman is at the door.

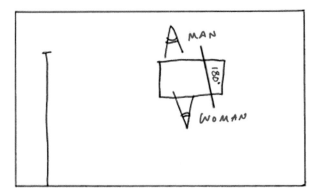

Fig. 8.50 Floor plan for Fig. 8.47, close-ups when the woman is seated.

Off-Camera Movement

The off-camera character should walk through all their blocking, matching any movement that might cause a reaction from the on-camera character: looking up when that character stands, looking deeper as the off-camera character walks away, etc.

Cutting into Moving Actors

If you are looking for a smooth cut between shots of a moving character, make sure to match their pace and blocking.

WHEN THE CAMERA MOVES THE LINE

When a camera move shifts the 180° line, the coverage should follow that shift. Note the moment exactly in relationship to the dialog and action and make sure the director and DP are aware of the change.

In the following example, we have two characters talking to each other as the camera moves from left to right.

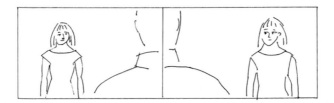

Fig. 8.51 A moving shot that starts over the left shoulder and ends over the right shoulder.

Fig. 8.52 Matching coverage on the man.

We need two shots for coverage on the man: one that matches the moving camera's first position and one that matches the last position. This coverage commits the editor to using the moving camera as it travels behind the man. It is the only coverage where the transition happens within a shot, not on the cut.

Fig. 8.53 Floor plan for beginning and end positions.

THE POWER OF JUMPING THE LINE

There are times when it makes sense to jump the line.

Jumping the Line in Action Sequences

The most common place to jump the line is in action sequences. When filmmakers want viewers to be surprised or disoriented, the slight confusion caused by a break in 180° agreement may be the perfect thing. Below is an example of jumping the line as our hero falls from a tall building. The break in visual flow not only makes the sequence more exciting but also prolongs the fall.

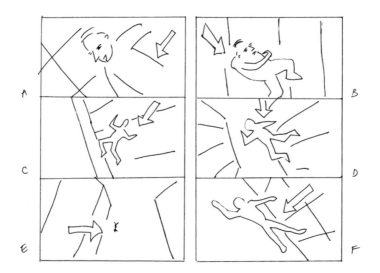

Fig. 8.54 Jumping the line in an action sequence.

Tension and the Line

Breaking the 180° line is often useful, but it should not be done arbitrarily. The power of breaking the 180° line comes from the 180° rule being enforced elsewhere in the movie. If the rule were to be thrown out altogether, the effect of breaking it would not carry the sense of disorientation that we find so helpful in certain situations.

Look at the bloody battle scene in the middle of *Braveheart*. It is mayhem, over-the-top berserk. The filmmakers use the 180° line to heighten the chaos. First, they construct and reinforce a strict directional orientation. For a full 15 minutes before the clash, Braveheart's tribe is on camera right, facing the enemy on camera left. Then all hell breaks loose. When the battle is won, Braveheart addresses his tribe, which has regrouped again on camera right. The formalized standoff before the battle and the tribe's return to wholeness after winning increases the feeling of pandemonium in the heat of the battle.

Jumping the Line in Dramatic Sequences

Disorientation may be useful in quieter scenes as well. If it is done carefully and deliberately, a new 180° line can express a sharp shift in the emotional dynamics.

Here's an example: We have two people, Mr. A and Mr. B, standing by a door. They are talking about another person, Mr. C, who is not present; he might be a lover, a boss, or a suspected killer.

Unexpectedly, a door opens and Mr. C comes in. The tone of the scene has shifted profoundly. A great way to express this shift is to jump the coverage to the other side of the line.

When we suddenly change the 180° line, the viewer gets a little visual jolt. This grammar is perfect for the moment of shock and disorientation that comes when you are surprised, embarrassed, or frightened. In another situation it might be confusing or annoying.

Fig. 8.55a Two-shot, CU Mr. A and CU Mr. B.

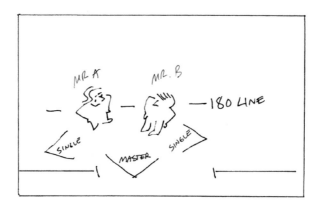

Fig. 8.55b Floor plan of Fig. 8.55a.

Fig. 8.56a Three-shot from across the line.

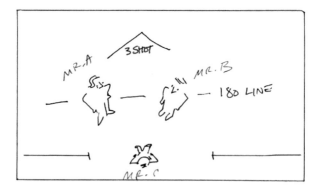

Fig. 8.56b Floor plan of Fig. 8.56a.

WHY THE LINE IS ELUSIVE

The 180° line is pretty easy to understand. Why does it cause so many arguments on set? The main reason is that editing, at this point, is theoretical. Another big issue is the matter of style.

Theoretical Editing

Like everything else in continuity, the 180° rule only matters on the cut. If there is no cut, there is no need to think about the 180° line.

If only one cutting choice is possible, there will be no argument about the line. A complex scene usually has many cutting options. Each crew member may have a different (and reasonable) idea about how the scene should be cut together.

A technically strong director will have a (at least basic) cutting plan, which the crew will be able to implement with no problem. A technically inexperienced or disinterested director may depend on their crew to work this out. This is when most of the long talks about the 180° line take place.

If you are in this situation as a script supervisor, you can help the director see the options and work though how to get the media that will deliver the scene that they are looking for.

First, comb the scene and mark the most important dramatic beats. I group the action and dialog into beats by drawing brackets on the side of my set script. Next, imagine you are watching the action as a play. What do you want to be looking at for each beat? What angle is best to see that action? When do you shift from one view to the next? Make a plan, go over it with the director, and make adjustments according to the director's wishes.

Draw up a 180° line for each dramatic beat. Match the eyelines on each probable cut. When the line shifts, figure out a smooth and meaningful way to get to the correct side of the line. This may happen naturally, or it may involve a slight camera move, change of an actor's blocking, or a neutral cut-away that can bridge the two different 180° lines.

Style

Another cause of 180° line discussions on set is style. Like all the other film grammar choices, the use of the 180° line has a flavor. A rough documentary style of shooting, or projects that focus on frenetic action, can get away with loose 180° line adherence. Quiet dramas that depend on intense emotional relationships and subtext cannot.

Some directors and lots of cinematographers feel that the 180° rule can be ignored when there are enough geographic markers to keep the characters physically oriented. They may prefer a camera position that has a nicer background to one that matches eyelines.

I agree that geographic markers might be enough in a casual scene when the characters are all doing their own thing. That plan falls apart when dramatic tension is high. There is emotional power in matching eyelines that goes beyond not getting geographically disoriented. If two people are talking to each other through a doorway, we know exactly where they are. If they are confessing their love for each other, it would be ridiculous if the eyelines didn't match.

NOTES

1   Other things that affect the depth of field are aperture and the distance between camera and subject.

2   A camera that booms up moves vertically. A camera that tilts up stays in one place and pivots upward.

3   When matching the speed of the cameras you may have to compensate for frame size. A close-up may feel faster than the same speed on a wider camera.

4   The cut from frame A to frame B would also work if frame B was a two-shot from behind, the boy on the right, mom on the left. The consistent travel direction, left to right, will carry us over the cut.

Chapter 9
A Day on Set

Each day on a movie set is different, but, to get an idea of what it is like to work as a script supervisor, here is an example of a typical day on set.

THE CALL SHEET

The evening before, each crew member will receive a call sheet for the next day. This is a one-page (double-sided) schedule that summarizes the day's work. It includes a wealth of information: what scenes will be shot, the address of the shooting location, who will work that day, what time each cast and crew member should be there, what major equipment has been ordered, etc. It is the place that will tell you about the day's special production elements, things like rain towers, firearms, child actors.

A call sheet may have attachments, such as a map of the location, safety information, or an invitation to a wrap party. It is a good idea to look over the next day's call sheet before you leave set, as long as you can do it without extending your wrap time.

ARRIVING

Breakfast

If the production offers breakfast before work, the crew is expected to come early to eat before call. It is a good idea to have a hearty breakfast. The next meal break will be at least six hours after call and often much longer. The first meal is always called breakfast, even if it is served at 4pm and is hamburgers.

Call Time

For most crew members, a 7am call means that they should be at their truck or staging area at 7. Script supervisors are expected to be on set, ready to work, at 7. That means that script supervisors have had breakfast, gone to the truck to get the day's notes and equipment, and have done enough prep to be ready for the first scene of the day. Depending on how much prep was done the night before, this means getting to set 15 to 45 minutes before call.

There are some days when I can't get to the truck before crew call. Some drivers won't open the truck before call. Sometimes the truck is parked too far

> The script supervisor is expected to be **on set, ready to work, at call**.

away from set. If I think that might happen, I take whatever equipment and notes I need for the first blocking rehearsal home with me the night before.

The Truck

On American crews, the script supervisor is on the camera truck along with the cinematographer, the digital imaging technician (DIT), camera operator, camera assistants, loader, and still photographer. If the production is small, the sound department and video assist team may be on the camera truck as well. On a huge production, or if the camera department has lots of gear, the script supervisor may travel with the production department, sometimes getting a desk or room in the same trailer as the ADs and PAs.

In England, we are on the prop truck. There, it is part of the prop department's job to provide the script supervisor with a worktable on set, just as they provide director's chairs for other crew members.

The A-camera second assistant will design the set-up of the truck and the loader will manage it day to day. Bring your gear to the truck a day before shooting starts to find your place on the truck. If you have a generous camera crew, they will give you a bit of bench to use as a desk.

> **Bring your gear** to the truck a day before shooting starts.

SETTING UP FOR THE DAY

Notes

Before call, set up your working script for the day.[1] If you are working on paper, mark the day's scenes so you can find them quickly. I clip a large, plastic coated paperclip at the top of the first page of each scene.[2] I punch the day's call sheet and put it in my book as the first page, since I refer to this page more than any other. I take the day's clean script pages from my final lined script and add them to a holding section in the back of the on-set notebook, along with enough blank forms for the day. I fill out the "taken previously" information on the daily production report and add a blank editors' log. I like to put these in the front of the notebook, right behind the call sheet. I will go to them often throughout the day so they should be very easy to find.

If something weird happens and you can't set up your book before call, at the very least grab your set book and a stopwatch. These two things are essential. Never show up on set without them.

> Never show up on set without your **set book and a stopwatch**.

Setting up your book when working digitally is basically the same, using different tools. If you are working on a PDF-based system, the day's scenes can be bookmarked, which is exactly the same as using a paperclip. A subfolder containing the day's work is useful for quick access to the day's script pages, notes, and reference material, and makes it easy to send your notes off at the end of the day. Make it a habit to have one folder with information organized by shoot day (everything that was recorded each day) and another organized according to type of note (a complete lined script and a complete set of continuity photos).

Working digitally has the benefit of keeping the day's work handy and all of your deep reference and history just a few clicks away. No more running back to the truck to get a binder when the director wants to see an old draft of the script or notes from last season's finale. Working digitally is so compact that some script supervisors don't use the truck at all. They carry everything they need in one backpack.

If your daily folder has lots of reference material and private notes, you will want a separate folder for the day's wrap notes. Set this up at the beginning of the day and you will have a ready place to export the notes for each scene as soon as it is complete. Make an email group called "daily wrap notes" or something similar with the addresses of all the people who should get your wrap notes. This list comes from the POC and will include the transfer house, editors, heads of production, the director, and others. Some applications have a feature to do this as part of their system.

As of this writing, script supervising applications are just starting to be able to share metadata with editing applications. This is likely one of the things you will have talked about with the assistant editor in preproduction. If so, include a folder for that information.

Finding Your Place in the Story

You need to be clear about what happens on today's story day as well as any action that impacts the day's scenes. Before call, I look over the day's work and any notes I may have added since preproduction to refresh my memory. I check the master breakdown for important continuity points and to remind myself of any elements that need to be matched back.

The more you know about the day's scenes and the continuity associated with it, the more valuable you will be to the production. If you have had a good prep, you will have a solid base.

Note to producers! A proper prep period for the script supervisor saves the production time and money.

Equipment

The equipment needed for paper and digital workflow is so different that I have divided this information into two sections. While reading, please keep in mind that almost no script supervisor uses exclusively one or the other. The equipment you will need will depend on which tasks you do with paper and which will be done digitally.

TOTAL PAPER WORKFLOW

I like to wear an equipment belt with a large pouch and a digital camera case. In the pouch is a second stopwatch, pencils, pens, white out tape and pen, erasers, a flashlight, and a pocket dictionary. Some script supervisors keep most of these things in a case near their chair. I find keeping everything with me saves time and makes me more mobile.

Good mobility is important. It makes it easy to speak privately with actors and crew members. If I have a question about the camera set-up or how a prop is set, I can get up and check it out myself instead of asking a question that will interrupt someone else's workflow. If, in the middle of a conversation, away from my chair, I need to check a note or photograph, I don't have to go back to my chair to get it.

Using a paper workflow has the advantage of self-sufficiency. For small productions on locations with unreliable internet service and sometimes no electricity, a paper workflow lets you work free of technical problems. Paper is the best way to start working as a script supervisor and a necessary backup system for experienced script supervisors who work digitally.

TOTAL DIGITAL WORKFLOW

There are a few situations when script supervisors are able to work at a desk all day, such as table-top and other commercials shot in a studio. Script supervisors on multi-camera live/live-to-tape shows (sitcoms, game shows, news programs, comedy reviews) usually work from a control booth. These are ideal situations for working digitally: you can be near the director and watch set while using a powerful laptop with a reliable network.

Working on a drama or comedy in a studio setting is almost as good. Your work station will move from scene to scene, sometimes set-up to set-up, but you will be out of the elements, with reliable internet and electricity. Studio sets are usually designed to have enough space for a director's monitor that will include a spot for you.

Working on location can be trickier; the more rustic the location, the harder it is to depend on electronic devices. You must plan for this sort of shoot, stockpiling extra batteries and backup drives, buying a rain shield, a tough case for your devices, and getting your equipment packages as physically small as possible.

Whatever your physical situation, your work priorities stay the same. The notes are second to your work watching set. We are not secretaries. We are film-makers. If your system takes your attention away from set, it is a bad system.

> **Our greatest value** to the production is not secretarial, it is seeing and understanding what is happening on set.

Working on location is where tablets (like the iPad) are a game changer. They are not as powerful as a laptop, and their applications can be fussy, but their size, portability, and storage capabilities make working digitally a great choice for experienced script supervisors.

See Chapter 3, "A Note about Digital Workflow," for a list of digital devices and applications that are available at this writing.

The Safety Meeting

At call, the first AD will gather the crew to go over the day's work. This is a brief meeting that will alert the crew to anything the AD thinks might help the shooting unit plan their day and work safely.

REHEARSING AND BLOCKING

Blocking and rehearsing are similar. Both are work done to develop the scene. Rehearsal is concerned with dramatic intent, while blocking is

> Blocking is concerned with **the technical elements** of the scene. The actors do not perform emotionally.

concerned only with the technical elements of the scene. A blocking is often called a "blocking rehearsal."

Private or Director's Rehearsal

Usually, the director will work privately with the actors for a bit, roughing out the scene. If the director comes to set with well-formed ideas about how to play a scene, this can take just a few minutes. If the director prefers to "find the scene" on location, the private rehearsal can take quite a long time. This happens more often when it's the first time at a new location or set.

Blocking or Blocking Rehearsal

When the director and actors have an idea about what they want from the scene, the first AD calls for a blocking rehearsal. A small group of crew members will join them—the DP, first AD, script supervisor, and sometimes the prop master. They will run through the action and dialog, feeling the physical space, finding how the space works best with the dramatic beats of the scene.

The DP will watch the blocking, imagining the best camera angles and lighting design to capture the scene. Together, the DP and director will make a plan for the coverage. They may ask the actors to adjust their action so that it works better for the camera. There will be time for more nuanced rehearsal just before the scene is shot.

Blocking for Department Heads

When the DP and director have decided on a shooting plan, the department heads as well as a few other crew members, such as the stand-ins, the boom and camera operators, the second AC, and the dolly grip come in. The actors do a blocking for them, moving through the action and saying the dialog without emotion. The second AC marks their positions and the director or first AD explains the shooting plan.

Various Blocking Styles

There is a lot of variation in blocking methods. Some directors like to decide the blocking in preproduction by making a storyboard or pre-vis.[3] If the director and the DP have made a shooting plan ahead of time, we will start the day with a blocking for department heads. The actors may or may not be present.

Other directors would never block a scene without knowing how the actors interact with the set. In contrast, Robert Altman liked to walk around and around the set in circles, all by himself, working out a plan in his head. After it was clear to him, he would share his plan with the cast and crew.

> There is a lot of **variation in blocking** methods.

The Shot List

If the DP and director have worked out the coverage before coming to set, the first AD should have a list that contains the shots they plan to make. Get a copy of that shot list. If they haven't, you should make a list on your own as you watch the blocking, and the coverage becomes clear. Don't count on the director telling you what the shots are—listen in. The first AD will be doing the same. Compare lists after the blocking to make sure you are in agreement, and nothing is missed. Present that list to the director and get their approval or make adjustments.

Either way, pay attention during the blocking as the director and DP talk about what shots they think might work. Think about how the shots will work together— how they might cut, where the 180° lines will be—ensuring that the dramatic beats will be well seen.

> Compare your notes with the first AD. **Make a shot list for the director's approval**.

However your director works, your job, during rehearsals and blocking, is to:

1. Time the scene.
2. Note any dialog (or other) changes, and make sure the changes are approved or corrected.
3. Alert crew members whose work may be affected by any changes that happen.
4. Remember where the actors are at the major moments in the dialog.
5. Make a shot list as the coverage develops.
6. Check that everything the director wants to express in the scene is covered clearly.
7. Think about what you saw in the blocking and how it might affect the continuity in this or related scenes.

The Most Current Script

Always make sure you have the most up-to-date script. If you are the only one on set with the most current changes, get a copy to the AD department so they can make more copies and distribute the changes to the cast and crew.

LIGHTING THE SET

The Crew Has the Set

When the blocking is done, the actors leave set for hair, makeup, and wardrobe. As the ADs say, "The crew has the set." This is when most of the lighting takes place. Even sets that have been pre-lit will need adjustment and refining based on the recent blocking.[4] The DP takes the lead, and the grip and electric departments have right of way on set. Our job during this time varies depending on a number of factors.

Continuity on Set

You may be needed on set to help the stand-ins remember where they should be. There may be some continuity to match with set dressing, props, effects, or light: the set dresser may need to know the time of day or date to set a clock or calendar, the window may need to be wet from the rain in a scene you haven't shot yet.

The set may be so small that it is impossible for you to be there and not be in the way. Then it is better for you to be someplace else. This is always tricky. You still need to keep track of what is happening on set. Check back from time to time. Things change as the work develops. It is a drag to come back to set and be surprised by something new that will not work with the cutting plan or time progression. A good AD can help by letting you know if there is an issue before things go too far.

> Even **when you can't be on set**, you still need to keep track of what is happening on set.

Review and Revise Your Breakdowns

This is a good time to check your continuity photos and review your breakdowns. Make sure you are current and clear about what happened (or will happen) in any scene that may affect (or be affected by) this one. If you see something that may be tricky, check in with the appropriate department. If you are nice about it, they will feel protected, not harassed.

Distribute the Shot List

If you made a shot list during the blocking, clean it up and distribute it to those who need or want one. This again varies from production to production. Ask the director who they think should have a shot list. It may go to all the department heads or just to the AD and DP. You should always keep one handy for yourself and to show the director (they will lose theirs). Mark off the shots as they are completed.

Running Lines

If an actor is having trouble remembering their dialog, offer to help them run their lines. It is less disruptive if this is done after they have been through hair, makeup, and wardrobe.

Power, Internet, Timecode, and Video Feed

This is a good time to set up your digital interface. If you will be working near the director's monitor, it should be easy to get a power outlet to power your devices, batteries, and whatever needs a charge. When that is not practical, set up a little charging station near an existing outlet.

There will probably be a few internet accounts set up for production. Get a WiFi name and password from the ADs. It is unprofessional to use bandwidth for anything other than work-related messages.

Most digital movie-making applications have a function to track timecode. Tagging media by timecode in your notes is a superpower. Follow the instructions for your specific application to sync the timecode on your device with the camera and sound departments. The timecode may be set to the time of day or elapsed production time.

You may or may not want a video feed directly into your electronic device. Some script supervisors use the video feed to save frame grabs, others feel it slows them down. If you prefer to use a video feed, work out the coordination in preproduction.

Set-Up and Roll Numbers

When you see that the camera and sound equipment is set up, check in with the second camera assistant and the sound mixer to confirm that you are all on the same camera roll and sound roll numbers. Do this before shooting every day. Now is also the best time to give them the set-up number. If you have a video assist operator, give them the set-up number too.

> Check the **camera and sound roll numbers** before shooting every day.

REHEARSAL

When lighting is complete, the actors are called back on set. Usually, they will go through the action once or twice before shooting starts. The actors will start to play the scene for emotion. There will probably be some technical adjustments as the crew adapts to slight changes in the action.

Representing the Editors

This may be the first time you see the action through the lens. Check for technical and matching problems. What are the important elements to match? Where are the most likely cut points? Which

> You **represent the editors** on set.

actors are having trouble with their dialog or action? If actors enter or exit, these actions should be clean.[5] You represent the editors on set. Imagine the media cut together and you will see if there are problems.

Overlapping Dialog

Overlapping dialog happens when more than one character talks at the same time. Overlapping dialog cannot be separated in post-production. This can become a problem when one character is on-camera and the other is off.

Here is an example: Say two characters are covered in two close-ups. Each character is mic'd when on-camera and not mic'd when off-camera. Usually this is fine. The editor will use the sound that matches the picture. But let's say these characters are having an argument. The first is trying to explain herself and the second character objects, cutting her off with overlapping dialog. If the off-camera character is not mic'd,

> Overlapping dialog becomes a problem when **one character is on-camera and the other is off**.

that dialog will be heard at a low volume, under the well-mic'd dialog of the first. This soundtrack will be unusable whenever the two voices are overlapped.

There are problems even if the off-camera character is mic'd. Now we hear both characters in nice full volume, but the relationship of the dialog is locked. Any cut we make that includes overlapping dialog needs an exact match; the two sides of the cut must agree in emotion, rhythm, accent, everything. Depending on the actor's consistency, this may or may not be possible. Even if it is possible, it is not ideal because it limits the cutting options.

The usual procedure in this situation is to run the scene a few times so that both players can find a natural rhythm to the dialog. This may happen automatically while shooting the master. When the actors have the rhythm, the off-camera actor starts or stops their dialog a few words short, leaving a quiet gap that keeps the on-camera dialog clean. When the scene is cut together, the editors use the clean dialog from both close-ups, overlapping them in post to restore the original energy and preserve the performances of the close-ups.

If the scene is too raucous for this technique, both actors are mic'd, they go at it with abandon, and the editors are left to find takes that match. This may mean using a performance that is not the first choice, cutting at a point that is not ideal, or filling in the no-good dialog with bits of ADR or dialog grabbed from other takes.[6] Thankfully, when a scene is so wild that the dialog must be overlapped, the action and coverage is usually raucous as well, and a more forgiving editing style is possible. As all things in film grammar, overlapping has a certain power and must be used appropriately.

Checking the Dialog for Accuracy and Content

During rehearsal, make sure the dialog is correct, or as correct as the director wants it to be. Some directors are strict about actors saying the dialog exactly as written. Others like to give them room to play. The first few times the actors change some dialog, let the director know, and you will get a feeling about how closely the director wants to follow the script. Be sure to let them know when dialog changes the meaning of the moment.

Make a note of any dialog that deviates from the script. If there are massive amounts of improvisation, it will be impossible to write down everything. Concentrate on getting the major beats of the ad-lib and any memorable phrases. Think about how the changes will affect all the related action.

If you are working on paper, keep your rehearsal notes very light, in pencil, or write an "R" next to them. If you are working digitally, depending on the application you are using, you can distinguish rehearsal notes by writing them

> **Think about how the changes will affect all the related action.**

in a different color, making a rehearsal layer, or recording them as private notes. It is useful to distinguish rehearsal notes because, until the scene is recorded, there is no match.

If an actor forgets a line, they will call, "Line, please," and the script supervisor will feed them the first few words of the missed line.

The Dialect Coach

If one of your actors is using a non-native accent, you may have a dialect coach on your crew. Have a short conversation with this coach to understand what the dialect issues are.

The dialect coach will make detailed notes about when and how the accent is good and bad. I like to flag the most important notes in my comment column. Usually it is just a note that says "Best for dialect" or "NG for dialect." A thumbs-up or a slight shake of the head from the dialect coach, seen from across the room, can give you immediate feedback and make it easy to include a note before moving on to the next take. Check in at the end of each set-up to get the definitive dialect notes for that set-up.

The Master Shot

Traditionally, the first set-up of a scene is a master shot. Shooting a master first helps everyone get their bearings and understand the scene as a whole, making it easier to shoot the smaller bits out of order without getting confused.

Set-Up Notes

Between rehearsal runs, if the action seems consistent, I start my notes with the two basic descriptions of the set-up. These are the "action" part of my facing pages and the "set-up" line on my lined script.

The player's action or the camera movement may change a bit from take to take as the set-up develops. This is one reason that, when working on paper, I like to use pencil instead of a pen. Notes in pencil should be dark enough to photocopy well. Using a soft lead will help with that. If you are working digitally, it is easy to make revisions.

Rehearsing on Film

Some directors like to "rehearse on film," shooting the first take with no rehearsal, while the actors are freshest. This can be useful for performance but complicated for the crew, as we have to work the scene blind, while also learning it. There will be some technically bumpy spots. That's the nature of rehearsing on film. A director, actor, or producer who complains about the bumps does not understand what rehearsing on film means and will just have to live with it. Don't feel bad; that's their problem.

> There will be some bumpy spots. That's **the nature of rehearsing on film**.

ROLLING FILM (AND OTHER MEDIA)

Going on Bells

Shooting stages are usually full of echoes. Moving anywhere on stage during a take can ruin the soundtrack and distract the actors. Production rings one long bell to let everyone know we are about to roll. Everyone who is not directly involved in capturing the shot stops working, is absolutely still and quiet until two short bells signal that the take is over and work can resume. In addition, a red light is mounted outside every door that leads to the stage. The red lights are turned on with the bells telling anyone who might have missed the bells not to open the door.

When we need quiet to rehearse, we follow the same procedure.

Where You Sit

PROXIMITY

Script supervisors are always next to the director. This is so the director can give us notes in a quiet way. I always prefer to be in the room with the actors. But this is not the script supervisor's decision. We go where the director goes, as per their preference. Most directors also prefer to be close to the actors when possible. If space is tight, we may be squeezed into a corner or under a camera. If the set is really tiny, we will be moved off set.

When the camera department trans-
mits a video feed, we may be able to get
that feed on a small handheld monitor. If
we are working on a laptop or tablet, the
feed might come right into our device.

> Script supervisors are
> always **next to the
> director**.

VIDEO VILLAGE

Some directors, especially those working with lots of cameras at once, prefer
to watch the scene from an array of monitors, one for each camera. In this
case, the prop department sets up chairs for the director and script supervisor facing the monitors. This is "video village." It can be built on or off
set. There may be additional chairs for producers, the DP, and department
heads. This assembly can get large, populated, and distracting. If the director likes a quiet work station, "video village" is mover farther away and the
"director's monitor" stays put.

WATCHING FOR THE CREW

When the set is difficult to access because of small space, restricted video
feed, or intimate action, the script supervisor becomes the eyes for the crew
members who cannot watch the action. A crew member who is closed out
should let you know that they will not be watching, and alert you to any special continuity concerns.

SILENCE

Because script supervisors are in the middle of the action, it is important
that we do our work as quietly as possible. Chatting should be minimal.
Take your cue from the director. Some directors like to have a very quiet
set, others like some liveliness. Turn your script pages quietly during a take.
Make sure all your devices are silenced.

PRIVACY

Be careful about what you say while at the
monitor. Video village has a microphone
that goes to the video playback operator,
so that you and the director can ask to see
playback. That sound may go to the operator's headphones or be broadcasted on

> What seems like a
> **private conversation** at
> the monitor is often quite
> public.

a speaker at their work station. What seems like a private conversation at the monitor is often quite public.

SLATING

History

Originally the slate was a piece of real slate, as in blackboard, with wooden clapping sticks fashioned along the top edge. The camera assistant would write the set-up information with chalk for each take. When the sticks were hit, they provided a one-frame event that the editors could use to match the picture (the frame the sticks hit) and sound (the smack of the sticks hitting). Once the sync between picture and sound was established, the picture "work print" and sound "magnetic film" (or "mag track") would be given a matching "edgecode," a series of numbers printed along the edge of the film and mag track every six inches, that could be used to keep the media in sync after the slates were cut away.

Timecode

Today we have timecode to keep the picture and sound in sync. This is an electronic code that is broadcasted and embedded in both the picture and sound. The numbers of the code tally a running time of hours, minutes, seconds, and frames. The timecode may be set to correspond with the time of day, or to start at *00:00:00:00* at the beginning of the shoot day.[7]

Now, basic slates are made of whiteboard and marker. We also use smart slates, which are whiteboards with the addition of an LED display. When the clapper bar is lifted, the LED displays the running timecode. When the board is clapped, the final timecode number pauses for a few frames, making it easier for the editors to spot. Smart slates can be programmed by the ACs to display other information about the shot after the clap, like date, scene and take number, camera roll, camera speed, etc.

As I said earlier, timecode is super useful. It is essential for taking notes on live/live-to-tape shows, and a lifesaver for pinpointing a particular moment in long takes of repeated action, or documentary-style shooting.

Some digital applications can grab timecode via WiFi. Some can even program the information on the smart slate's LED display, like the scene and take number. Other applications require you set the timecode yourself by capturing a photo of the slate and tagging the photo. Once the timecode is entered into your digital device, you can pin timecode to your notes.

If you are working on paper, you can use timecode by having a timecode reader near you. A glance at the reader will get you close enough to be very useful.

Check with the sound department to make sure the timecode has been set before you import it into your system. It is essential that the timecode is correct and synchronized among all departments (camera, sound, video assist, DIT, and script). This is known as "jamming the slate." The timecode on the slate is usually set in the morning and reset after lunch.

Phonetic Alphabet

When the camera assistant calls the set-up, the letters in set-up names are not called as single letters but as whole words, as in a military phonetic alphabet. This is so that similar-sounding letters will not be confused. A set-up named "35B" will be called as "Thirty-five bravo."

Traditionally, camera crews use the military's system, but this is not universal. Many camera departments have fun making up their own words that have something to do with their crew, location, or story.[8] You can do this as long as the words you are using distinguish each letter and it is not distracting to the actors.

Table 9.1 shows the official NATO phonetic alphabet.

Table 9.1 The NATO phonic alphabet.

A Alpha	**J** Juliette (We also use Jackson)	**S** Sierra (We also use Sam)
B Bravo (We also use Baker)	**K** Kilo	**T** Tango
C Charlie	**L** Lima	**U** Uniform (We also use Universal)
D Delta	**M** Mike (We also use Mary)	**V** Victor
E Echo	**N** November (We also use Nancy)	**W** Whiskey
F Foxtrot	**O** Oscar (We don't use O)	**X** X-ray
G Golf	**P** Papa (We also use Peter)	**Y** Yankee
H Hotel	**Q** Quebec (We also use Queen)	**Z** Zulu (We also use Zebra)
I India (We don't use I)	**R** Romeo (We also use Roger)	

Checking the Set-Up and Take Number

Look and listen for the set-up and take numbers as they are called to make sure the camera assistant has the right information on the slate and is saying it correctly. I like to get in the habit of looking at the slate before the assistant steps in front of the camera. Often you can get in a nice professional rhythm with the assistant flipping the slate toward you, just before they call it, so you can read it and give a nod of approval.

If the number is wrong, you need a way to communicate that across the set. Yelling out the number is a last resort. Most crews use a one-handed signal that makes this communication easy. In this system, the numbers 1–5 are the fingers on one hand held vertically. The numbers 6–10 are the same fingers held horizontally. Zero is an "o" made with the thumb and forefinger. Only using one hand is a big advantage, as you usually don't have to put things down to signal.

> Most crews use an easy, **one-handed signal** to communicate about numbers.

Calling the Slate

When it is time to start shooting, the first AD will call "Picture's up!" then "Rolling!" The sound mixer will call "Speed!" when their recorder is ready. Then the second camera assistant will call the slate number, and get a nod from the first camera assistant as the camera reaches speed. On the East Coast, on the first take of each set-up, the second camera assistant will call the set-up name, the take number, say "Mark!" and clap the slate. After that, they will call the take number only, say "Mark!" and clap the slate. On the West Coast, the second camera assistant will only say "Mark!" for all takes, and clap the slate.

The prevailing opinion on the West Coast is that all that talking is inelegant—it clutters up the dailies and is not necessary since the sound mixer pre-slates each take. On the other hand, many assistant editors find the extra information in the East Coast method to be a helpful safety net. If I am working with a mixed coast crew, I ask the assistant editor if they have a preference for calling the slate and try to talk the camera crew into supplying what the editors want.

> I ask the assistant editor which slating system they prefer and try to talk the camera crew into supplying that.

If you are working with a smart slate that includes this information after the clap, or digital files that include the information as metadata, calling the slate is not so important. On a low-tech production, the editors usually prefer the East Coast style. Audio pre-slates are often trimmed off the takes.

Tail Slates

A tail slate is just what it sounds like, a slate recorded at the end of a take instead of the beginning. Tail slates are used when a slate can't be clapped at the start: if there is no room in a tight frame, if the camera is too far away at the beginning of a crane shot, if the camera starts underwater, or after a long pre-action. Tail slates are also used to correct a mistake made in a head slate. The tail slate is held upside down so that it isn't confused with a head slate for the next take.

> The tail slate is **held upside down** so that it isn't confused with a head slate for the next take.

Correcting a Mis-Slate

If there is time, a mis-slate that has already been recorded is corrected on camera. To do this the AC will slate again, holding their hand over the slate. The hand is taken away as the camera rolls, revealing the corrected information. Another way to show that a slate is a correction is for the AC to point to the specific information that has changed on the slate as the camera rolls. This should be noted on your facing page as a corrected slate. If there is no time to correct it on camera, make a note in the comments column on your facing page that says, for example, "mis-slated as take 2."

MOS Slates

An MOS take has picture but no sound. There is a common story behind the abbreviation that says it came from the influx of German filmmakers in Hollywood just as movies were starting to record sound: the Germans would say "Mit out sound" which was shortened to "MOS." Really, the term MOS started because sound was originally recorded on the side of the film negative as a black-and-white optical strip. MOS was short for "Minus optical sound." The joke about the Germans was so good that it stuck.

An MOS shot is slated on a traditional slate with the AC's hand covering the sticks or holding the slate by the top stick only, showing that the sticks will not be hit. A smart slate for an MOS shot is held by the top stick, open, so that the metadata runs on the display. "MOS" should also be written on the whiteboard and/or programmed into the display on a smart slate.

Slating Multiple Cameras

If there is more than one camera shooting, each camera will be named before the mark, as in "A-mark" and slap, "B-mark" and slap. If it is unusual on your project that only one camera is running, the assistant may say "A-camera only. Mark," and slap.

When more than one camera is looking in the same direction, they may be clapped at the same time with the same slate. This is called a "common slate." Each camera will be given a separate camera ID ahead of time, similar to an MOS slate, picture only, no sound. When it is time to record the take, one slate with the names of the common cameras written on it will be hit. The AC will call it as "Common mark!" and clap, or if there are some cameras that are common and some not, the AC will name the cameras, "A and D, common mark!" and slap.

> Common slate: When more than one camera is **looking in the same direction**, they may be clapped at the same time with the same slate.

Pick-Up Slates

Sometimes a director will want to shoot just part of a set-up. Usually this is after a few takes that are good except for one section of the action. In this case, the crew will do a pick-up of the take.

Some script supervisors make this a new set-up. I don't. Editors tell me it is useful to know that this media is the same set-up as the original, and therefore does not provide another coverage choice. In my preferred system, if we have five full takes, then shoot a pick-up, that new take is called "Take six, pick-up." The take is written as "6PU" on the slate and in my facing pages. I mark a pick-up on my lined script whenever it starts or ends at a different time than the rest of the takes. See the line for set-up 53A in Fig. 6.3 (page 118) for an example.

Hand Slates

Once in a great while, you shoot a take when there is no slate. Maybe the slate is broken, can't be found, or is miles away. When there is no other choice, an inventive AC, AD, or actor can make do with just their hands.

The take number is shown by how many fingers are held up to camera. If there is sound, the impromptu slater can voice "Take five!" and clap their hands in front of the lens. This gives the editors something to go on. It shows where the new take starts, gives it a take number and maybe even a frame where picture and sound can be put in sync. It is not ideal, but a hand slate is way better than nothing. The most helpful hand slate will be a clap that moves side-to-side in relation to the lens so that the camera can see the exact moment the hands meet.

NOTATING TIMECODE

Most digital workflow applications can automatically sync timecode to your notes. If you're working with digital camera files and a pen and paper workflow, timecode is still really valuable.

If you are shooting straight to a digital file, the editors may ask for a notation of the timecode at the clap. I note that code as the first entry in the comments column on my facing page. I find it helps to write down the hours and minutes on the code a bit ahead, and fill in the seconds at the moment of the clap. I don't bother with the frames.

Notating timecode can be very helpful during documentary style shooting or long takes of repeated action to pinpoint a particular moment in the middle of the action. On *Life of Pi*, we had takes that lasted 30 minutes or more. By writing down the timecode when something interesting happened or when Ang liked a moment of performance, the editors were able to get to it quickly. See Fig. 6.12 on page 131 for an example of using timecode with a paper workflow.

> Timecode can be very helpful to pinpoint a particular moment in **a long run of the action**.

To note timecode, you will need to see the timecode during the take. It is possible to display the timecode on the monitors. If that is too distracting to the director, you need to do something else. Sometimes the video playback operator can give you a dedicated monitor or the camera department may have an extra slate that can be jammed to sync and placed within easy view. If you have a smartphone, there are apps that can be jammed and will display a timecode in sync.

TIMING THE TAKE

We time the take from the director's "Action!" to "Cut!" There are situations when you need to time something within a take as well: the duration of a dolly or crane move, a bit of action that has to work with a pre-recorded piece of sound, some action from another scene or location. You can use the split timing on your stopwatch or device to temporarily freeze the numbers on its display. Record that time, and when you hit the split timing button again, the watch will go back to the running time that has continued even as the readout was stopped. Of course, your watch or device must be completely silent.

FIRST SHOT OF THE MORNING

Note the time of day as the first "Action!" is called. The second AD (or DGA trainee) will want to know this right away, so they can call it into the office. I jot down the time at the top of whatever script page I am on so I don't have to leave that page as we are starting to shoot. When the take is over, I record it on my script supervisor's daily report.

NOTES FOR EACH TAKE

Mark dialog misses or changes in the scripted dialog with a small number to note the set-up and take. Mark important action or variations of action on the set-up's line on the lined script, with a small number noting the take. Here's where your private matching notes mentioned in Chapter 6, starting on page 185, become useful. Use layers or private notes if you have those options in your digital workflow.

In the comments column of your facing page, mark any important distinction of this particular take. Was there any dialog that was skipped, mangled, or repeated? Was there any action that happened at a different time or in a different way?

Think of what the editors may want to know: for instance, if there was a false start (usually noted as "FS") that explains an unusually short or long running time for the take.

Think about what the director will want to remember: for instance, this take is particularly good for a certain section of dialog. I use a star to note a favorite take in general and also for a specific section that the director really likes. The star stands out from a page of letters, making it easy to see what the favorites are in a quick glance. If you have numbered the dialog lines or dialog sections, it easy to be specific by writing: "Best for lines 34–46" or "NG for dialog 5."

CIRCLED TAKES

When I started as a script supervisor, every movie was shot on film. All the film stock we exposed was developed, but only selected takes were printed. When a director wanted a take to be printed, that take's number was circled on the facing page (and editors' log). This was a very important distinction, as the negative would be divided into the A-roll, the footage to be printed and used, and the B-roll, the footage to be put in deep storage. It was a big deal to dig up some footage from the B-roll, and there was no way, other than our notes, to tell what was on an unprinted take.

Those days are mostly over. Even projects that are shot on film are transferred to video instead of printed as work print. Usually it is cheaper to transfer everything than to start and stop the transfer for selected takes. Now all takes are available for review, making the careful noting of circled takes much less critical.

I still circle takes, though. The notation is useful to highlight the director's preferred takes. I have added a couple of other notations to the circle, since the old "print" or "no print" distinction has lost its meaning. I make a slash on the bottom right of the take number, a sort of quarter circle, on the takes that the director kind of likes. You can use a comma if you use a keyboard. This is a take that is not preferred at the moment, but later may be. If that does happen, I extend the slash the remaining three-fourths to make it a circled take. I note a star, as I've said, on the very favorite takes. Sometimes the star also serves to mark which takes will be shown in dailies. Sometimes I use a double circle for this (see Figs 6.10 and 6.34 as examples). If a take is no good (usually marked as "NG") include why it is NG. If it is NG for picture, it still may be good for sound and vice versa.

> Circle takes to highlight the **director's preferred takes**.

LENS INFORMATION

When we have shot a few takes and the director and DP seem happy with the technical set-up, it is time to fill in the lens information on the facing page. Look for a moment between takes when the second assistant camera person is not busy.

The second assistant keeps a book with notes about each set-up: the lens's focal length, aperture, focus distance, the camera height, and filters, if there are any. If the set-up will be used as part of a visual effect composite, the exact degree of the camera's tilt will be noted. If there is anything unusual about the camera speed or shutter opening there will be a note for that too. Some assistants prefer to tell you the information between takes, some like to hand off the book at the end of each set-up. I do whatever they like.

CONTINUITY PHOTOS

How to Think about Continuity Photos

It is a good idea to take a wide photo of the set from the camera angle of the master shot.[9] This gives you an overview that could contain information not in any of the captured footage. Do this before the first take, if the scene has been worked out. If your production usually makes some adjustments during the first few takes, wait until the scene has settled in.

Most digital devices can accept the camera feed, either by WiFi or cable. If you are set up for that, grab frames during the action when you need to document some detail within the action. If you are working on paper, you can take a picture of the image on the monitor. It will not be the best quality, but if the image is not too dark it can show basic framing and blocking. Make sure your camera is silent.

I try to get at least one full body photo of each "look" of each character, then another picture if something has changed, or when a detail becomes important.[10] I take pictures to record the actors' positions on set, any tricky costume or hair situation, and for the positions of important set dressing and props. If there is a fight, stunt, or another unpredictable action, I take a photo at the end of each take to record how everything landed. This could include set dressing, props, makeup, hair, costume, or whatever is in play. Again, a wide overview may give you more information than the captured footage, making it easier to reconstruct a matched moment. All departments should know how the scene starts. You will usually have a better view of what happens during the scene.

Organizing Your Pictures

Whatever application you are using to organize your continuity photos, title your photos by scene number. Add *000*s as placeholders (for example, *Sc. 003*), and your photos will automatically sort in scene order in any application. Depending on your project, you may also want to include the story day. Check the box that says *Use title* when you are exporting, so that these new names will be what the photos are called.

If you are working digitally, title your pictures right away. If you are working on paper and using a separate device to take pictures, use a device that lets you write the scene number on the image. If you can't do that, you will need a system to remember which scene (and sometimes take) each picture reflects. Take a picture of the scene number at the start of each scene. This can be a picture of the slate or a close-up of the scene heading in your book. Export your photos sorted by capture time, and your pictures will line up after your scene notation.

Continuity pictures can be included as part of your daily production folder. Back them up on a separate device in a folder that contains all the pictures for the project.

Most digital applications have the ability to include continuity photos on a page along with the script notes. This is helpful in some situations. They are great for commercial production reports, which are often glossy presentations made with the agency and clients in mind. They can be useful for explaining dramatic moments that are better defined by pictures than words. As a rule, feature editors would rather not have continuity photos embedded in the facing pages and editors' daily logs. Feature editors know the footage, so for them, the photos are clutter.

Digital Capture and the Crew

The ability to capture digital photos and camera feed presents choices that we script supervisors need to make. I know one script supervisor that records the video feed of every take, and selects a few frames to keep as continuity photos. I know another that will not accept the video feed because that is someone else's job and feels that it distracts her from doing her more important work. Another records frame grabs for herself but will not share them. All these choices are legitimate and depend on your crew and the nature of your project.

For a simple project with a small non-union crew, like a student movie or internet project, a script supervisor may be the logical person to double up as the video recorder. This is not appropriate for a professional, fully staffed production, which demands more of your script supervising skills.

However you decide to play this, remember that your job is not to record the frame, but to see and understand the frame. Sometimes recording the frame can help you see it, sometimes it takes time away from that more important task.

DRAWING SET-UP FRAMES

I draw my set-up frames anytime I have a moment. If the set-up is very complicated, full of camera moves or lots of characters coming and going, I draw something very rough and wait until the set-up is finished to make more detailed frames. I look for a moment when no one else needs the video playback and ask the operator to play back the favorite take for me, stopping and starting so I can draw each important configuration. If you are working digitally, it is easy to make adjustments and add details to your set-up frames as your understanding becomes more detailed; even better if you are working in layers.

WHAT TO LOOK AT

One of the most difficult skills of our job is to know when and where to look during a take. We need to follow the dialog, watch the action (often of many people at once), and make notes on the page, all at the same time. Some takes have two or more cameras looking in different directions. You can't always do everything at once. Knowing what the most important elements of the set-up are will help you see what you need. If it is essential that the dialog is exact, put your attention there. If you think there will be a lot of critical cutting, make sure the matching works at those points. This is where your understanding of the language of filmmaking comes into play. The more you know about filmmaking, the better you will be at this.

> Knowing what are the **most important elements** of the set-up will help you see what you need.

Some directors will want all dialog to be said exactly as written. Others are fine with any dialog as long as the story points are hit. Know what is important to your director and make sure you have that covered.

Some script supervisors can memorize dialog. That, of course, is a big help. I can't. I tend to split my looks between the written dialog and the action on set, making notes without looking at my writing. I have to clean up some notes after, but it is worth it to me. If the dialog is so fast and complicated that I can't write notes during a take, I will make a dash in the exact place in the dialog, along that set-up's line, and bend one finger for each note. That way, at the end of the take I know I have a certain amount of things I need to remember and will find a dash on the page for every one of them. I write these notes between takes.

> If ad-libbing is extreme, **treat the scene like a documentary** shoot.

Tracking everything is easier if the actors are consistent. If there are a number of actors ad-libbing dialog and action, you just can't get everything down. If ad-libbing is extreme, you have to treat the scene like a documentary shoot. Listen for the general trend of the ad-lib and any standout phrases. Note in which take a new trend is introduced and when it works well. I will look more often than usual at my page if I have to write this much.

NOT MATCHING WELL

In a situation of major ad-libbing, the action and dialog will not match very well. That's OK, as long as everyone acknowledges this, and the set-ups provide the sort of coverage that will let the scene be cut together. Make sure to shoot singles and clean cut-away shots that the director will actually want to use. A second camera getting closer reaction shots of principle players can buy a lot of freedom from matching. Keep in mind that continuity only matters on the cut.

> **Singles and clean cut-away shots** are helpful for scenes that have major ad-libbing.

Make notes of things you know, not what you guess. A few unreliable notes will discredit dozens of good ones. If you want to leave a clue to some situation you aren't sure of, make sure to add some "??" to flag it for the editors. This is not good form for traditionally shot scenes, but when the ad-libs are too chaotic for you to do the proper research, it is the best you can do, and better than nothing.

DELIVERING OFF-CAMERA DIALOG

Sometimes a set-up will be shot when one of the off-camera actors is not present. The script supervisor may be asked to read the absent actor's lines. This is no problem on a master-only scene or if the off-camera dialog is minimal. When there is lots of off-camera dialog and complicated, critical matching, it is OK to ask if someone else can read the dialog.

People sometimes forget how much script supervisors do during a take. I once worked for a director who didn't like my off-camera performance. It drove me crazy. I talked to him after, and he was shocked to realize that I was not just reading the dialog, but also doing my full job at the same time.

GIVING NOTES TO ACTORS, DIRECTORS, CREW MEMBERS

Deciding when to give notes can be tricky. Some actors like to hear dialog corrections early, before they have fully refined their performance. Others start with subtext, circling in on the text, and will want to be specific about the dialog only after they get close to the right performance.

Directors vary in their work styles, too. Some don't want to think about the details until the big issues are solved. Others will hate to have an adjustment thrown at them late in the game. Try what you think is best, pay attention, and adjust until it feels right.

One hard rule, however, is to never assume you can give notes to the actors directly. If an actor has missed some dialog or action, tell the director. The director will decide if the miss is important and if this is a good time to tell the actor.

> **Never assume** you can give notes to the actors directly.

After you have forged a strong and trusting relationship with the director, they may give you the authority to give notes to the actors as you see fit. Even then, I will always check in with my director before approaching the actor, saying something simple like, "I have a matching note for Phil." This gives the director a chance to stop you if they feel the time is not good.

The relationship between actor and director is complex and intimate. A good script supervisor will help maintain and protect that relationship. I have at times been the fall guy in front of an actor so that the director doesn't look bad. The director should quietly acknowledge that this happened, and your relationship should not become abusive.

Giving notes to other crew members is different. Almost always, sooner is better. Hold back if they are working something out; however, if there is a mistake in a prop, costume, etc., don't delay in talking to the responsible person. No one wants to have a good take blown because something under their responsibility wasn't right. Be polite, of course. Don't call out across the set. Get out of your chair, go and talk to them using a soft and respectful tone. I often ask them if they have noticed whatever it is that I think is wrong. Sometimes there is a good reason for the mismatch, a reason that is also best explained privately.

Never ever call cut. No matter what is happening. The hard rule is to wait until after the take to tell the director what went wrong. If you have a tight working relationship with the director, and you are in a very long take where the problem is being repeated, you can catch the director's eye to indicate there is a problem. It is up to them to ask you what the problem is.

The only exception to this is for a take that has a dangerous or one-time-only action, when a building is going to blow up, or many vehicles will be in a crash. If something is out of continuity at the start of a set-up like that, tell the director while there is still time to stop the explosion. Even here, don't yell cut.

MOVING ON TO THE NEXT SET-UP

Before You Move On

WHAT YOU NEED FROM THE SCENE

While shooting any set-up, be mindful of what that set-up needs to accomplish. What factual information must the scene deliver? What dramatic points need to be hit? If the director has asked for an alternative performance or camera variation, make sure you have it before moving on.

TV AND AIRPLANE DIALOG

As was explained in Chapter 3, some projects need alternate dialog to play on airplanes and in some television markets. In these takes, adult language will be replaced with soft curses or other alternate words. An ID of "TV" will be added to the take number, for example, "take 8TV." Some projects will fulfill this requirement by recording the new dialog as wild track only. Add the TV notation in the description of this wild track.

Wild track for TV coverage may be recorded after the take or after the scene is completed. It is easier to get a good match if this alternate is recorded before the crew moves on to the next set-up. Your producer will know what you need to deliver, but you have to track it and remind the first AD at the right time. If a set-up needs an alternate take and you can't get it on set, make a note in the facing pages and on the owed list.

Getting and Distributing Information

When the director is satisfied with the takes for this set-up, the first AD will call "Moving on!" Before the director gets too involved with the next set-up, make sure you have their notes for the work that you have just completed. Which takes are circled? Is there a favorite? If the scene was played with variations, which one should we match?

The second camera assistant will want to know which takes are circled so they can be marked on the camera report. You can do this verbally, or you can take a camera report for each roll, drive, or card and circle the takes on the report yourself. Some assistants put the lens information on the camera report, and you will use that to fill in the lens column on your facing pages.

The sound department will need the circled takes too. Some sound mixers will take the information themselves, some have their cable person do it. The video playback operator will want to know the circled takes and, if there is one, the favorite take.

The camera assistants and the sound mixer should tell you every time they change a roll or drive. These are important notes for both the facing pages and editors' daily log.

Completing Your Notes

While the set is being prepared for the next set-up, I check over my notes for the last set-up and complete whatever is not done. Most commonly this includes cleaning up my facing pages, filling out the editors' daily log, updating my final lined script, and checking off the shot list. If we are shooting elements for a visual effect composite, I will line those boards now.

> Take a moment to imagine the new footage cut into the movie.

I take a moment to think like an editor and imagine the new footage cut into the movie. There is often a new detail that I need to track, adjusting my breakdowns to stay current.

Prep for the Next Shot

Preparing for the second set-up of a scene is a bit different from prepping for the first. There is now action and dialog to match. Think about where the possible, and the most likely, cut points will be. What is necessary to match and what is not?

Very often something happens in the first set-up that increases your understanding of a story point or character. When this happens, small details in other scenes are revealed as more significant elements in the narrative. Take a moment to adjust your understanding of the story and make a note on the affected scene to remind you later.

Turning Around

In a traditionally lit set, there will be a general lighting plan for all the coverage of a scene. The lighting will usually be adjusted for each set-up. Set-ups that are seen from similar angles need less adjustment than those that look in the opposite direction. Because of this, after the master, we traditionally shoot all the coverage in one direction, then turn the camera around and shoot all the coverage in the opposite direction.

Turning around and relighting the set takes time. Once you turn around you don't want to go back. Therefore, it is important that all the set-ups looking in the first direction are complete and satisfying before the work of turning around starts. Anticipate the turn around and check your shot list to make sure you are getting everything you need before the AD calls, "Turning around!"

> Once you turn around **you don't want to go back**.

Because relighting for the turn around takes time, this is a good chance for script supervisors to do some work that takes more time than we usually have between set-ups. It may be incorporating the changes that happened on set into the script as shot, backing up photographs, revising a break-down, or going to the truck to get something you will need later. It is also a good time to get a cup of coffee or go to the bathroom. Make sure to tell an AD or PA whenever you leave the set.

MOVING ON TO THE NEXT SCENE

When the director is satisfied with all the takes and set-ups for the current scene, the AD will announce that the crew is moving on to the next scene. We script supervisors do the usual things that we would do after every set-up is complete, plus a few more.

We check the shot list to make sure all the planned coverage has been taken. Sometimes insert or cut-away shots are saved for a second unit shooting crew. If there are shots like this, add them to your owed list. This could include wild track like TV dialog, off-camera dialog, special sound elements, or atmospheric sounds.

Besides completing the notes as we do after each set-up, we also credit the scene, master time, and pages count. Depending on your workflow, this may be recorded directly on your script supervisor's daily report or in your scene information, to be exported as part of your daily report as it is generated.

The master time for each scene is different from the running time of the master shot. A scene's master time is how long we think that scene will run if it is cut for pace and all the dramatic beats are included. Sometimes this is as simple as trimming the extra time off the head and tail of the master shot. Other times, you have to drop time for shoe leather. An example of this is a wide shot of someone walking all the way across the street, up the steps, and then ringing a doorbell. This sort of shot will usually be

> **A scene's master time** is how long we think that scene will run, cut for pace, with all the dramatic beats included.

cut short, to a closer shot at the door. If you have no master shot in a scene, add together the sub-masters, using the takes that are most likely to be used for each leg of the action, keeping the pace of your project in mind.

LUNCH

Lunch is the first meal break of the shooting day, whatever the hour. When lunch is called, note the time of day. The crew's meal penalties will be calculated according to your record. Make sure your time of day is accurate.

Most productions require a lunch report, which is a summary of the production's progress in the first half of the day. Some production departments will have a form they will want you to fill out. You can also make your own. Many digital applications have a function that automatically tallies selected information into a lunch report and will email that report when prompted. Check with the POC in prep to find out what information the production wants on the lunch report. Usually it is a list of how many scenes, pages, set-ups, and how much master time was shot, as well as the time of the first shot and the time of day that lunch was called.

When you start shooting again after lunch, note the first "PM shot" in your script supervisor's daily report.

THROUGHOUT THE DAY

Comb through Your Story

A sophisticated movie story has thousands of meaningful beats. Some are so tiny they can be easily overlooked. If a script supervisor keeps reviewing the action on the written page as well as how it develops on set, they can be a big help in tracking and recording these little beats.

Reloading the Camera

One of the worst things that can happen on set is when the film, drive, or card runs out in the middle of a wonderful take. The second AC (and/or the DIT) tracks the progress through each load and replaces the magazine or drive before this can happen. Your timing of each take can help. Besides timing every rehearsal and take, pay attention to the pre-roll and end roll. The assistant will ask you, "How long does this run?" Answer with the longest time you have, and add ". . . action to cut" as a qualifier. Also mention if the head or tail rolls are running particularly long.

Film Break

Sometimes we will send the morning's work to the lab or transfer house before the end of the shooting day. We call this a film break. The camera and sound reports must be complete before the media leaves the set. You should hear that a film break is coming well ahead of the fact, so you have time to complete the necessary paperwork. You do not want to be checking the camera and sound reports at the same time you are shooting a new set-up.

If you are working digitally, you will email or post the in-progress editors' log, so the lab will have those notes when they receive the media.

Notating Playback

Make sure to identify any playback that is used in a scene. This could be a song played by a band or on a radio, pre-recorded off-camera dialog, a picture on a TV, or a rhythm track that actors will use as a guide while shooting. Most likely there will have been different versions prepared, so get all the identifying information the editors will need to find the exact material. This could include the name of the piece, its writer and performer, what take or what section of the piece was heard or seen. If different versions are used throughout the day, note when the changes were made.

False Starts and Series Takes

When something goes wrong in a take, the director may ask the actors to start again. If this happens before any dialog has been spoken, it is a false start. Note "FS" at the start of your comments column on the facing page. If you cut camera, that is the entire notation. If you keep the take running, and the next try works, add "+ full take" so that the note reads, "FS + full take." This is one full take that also includes a false start. The timing of this take will be longer than the others.

If the director asks the actors to repeat all or part of the action more than once, without cutting camera, this is a series take. There will be one take number for all the action. A subset of numbers will be added in the "Comments" column, one for each time the action starts again. This includes a new series number for parts of the action and any subsequent false starts. If you need to make a matching note on a series take, use a decimal. The third pass of take five would be noted as take 5.3.

If the take is long with multiple starts, a series notation will not be accurate enough. Use timecode to pinpoint the start of each new pass. If timecode is not available, take the time from your stopwatch and note how much time has elapsed since action was called.

WRAP

The work at the end of the day is similar to the work at lunch, with a few additional tasks.

Immediate Concerns

When the first AD calls "That's a wrap!" note the time of day in your script supervisor's daily report. Catch the director before they leave set to get the prints for the last set-up and any last notes for the editor. Next, get the last camera and sound reports. The camera and sound departments will need their circled prints before they can wrap. The sooner you can get those to them, the better.

End of the Day Notes

Clean up your facing pages, complete your editors' daily log, and add the day's progress to the script supervisor's daily production report. All these notes are needed immediately.

If your lined script can be ready to go in a few minutes, finish that. If scenes need to be rewritten to include changes that happened on set, that work can be done off set and handed in with tomorrow's notes. The goal at wrap is to get the truck packed and the notes handed in as soon as possible.

If you are working in a digital workflow, this is your big payoff. Check the day's wrap notes folder to make sure everything is there and complete. You can email your daily notes or post them to the cloud with one click.

If you are working on paper, the notes have to be scanned or copied. I always do this myself. It is very rare that I hand off my originals to someone else.

There are many scanning programs that will work with a smartphone. Look for one that will square the perspective and take out the shadows. You will have to shoot your notes page by page and the cleanup process can take some time, so if you can, do this throughout the day after each page is complete.

If you are working in a total paper workflow, you will need to photocopy your notes. There will probably be a copy machine on set with the PAs. If not, you may have to go to the production office. Make a copy of everything, hand the copies to the POC, and keep your originals. The POC will distribute the editors' log to the film lab or transfer house, the daily report to production, and everything to the edit room.

Dailies

Selected takes will be processed, color corrected by the DP, and posted online. The POC will get you a link and a password that will allow you to see them. During the shoot, I watch the set more than the monitor, so seeing dailies is always informative. Watching dailies is work done off the clock, but I always try to make time.

A few productions still screen the dailies at the end of the shooting day. If your project will have a theatrical release, it is informative to see the media projected on a big screen. The ritual of the crew sitting together and reviewing the group effort builds cohesion within the crew and is especially valuable when shooting on location.

> **Seeing dailies is always informative.**

Homework

It is customary for script supervisors to get one hour of paid homework each day, off set. This is time spent finishing the day's notes, incorporating changes into the script and breakdowns, planning and setting up for the next day's work.

When you arrive on set the next morning, you should be up to date with your notes and breakdowns, and be ready to start the new day's work.

THE END OF THE JOB
Final Notes
Although you have turned in your notes day by day, you will send in a whole, completed, final book at the end of a shoot.

On a feature, script supervisors get at least one day to clean up our notes and distribute the final book. If production has been a wild ride, you should be able to get more time to sort things out. Your final book contains the final lined script, facing pages, script supervisor's daily reports, editors' daily logs, and whatever breakdowns may be useful in post-production. Talk to the assistant editor to find out how they have been working with your notes and organize your final book in folders however they like it. The POC will give you a list of people who should be in the last group email or posting.

If you are working on paper, your book must be scanned or copied. Production will tell you what format they want to use in post-production. Usually, the editors get the original book and one copy, the post-production coordinator gets a copy, and I keep a copy for myself. The continuity photos are exported to thumb drives and handed in with each script. I keep a copy of those as well.

Hang Out with the Editors
If your editors are game, it is a great idea to spend a little time in the edit room, especially when you are starting out. You will get a better idea of what happens to your notes after they leave you, and see some of the technical problems they deal with when the media is not perfect. If this is impossible during the shooting schedule, try to go after principal production. Bring nice snacks to show your appreciation.

NOTES
1   The difference between a working script and a final script is shown in Chapter 6 on pages 176–185.

2   If you like to work with a book that has only the day's pages, you will need to find and pull those pages.

3   A "pre-vis," short for "pre-visualization," is an animated storyboard. It shows the set, action, blocking, camera position, angle, lens, and a rough timing of a scene or sequence. It is used to work out the details of production in advance so action that is expensive to shoot can be designed in the most economical way.

4 To "pre-light" a set is to rough in the lighting before the blocking.

5 A clean entrance starts on a moment of empty frame. A clean exit holds on an empty frame for a beat after the actor leaves.

6 ADR (additional dialog recording) is when an actor is recorded, usually during post-production, as they watch the cut scene and recreate their dialog, or sometimes perform new dialog.

7 A timecode reading *09:15:30:10* shows a time of approximately 9:15am. Do not use the timecode as the official time of day in your production report. It is not always correct.

8 For an extreme example of made-up slate calls, see the compilation slates from *Inglourious Basterds* on YouTube.

9 This should be a series of photos, if the camera is moving.

10 A "look" is a continuous design of costume, hair, and makeup. Each department will be tracking the details of their work. If they are present and doing their job, you will be their safety net only. Glance at your picture whenever an actor comes back to an established look.

Chapter 10
The Big Picture

Here are a few unrelated but important points before I wrap up.

PICK YOUR PROJECTS, FOLLOW YOUR LEADER

A film crew is a crazy combination of opposites, a group of artists, free-thinkers, and entrepreneurs who willingly fall into a tight chain of command and follow their leader: the film's director. We work long, harsh hours in extreme physical conditions. It is not uncommon for us to work to the point of exhaustion. To do this and have a happy life, we must know why we are there and remember it.

The work is interesting, for sure. Some directors are an inspiration and some companies are a joy to work with. Still, near the end of a 15-hour day, in a 70-hour week, the urge to grumble becomes almost unavoidable. It is important to fight this as best you can. Spending long hours with a crabby crew is torture. Don't contribute to a bad atmosphere. If you are working for the money, count it up and think about how it will make your life better. If you are there because you believe the project is likely to be a cinematic beauty, imagine how proud you will be when it plays. Make deals you can live with and take responsibility for those decisions. Don't let the production company change the contract mid-job.

Before you make your deal, do some research about the producers and production manager on the project. A few calls to crew members who have worked with them will tell you if they are trustworthy and supportive of crew or not. Say yes to the good ones. This will not only be good for the current work, but can lead to more good work in the future.

If you find yourself on project after project that makes you unhappy, consider finding a new position. Use your connections you've made on set to see what's available. Maybe there's another position on the crew that suits you better. Maybe you should work off set. It's possible you will be happier with a job outside the film industry.

As I write this, our industry is in an important conversation about how to regulate our working conditions to be less punishing, dangerous, and unhealthy. It is too early to know how that will work out. I encourage you to join this conversation and do whatever you can to improve working conditions.

ACTORS ARE ANGELS

In your work as a script supervisor, you will come across touchy actors: actors who need absolute quiet, actors who freak out when given a note, actors who make it difficult for you to do your job as the director is asking you to do it. It's hard to know how to deal with people like this.

My recommendation? Take an acting class. Take a bunch of acting classes. Actors work with the crew, but the kind of work they do is very different from ours. Even the most community-minded, the ones with the most gracious set presence, need something we crew people don't need. Their job is, more or less, to bare their souls. And that work is the reason we love movies.

In real life, it is rare to see what makes people tick. An actor's job is to show us exactly that. It is scary to be emotionally visible, but accomplished actors have figured out how to do this every day. Trying to do it yourself is the best way to understand a little about that. Once you get what this feels like, you will be able to recognize when you can approach an actor and when you should wait for a better moment. I cannot overstate the importance of this.

WORKING OUTSIDE AND WITHIN TRADITIONAL STUDIO STRUCTURE

At some point, most professional projects are pitched to a studio, network, or streaming company. Usually, a writer, director, or producer pitches a project to one of these companies. If the company takes the project, they finance it, own, and control it, becoming the legal author of the project. The original filmmakers keep very little control.

The more developed a pitched project is, the better chance it has to survive the studio process intact.[1] This dynamic is a powerful incentive for making projects as complete as possible before looking for a corporate partner.

Micro-budget spec projects, shot with a small crew, can be a valuable component for the pitch. These independent, pre-studio projects are great opportunities for new script supervisors to practice their skills in a low-risk atmosphere. Transitioning from training work to professional work can be tricky.

Below the Line Crew: Transitioning into the Studio System

Working on a film crew, even for free—especially for free—gives you a heady feeling of solidarity. Everyone makes the movie, everyone's work is appreciated. Once a studio is involved, all that can change.

Studios, networks, and streaming corporations are structured to recognize individual filmmakers, not teams. Writers, directors, producers, and sometimes lead actors are recognized by the studios as creative leaders, referred to in the business as "above the line." Script supervisors are not in this category. We are considered "below the line," not creative leaders. No matter how much we have contributed to the development of a specific project, our time and work investment will not pay off for us like it might for above the line filmmakers. If that project gets financed by a studio, we will most likely be replaced by a script supervisor with more experience.

This doesn't mean that this work is not worth doing. The work will help you build skills, experience, and your professional reputation. But protect yourself. Don't assume that your investment in a project will be returned—unless it is in writing. Even if your project gets studio financing, the attached above the line filmmakers may not have the power or control to bring any crew members with them.

You can help your chances by building your individual professional legitimacy. Diversify your work partners and experiences. This will strengthen your professional reputation, introduce you to more people making movies, and give you more possibilities of work.

Working Independently of the Studio System

Easy access to digital filmmaking equipment is opening up some exciting new possibilities for financial models that skip the studio system altogether. Independent producers and filmmaking collectives are experimenting with crowdfunding, independent branding, fan-based patronage, and selling subscriptions to superfans. It is too early to know where this is going, but it may soon be possible to be part of a filmmaking collective that is structured something like a small press or niche business and skip the corporate gatekeepers altogether.[2]

CHANGING PRODUCTION DYNAMICS

Smartphones: Everyone Makes Movies

Most of us have a movie camera in our pocket. And we use it. We make and watch moving pictures all day long, capturing things we want to remember, sending visual notes to friends and relatives. Film literacy is becoming as fundamental to our culture as reading and writing. This is a wonderful development, making it possible for more diverse voices (aesthetically as well as experientially) to be heard. For professional filmmakers, fewer technical and financial barriers means more time to develop a personal aesthetic or a specific project.[3]

Balancing Filmmaking and Data Management

As motion picture literacy is becoming more central to our culture, professional movies are using more complicated, experimental, and expressive film grammar. To keep up, script supervisors need a deeper, more nuanced and creative understanding of the language of filmmaking. At the same time, the switch to digital filmmaking has added so much data management to our craft that our more important work as filmmakers is in danger of getting overwhelmed.

Each project has a different balance point between these tensions. More creative projects will be served best by a script supervisor with a deep understanding of film craft. Formulaic, fast-paced, and high-volume projects will benefit from a script supervisor with excellent data entry skills. It is essential that these two opposing skills are recognized for what they are, not lumped together and confused. For projects that demand both, it is helpful to have two script supervisors: a head who will engage in the filmmaking aspects and an assistant to handle the data management.

UNIONS, A LIVING WAGE, AND ART

Why Join the Union?

Unions are essential for economic health. Working on micro-budget projects for little or no pay is a fine way to practice your skills, but it will only get you so far. If you are working on a production where people are getting paid for their work, your pay should be equal to the other department heads. When you feel professionally competent and want work that can support you financially, it is a really good idea to join the *International Alliance of Theatrical Stage Employees* (IATSE). The union has low-budget contracts for small movies, which are good for making the transition to more skilled, and better paying, work. There are local chapters in New York (Local 161) and Los Angeles (Local 871), as well as smaller locals around the US and Canada. Contact the one near you and ask if they have programs to support script supervisors who want to become members.

The corporations that own studios, networks, and streaming services care more about share prices and data mining than producing quality motion picture entertainment. For them, movies are widgets to make as cheaply as possible. They do not care about art. They do not care about the health and safety of the crew. They exploit our passion for the work we love by paying us under market value whenever they can, and pocketing the difference. The only way crew can be in dialog with them is to organize and bargain collectively.

If the union seem incompatible to the way you think about your work life, join anyway, then work to shape it into an organization that serves you better. It is impossible for exhausted, demoralized filmmakers to do their best work. Unions are art's best defense.

Creative Producers

Hands-on, creative producers, dedicated to making quality motion pictures, are another thing completely. They are part of the crew and full partners in developing, shooting, and finishing meaningful movies while negotiating with corporate executives. Try your best to recognize the good ones and work for them as often as you can. They are our friends and allies.

THE GIRL THING

Legacy

When our craft was first defined, the script supervisor was one of the few crew positions open to women. This was a time when women who loved medicine became nurses and women with business skills became executive secretaries. Look at the movie stills from early Hollywood: the only women near the camera are script supervisors. Script supervisors were the women of the time who knew how to make movies. In those days, it was affectionate to call us "script girl."[4] We were valued, but not full members of the shooting team.

That beginning has consequences to this day. We started out getting paid less than men with similar responsibilities. This gap continues to widen, as union contracts have a cost-of-living increase that's granted by a percentage of our salaries. We do not get sizable kit rentals, residuals, or points as other department heads do.

Being Supportive and Assertive at the Same Time

When script supervisors practice our craft elegantly, we are invisible. We watch and understand the work on set, helping when we can, staying out of the way until we have something to contribute. A set persona that is deferential helps us do the work, but makes it harder for us to stick up for ourselves.

This is how all women were expected to work a century ago. And for us, it is often still expected.[5] The minute I started working as a still photographer, and no longer needed to be extremely deferential, I found it much easier to ask for what I wanted.

Changing Gender Hires

The baked-in sexism of our craft, and our industry in general, is not over, but it is getting better. More men are script supervisors. More women are directors, producers, and crew members in every department. My hope, as with almost everything, is in the next generation. Filmmakers who grew up with a higher expectation of equality may be more empowered to demand it, and to grant it to others.

NOTES

1   A script alone can be caught in rewrite hell for years. A script with a proof-of-concept short presents a more specific creative vision. A finished series pilot with a bible is better still. With a completed feature film, the only thing left to talk about is distribution.

2   For more about this, see Kevin Kelly's influential essay, "1000 True Fans."

3   See *How To with John Wilson* for an inspiring example of personal aesthetic, made possible by accessible technology.

4   Today, some people think it is affectionate to call us scripty. It's not as demeaning as script girl, but still way too patronizing for most people in our profession, myself included.

5   Production office coordinators (also traditionally a woman's position) are in a similar situation.

Index

Page numbers in italics refer to figures. Page numbers followed by 'n' refer to notes.